PRAXIS II: PARAPRO TEST PREP (0755 & 1755)

OTHER TITLES OF INTEREST FROM
LEARNINGEXPRESS, LLC

Algebra Success in 20 Minutes a Day

Geometry Success in 20 Minutes a Day

Grammar Success in 20 Minutes a Day

Practical Math Success in 20 Minutes a Day

Reading Comprehension Success in 20 Minutes a Day

Vocabulary and Spelling Success in 20 Minutes a Day

Writing Success in 20 Minutes a Day

PRAXIS II: PARAPRO TEST PREP
(0755 & 1755)

LEARNINGEXPRESS®

NEW YORK

Printed in the United States of America

9 8 7 6 5 4 3 2 1

First Edition

ISBN-10 1-57685-733-6

ISBN-13 978-1-57685-733-5

For more information or to place an order, contact LearningExpress at:

    2 Rector Street

    26th Floor

    New York, NY 10006

Or visit us at:

www.learnatest.com

ABOUT THE AUTHOR ▶

Russell Kahn is a developer, writer, and editor of educational publishing products. He has developed scores of test prep guides and authored products for both children and adults. He is currently working toward dual master's degrees in education from Montclair State University. He lives in Montclair, NJ, with his wife and two children.

CONTENTS ▶

PRAXIS II: PARAPRO TEST PREP
(0755 & 1755)

INTRODUCTION: THE PARAPRO ASSESSMENT

The No Child Left Behind Act (NCLB) of 2001 required all instructional paraprofessionals to do one of the following:

- complete at least two years of study at an institution of higher education;
- obtain an associate's (or higher) degree; or
- meet a rigorous standard of quality and demonstrate this through a formal state or local academic assessment.

As a result of this legislation, ETS created the Praxis® II: ParaProfessional Certification Assessment (also known as "ParaPro Assessment"). Most states now accept the ParaPro Assessment as a qualifier for prospective (and practicing) paraprofessionals.

About the ParaPro Assessment

The ParaPro Assessment contains three sections, each of which contains 30 multiple-choice questions. The sections cover the following three subjects:

- reading
- writing
- mathematics

However, NCLB stated that the assessment must test both the knowledge of these subject areas and the ability to apply reading, writing, and mathematics skills to the classroom. Therefore, some of the questions in these sections will test basic skills and knowledge of the subject; some will test the application of these skills in the classroom. The following table shows the approximate breakdown of the questions.

Approximate Breakdown of Praxis II: ParaProfessional Certification Assessment	
Section 1: Reading	**30 Questions Total**
Basic Skills & Knowledge	18 Questions
Application of Skills for Classroom Use	12 Questions
Section 2: Mathematics	**30 Questions Total**
Basic Skills & Knowledge	18 Questions
Application of Skills for Classroom Use	12 Questions
Section 3: Writing	**30 Questions Total**
Basic Skills & Knowledge	18 Questions
Application of Skills for Classroom Use	12 Questions

Fifteen questions on the ParaPro Assessment (five questions per subject) will not count toward your score. However, you will not know which items won't count, so be sure to answer every question to the best of your abilities.

The Timing of the ParaPro Assessment

You will have 2.5 hours to complete the ParaPro Assessment. Because there is a total of 90 questions on the test, that gives you an average of 1 minute and 40 seconds per question—or 50 minutes per 30-question section.

Keep in mind that you can choose where you what to spend your time. For example, you can spend more time on one section than on another. This can be helpful if you would prefer to spend more time on one area, such as the math problems or the reading passages. Use the practice test in this book to determine how you want to adjust your time for each section. Choose the pace that makes the most sense for you.

The Scoring of the ParaPro Assessment

Each question on the ParaPro Assessment is worth the same number of points (other than the 15 questions that don't count at all). ETS takes the number of questions you answered correctly and translates it to a score from 420–480. Most students usually get a score in the range from 460–475. You will also get specific scores for the three sections on the test.

There is no guessing penalty on the ParaPro Assessment. That means you will *not* get points taken away for getting a question wrong. In other words, you should absolutely answer every question—even if you're not sure of the answer.

The passing score for the ParaPro Assessment varies, depending on your state or school district. For example, Virginia requires a minimum score of 455; North Dakota requires a score of 464. Contact your school or school district to find out what score they require.

Online vs. Paper-and-Pencil ParaPro Assessment

The ParaPro Assessment is offered as both a paper-and-pencil test and an online test. You can choose which format you'd prefer to use to take the test. The paper-and-pencil and online ParaPro tests are identical; they have the same questions, and you will have 2.5 hours to take either test.

Most test takers opt for the Internet-based test. The online test is generally more convenient. You do not need to pre-register, and can take the online test whenever the school district offers it. The paper-and-pencil test, on the other hand, is offered only a few times per year.

Another benefit of the Internet-based test is the immediacy of the results. Test takers can see their unofficial score on the screen right after taking the test. (The official score report arrives about two weeks later.) With the paper-based test, it takes about four weeks after the test to get the score report.

Some people are more comfortable writing their answers with a pencil on paper. The online test, however, does not require a great degree of computer savvy. If you are comfortable using a mouse and a web browser, you will likely feel at ease taking the online test. The following image shows what the screen will look like during the online test:

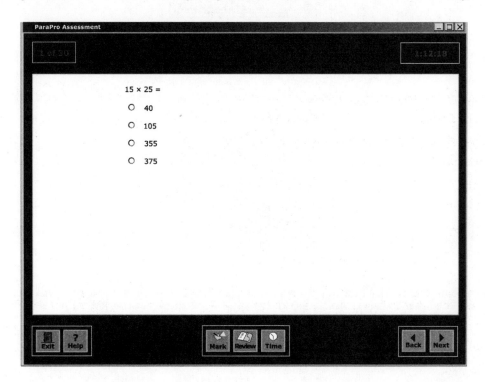

The questions on the ParaPro Assessment will always appear in the white area of the screen. To choose your answer, use the mouse and click on the circle next to the answer. If you want to change your answer, just click on another circle. The program will automatically change your answer. (It is impossible to accidentally select two answers.)

The buttons on the ParaPro Assessment will always appear in the black border of the screen in the layout shown on the previous page. The buttons serve the following functions:

This button will end the test and calculate your score. It will ask you if you are sure before exiting.

This button will give you help on taking the ParaPro Assessment. It won't give you help on the content of the questions, of course.

This button can be used to mark a question for review at a later time. The top of the screen will then say "Marked." Click the button again to unmark the question.

This button will show you a list of every question on the test—and whether you have seen, marked, or answered each one. You can use this to ensure that you have answered every question on the test. You can click to any question on the test from this review.

This button hides or shows the clock at the top-right corner of the screen. The clock will count down from 2:30:00 and cannot be paused once the exam begins. When there are 10 minutes left in the test, the clock will remain on the screen until the end of the test.

This button brings you back to the previous question in the test.

This button sends you to the next question in the test.

How to Register for the ParaPro Assessment

To register for the paper-based test, you need to complete a registration form—available online at the ETS website, *www.ets.org/PRAXIS*. A PDF of the registration form may be found at *www.ets.org/Media/Tests/ParaPro_Assessment/13223reg.pdf*. You can also call 1-800-537-3161 (8:00 A.M. to 7:00 P.M. EST Monday through Friday) to request that a registration bulletin be mailed to you.

The online test is scheduled by your school district. Contact your school or school district to register for the online ParaPro Assessment.

What to Bring to the ParaPro Assessment

You will need to bring identification and your admission ticket to your ParaPro Assessment. Be sure to also bring several sharpened number 2 pencils and erasers. You will not be allowed to use a calculator, cell phone, mechanical pencil, or other electronic device.

Special Accommodations for the ParaPro Assessment

ETS offers some accommodations for students with disabilities. For example, students may have extended time or additional rest breaks. Some students may take the ParaPro test in a large print, Braille, or audio format.

You can view the testing arrangements and registration procedures on the ETS website, *www.ets.org*. Or to find out if you are eligible for the special accommodations, you can contact ETS Disability Services directly:

Phone: Monday–Friday 8:30 A.M. – 4:30 P.M. Eastern Time
1-866-387-8602 (toll free) from U.S, U.S. Territories*, and Canada
1-609-771-7780 (all other locations)
TTY: 1-609-771-7714
Fax: 1-609-771-7165
E-mail: stassd@ets.org
Mail: ETS, Disability Services, PO Box 6054, Princeton, NJ 08541-6054

BECOMING A TEACHING ASSISTANT/ PARAPROFESSIONAL

CHAPTER SUMMARY

Paraprofessionals may have many names. They may be called "paraeducators," "teacher's assistants," "teacher's aides," "instructional aides," "instructional assistants," "educational assistants," or a variety of similar titles. Whatever the job title, the function is similar: playing a key role in the educational team for a student or classroom full of students.

What Paraprofessionals Do

There are paraprofessionals at almost every level of education, from pre-kindergarten up through high school. Paraprofessionals may work with children with special needs or disabilities, or even with gifted and talented students. You can find a paraprofessional in almost every educational setting imaginable. And the paraprofessional may be responsible for an almost unlimited number of tasks.

Paraprofessionals may be responsible for any or all of the following tasks (and more):

- grading papers, homework, or standardized tests
- making photocopies for the teacher
- putting bulletin board materials together
- providing one-on-one help for students
- supervising students between classes
- delivering lessons in small groups (or even to the whole class)

In general, paraprofessionals are expected to be available at all times for the classroom teacher and his or her students. A handbook provided by the school administration may also describe the precise job duties of the paraprofessional. You should be able to get a copy of this handbook from a school before starting a job.

Traits of Good Paraprofessionals

Because paraprofessionals spend their days in schools, it is essential that they enjoy spending time with children and have a strong desire to help them. In addition to helping students in the classroom, paraprofessionals must be willing to support the teachers who run the classroom. After all, additional terms for a paraprofessional include "teacher's assistant" or "teacher's aide."

Life in the classroom is rarely predictable, so good paraprofessionals must also be flexible, both for the sanity of the teacher and the students in the class. Materials in the classroom may be limited, so paraprofessionals are expected to be resourceful, using whatever tools they have for the benefit of the students. Lastly, paraprofessionals may work with many teachers in a school—as well as other paraprofessionals—so the ability to work well in a collaborative setting is essential.

Paraprofessional Facts

According to the U.S. Bureau of Labor Statistics, there were 1,312,000 paraprofessionals working in the United States in 2008. Of those employees, the median income was $22,240. The government agency estimates an approximate 10 percent increase in the workforce by 2016, so there should be additional job openings in the coming years.

Career Advancement

Some paraprofessionals use the job as a stepping-stone to a head teacher's position or another position within a school. Others are happy to spend their career as a parapro. Whatever you decide is right for you, you need to put yourself in a position to land that first job with a school.

Get Qualified

The fact that you're reading this book shows that you're serious about getting qualified. As mentioned in the introduction, the No Child Left Behind Act demands that paraprofessionals do at least one of the following:

- complete at least 2 years of study at an institution of higher education;
- obtain an associate's (or higher) degree; or
- meet a rigorous standard of quality and demonstrate this through a formal State or local academic assessment

Passing the Praxis II: ParaPro Assessment usually meets the third point above (depending on your state), but there is more you can do as well.

Depending on where you live, you may be able to attend specific college courses or training programs tailored for paraprofessionals. What better way to show that you are dedicated to your profession than to take a distinct course or training program for it? You should even be able to earn college credits through these classes as well.

Get Experienced

Most schools will not require any experience—and they will provide on-the-job training. However, some schools prefer to hire paraprofessionals with experience, especially schools with gifted students or students with disabilities. Volunteering at a school or youth group can provide a terrific opportunity to work with children and gain excellent parapro experience. This type of experience, even if it's unpaid, can help set you apart from other candidates applying for the same job.

Find a Job Opening

The best place to find a list of available jobs depends on your school district or state. For example, Wisconsin lists all its government jobs (including teaching jobs) on its job website, at *www.wisconsin.gov/state/employment/app*. Other states have a special site dedicated for teachers, such as Virginia's website *teach virginia.org* or California's site *www.teach california.org*. See the list of resources in the following section for additional websites.

Depending on the particular job market, you may find some difficulty finding an open position in an area that you want to work. Jeff Mills, a paraprofessional in New Jersey, says that finding a job "really takes persistence and not limiting yourself to a specific district." He recommends that prospective paraprofessionals send their resume and cover letter to all the districts in the area—and "use every contact you have."

It can't hurt to contact a school directly to see if there is a position available. You may want to work at a particular school, based on the location or the people who work there. Feel free to reach out to a school administration office or the human resource department for a school system if you want information about employment opportunities. You might discover opportunities that have not yet opened up to the public. Similarly, you may discover short-term opportunities (like filling in for a paraprofessional on leave) that may end up evolving into a more permanent position.

Job Hunting and Resource Websites

There are a seemingly endless number of job-hunting websites on the Internet. Some of the biggest and best are listed below, but don't limit yourself to them if you know other places to find job listings. There may be some regional job sites (including local newspapers) that can provide additional openings. A quick word of warning: some job opportunities listed on various websites might not be completely legitimate. Be cautious when conducting your search.

www.nrcpara.org

While not a job-hunting site, the National Resource Center for Paraprofessionals can provide invaluable information about the profession—including general information for job seekers. If you're new to the profession, this website is a good place to learn about becoming a paraprofessional.

www.teachers-teachers.com

Claiming to be the "The Internet's largest resource of teaching jobs" with connections to more than 1,500 school systems, this site also provides valuable links to state resources for teaching jobs.

www.aaee.org

AAEE, the American Association for Employment in Education, has focused on education employment since 1934. You can find information about jobs, job fairs, networking, and advice on job hunting on their site.

www.craigslist.org

Yes, you can also use Craigslist to find a used couch, but there are many teaching jobs listed on the site as well. Job listings are free or inexpensive to post, so many institutions like to list jobs there.

www.schoolspring.com

This website combines the educational job listings from across the country into one database with thousands of jobs. For example, if you are looking for a job as a paraprofessional in New Jersey, this site will connect you to job listing through *www.njschooljobs.com*, one of the state's best resources for educational jobs.

CHAPTER

2 ▶

THE LEARNINGEXPRESS TEST PREPARATION SYSTEM

CHAPTER SUMMARY

Taking any test can be tough. But don't let the written test scare you! If you prepare ahead of time, you can achieve a top score. The LearningExpress Test Preparation System, developed exclusively for LearningExpress by leading test experts, gives you the discipline and attitude you need to be a winner.

First, the bad news: Getting ready for any test takes work. If you plan to get a job as a paraprofessional and you don't have at least an associate's degree or two years of college, you will have to pass a test that shows you have the knowledge to work in the classroom. In most cases, that is the Praxis II: ParaPro Assessment. This book focuses on the reading, math, and writing skills that you will be tested on. By honing in on these skills, you will take your first step toward achieving the career of your dreams. However, there are all sorts of pitfalls that can prevent you from doing your best on exams. Here are some obstacles that can stand in the way of your success.

- being unfamiliar with the format of the exam
- being paralyzed by test anxiety
- leaving your preparation to the last minute
- not preparing at all
- not knowing vital test-taking skills like:
  - how to pace yourself through the exam
  - how to use the process of elimination
  - when to guess

- not being in tip-top mental shape
- forgetting to eat breakfast and having to take the test on an empty stomach
- forgetting a sweater or jacket and shivering through the exam

What's the common denominator in all these test-taking pitfalls? One word: *control*. Who's in control, you or the exam?

Now the good news: The LearningExpress Test Preparation System puts *you* in control. In just nine easy-to-follow steps, you will learn everything you need to know to make sure you are in charge of your preparation and performance on the exam. *Other* test takers may let the test get the better of them; *other* test takers may be unprepared, but not *you*. You will have taken all the steps you need to take for a passing score.

Here's how the LearningExpress Test Preparation System works: Nine easy steps lead you through everything you need to know and do to get ready to master your exam. Each of the steps listed below gives you tips and activities to help you prepare for any exam. It's important that you follow the advice and do the activities, or you won't be getting the full benefit of the system. Each step gives you an approximate time estimate.

Step 1.	Get Information	30 minutes
Step 2.	Conquer Test Anxiety	20 minutes
Step 3.	Make a Plan	50 minutes
Step 4.	Learn to Manage Your Time	10 minutes
Step 5.	Learn to Use the Process of Elimination	20 minutes
Step 6.	Know When to Guess	20 minutes
Step 7.	Reach Your Peak Performance Zone	10 minutes
Step 8.	Get Your Act Together	10 minutes
Step 9.	Do It!	10 minutes
Total		**3 hours**

You estimate that working through the entire system will take you approximately three hours, though it's perfectly okay if you work faster or slower than the time estimates say. If you can take a whole afternoon or evening, you can work through the entire LearningExpress Test Preparation System in one sitting. Otherwise, you can break it up, and do just one or two steps a day for the next several days. It's up to you—remember, *you're* in control.

Step 1: Get Information

Time to complete: 30 minutes
Activities: Read the Introduction.
If you haven't already done so, stop here, go back, and read the introduction of this book. Here, you'll learn all about the Praxis II: ParaPro Assessment, such as the length of the test, the number of questions, and the way that the test is scored.

Knowledge is power. The first step in the LearningExpress Test Preparation System is finding out everything you can about the types of questions that will be asked on the exam. Practicing and studying the exercises in this book will help prepare you for those tests. Topics that may be tested on the reading, math, and writing sections of the ParaPro Assessment include:

- main idea and supporting details
- inferences
- vocabulary in context
- arithmetic
- fractions
- decimals
- grammar
- punctuation
- spelling

After completing the LearningExpress Test Preparation System and the diagnostic test (Chapter 3), you will then begin to apply the test-taking strategies you learn as you work through practice questions in the above topic areas (Chapters 4 through 6). You can see how well your training has paid off in the practice test at the end of the book, which is based on the all the topics covered in this book. (You can also test your training with the online test!)

Step 2: Conquer Test Anxiety

Time to complete: 20 minutes
Activity: Take the Test Stress Test

Having complete information about the exam is the first step in getting control of the exam. Next, you have to overcome one of the biggest obstacles to test success: test anxiety. Test anxiety not only impairs your performance on the exam itself, but it can even keep you from preparing! In Step 2, you'll learn stress management techniques that will help you succeed on your exam. Learn these strategies now, and practice them as you work through the practice tests in this book, so they'll be second nature to you by exam day.

Combating Test Anxiety

The first thing you need to know is that a little test anxiety is a good thing. Everyone gets nervous before a big exam—and if that nervousness motivates you to prepare thoroughly, so much the better. It's said that Sir Laurence Olivier, one of the foremost British actors of the last century, was ill before every performance. His stage fright didn't impair his performance; in fact, it probably gave him a little extra edge—just the kind of edge you need to do well, whether on a stage or in an exam room.

On page 14 is the Test Stress Test. Stop here and answer the questions on that page to find out whether your level of test anxiety is something you should worry about.

Stress Management before the Test

If you feel your level of anxiety getting the best of you in the weeks before the test, here is what you need to do to bring the level down again:

- **Get prepared.** There's nothing like knowing what to expect. Being prepared will put you in control of test anxiety. That's why you're reading this book. Use it faithfully, and remind yourself that you're better prepared than most of the people taking the test.
- **Practice self-confidence.** A positive attitude is a great way to combat test anxiety. This is no time to be humble or shy. Stand in front of the mirror and say to your reflection, "I'm prepared. I'm full of self-confidence. I'm going to ace this test. I know I can do it." Say it into a tape recorder and play it back once a day. If you hear it often enough, you'll believe it.
- **Fight negative messages.** Every time someone starts telling you how hard the exam is, start replying to them with your self-confidence messages above. If the someone with the negative messages is you, telling yourself you don't do well on exams and you just can't do this, don't listen. Turn on your tape recorder and listen to your self-confidence messages.
- **Visualize.** Imagine yourself reporting for your first day on the job. Visualizing success can help make it happen—and it reminds you why you're preparing for the exam so diligently.
- **Exercise.** Physical activity helps calm down your body and focus your mind. Besides, being in good physical shape can actually help you do well on the exam. Go for a run, lift weights, go swimming—and do it regularly.

Stress Management on Test Day

There are several ways you can bring down your level of test anxiety on test day. To find a comfort level, experiment with the following exercises in the weeks before the test, and use the ones that work best for you.

- **Breathe deeply.** Take a deep breath while you count to five. Hold it for a count of one, then let it out on a count of five. Repeat several times.
- **Move your body.** Try rolling your head in a circle. Rotate your shoulders. Shake your hands from the wrist. Many people find these movements very relaxing.
- **Visualize again.** Think of the place where you are most relaxed: lying on the beach in the sun, walking through the park, or sipping a cup of hot tea—whatever works for you. Now close your eyes and imagine you're actually there. If you practice in advance, you'll find that you need only a few seconds of this exercise to experience a significant increase in your sense of well-being.

When anxiety threatens to overwhelm you right there during the exam, there are still things you can do to manage your stress level:

- **Repeat your self-confidence messages.** You should have them memorized by now. Say them quietly to yourself, and believe them!
- Visualize one more time. This time, visualize yourself moving smoothly and quickly through the test, answering every question right and finishing just before time is up. Like most visualization techniques, this one works best if you've practiced it ahead of time.
- **Find an easy question.** Skim over the test until you find an easy question, and then answer it. Filling in even one circle gets you into the test-taking groove.
- **Take a mental break.** Everyone loses concentration once in a while during a long test. It's normal, so you shouldn't worry about it. Instead, accept what has happened. Say to yourself, "Hey, I lost it there for a minute. My brain is taking a break." Put down your pencil, close your eyes, and do some deep breathing for a few seconds. Then you're ready to go back to work.

Try these techniques ahead of time, and see if they work for you!

Test Stress Test

You only need to worry about test anxiety if it is extreme enough to impair your performance. The following questionnaire will provide a diagnosis of your level of test anxiety. In the blank before each statement, write the number that most accurately describes your experience.

0 = Never   1 = Once or twice   2 = Sometimes   3 = Often

_____ I have gotten so nervous before an exam that I simply put down the books and didn't study for it.

_____ I have experienced disabling physical symptoms such as vomiting and severe headaches because I was nervous about an exam.

_____ I have simply not showed up for an exam because I was scared to take it.

_____ I have experienced dizziness and disorientation while taking an exam.

_____ I have had trouble filling in the little circles because my hands were shaking too hard.

_____ I have failed an exam because I was too nervous to complete it.

_____ **Total:** Add up the numbers you wrote in the blanks above.

Your Test Stress Score

Here are the steps you should take, depending on your score. If you scored:

- **Less than 3:** Your level of test anxiety is nothing to worry about; it's probably just enough to give you the motivation to excel.
- **Between 3 and 6:** Your test anxiety may be enough to impair your performance, and you should practice the stress management techniques listed in this section to try to bring your test anxiety down to manageable levels.
- **Above 6:** Your level of test anxiety is a serious concern. In addition to practicing the stress management techniques listed in this section, you may want to seek additional, personal help. Call your local high school or community college and ask for an academic counselor. Tell the counselor that you have a level of test anxiety that sometimes keeps you from being able to take an exam. The counselor may be willing to help you, or may suggest someone else you should talk to.

Step 3: Make a Plan

Time to complete: 50 minutes
Activity: Construct a study plan

Perhaps the most important thing you can do to get control of yourself and your exam is to make a study plan. Too many people fail to prepare simply because they fail to plan. Spending hours on the day before the exam poring over sample test questions not only raises your level of test anxiety, it is also no substitute for careful preparation and practice.

Don't fall into the cram trap. Take control of your preparation time by mapping out a study schedule. If you're the kind of person who needs deadlines and assignments to motivate you for a project, here they are. If you're the kind of person who doesn't like to follow other people's plans, you can use the suggested schedules here to construct your own.

Even more important than making a plan is making a commitment. You can't review everything you need to know for the ParaPro Assessment in one night. You have to set aside some time every day to study and practice. Try for at least 20 minutes a day. Twenty minutes daily will do you much more good than two hours on Saturday.

Don't put off your studying until the day before the exam. Start now.

Even 10 minutes a day, with half an hour or more on weekends, can make a big difference in your score—and in your chances of making the grade you want!

Schedule A: The 30-Day Plan

If you have at least one month before you take your test, you have plenty of time to prepare—as long as you don't procrastinate! If you have less than a month, turn to Schedule B.

TIME	PREPARATION
Day 1	Skim over any written materials you may have about the ParaPro Assessment. Learn the specific content that you need to brush up on to prepare for the test. Read the Introduction and the first chapter of this book.
Day 2	Take the diagnostic test (Chapter 2) and score yourself. Be sure to take the test during one 150-minute session, just like the actual test.
Day 3	Review any questions on the diagnostic test that you answered incorrectly. Make note of which chapters review the skills contained in these questions.
Days 4–7	Read Chapter 4, "Reading Skills and Knowledge." Take care to read the vocabulary terms that you will be expected to know for the reading section of the test. If you need to, make index cards for unfamiliar items. Finally, practice these basic skills by working through the practice questions.
Day 8	Review any Chapter 4 concepts that you feel are necessary for you to brush up on.
Days 9–12	Read Chapter 5, "Math Skills and Knowledge." Take care to read the math vocabulary terms and symbols that you will be expected to know for the math section of the test. If you need to, make index cards for unfamiliar items. Finally, work through the practice questions.
Day 13	Review any Chapter 5 concepts that you feel are necessary for you to brush up on.
Days 14–17	Read Chapter 6, "Writing Skills and Knowledge." Take care to read the vocabulary terms that you will be expected to know for the writing section. If you need to, make index cards for unfamiliar items. Finally, work through the practice questions and score yourself.
Day 18	Review any Chapter 6 concepts you feel are necessary for you to brush up on.
Day 19	Take the practice test at the end of this book. Be sure to take the test during one 150-minute session, just like the actual test. Score yourself.
Days 20–21	Review any incorrect answers from the practice test, and then go back to the chapters covering skills that you might have missed on the practice exam.
Day 22	Take the online practice exam.
Days 23–24	Review any incorrect answers from the online practice exam, and then go back to the chapters covering skills that you might have missed.
Days 25–26	Review any concepts that you feel are necessary for you to brush up on. Work through similar questions in the appropriate chapters.
Days 27–29	Continue to review the chapters that contain the topics you were weak on during the practice exams.
Day before the exam	Relax. Do something unrelated to the exam and go to bed at a reasonable hour.

Schedule B: The 14-Day Plan

If you have two weeks or less before the exam, you may have your work cut out for you. Use this 14-day schedule to help you make the most of your time.

TIME	PREPARATION
Day 1	Read the Introduction and Chapter 1. Take the diagnostic test in Chapter 2.
Days 2–3	Read Chapter 4, and complete the practice questions.
Days 4–5	Read Chapter 5, and complete the practice questions.
Days 6–7	Read Chapter 6, and complete the practice questions.
Days 8–9	Take the practice test at the end of the book and score yourself. Review all of the questions that you missed.
Day 10	Review any concepts you feel are necessary for you to brush up on. Work through similar questions in the appropriate chapters. Study the Appendix material.
Days 11–12	Complete the online practice exam and score yourself. Review all of the questions that you missed.
Day 13	Review topics as necessary, based on the questions you missed on the practice tests. Then, after reviewing the underlying concepts, look at the questions you'd missed and make sure you understand them this time around.
Day before the exam	Relax. Do something unrelated to the exam and go to bed at a reasonable hour.

Step 4: Learn to Manage Your Time

Time to complete: 10 minutes to read, many hours of practice!

Activities: Use these strategies as you take the sample tests in this book

Steps 4, 5, and 6 of the LearningExpress Test Preparation System put you in charge of your exam by showing you test-taking strategies that work. Practice these strategies as you take the diagnostic and practice tests in this book, and then you'll be ready to use them on test day.

First, take control of your time on the exam. The Praxis II: ParaPro Assessment has a time limit of 150 minutes, which may give you more than enough time

to complete all the questions—or not enough time. It's a terrible feeling to hear the examiner say, "Five minutes left," when you're only three-quarters of the way through the test. Here are some tips to keep that from happening to you.

- **Follow directions.** If the directions are given orally, listen closely. If they're written on the exam booklet or on the computer screen (for the online version of the exam), read them carefully. Ask questions *before* the exam begins if there is anything you don't understand. If you're allowed to write in your exam booklet, write down the beginning time and ending time of the exam.
- **Pace yourself.** Glance at your watch every few minutes, and compare the time to how

far you've gotten in the test. When 50 minutes has elapsed, you should be about a third of the way through the test (or completely through one 30-question section), and so on. If you're falling behind, pick up the pace a bit.

- **Keep moving.** Don't waste time on one question. If you don't know the answer, skip the question and move on. Circle the number of the question in your test booklet in case you have time to come back to it later. If you're taking the exam on a computer, the computer will keep track of the questions that you've skipped—and as long as you have enough time, it will allow you to come back to those questions.

- **Keep track of your place on the answer sheet.** If you skip a question, make sure you skip it on the answer sheet, too. Check yourself every 5–10 questions to make sure the question number and the answer sheet number are still the same.

- **Don't rush.** Although you should keep moving, rushing won't help. Try to keep calm and work methodically and quickly.

Step 5: Learn to Use the Process of Elimination

Time to complete: 20 minutes
Activity: Complete worksheet on using the process of elimination

After time management, your most important tool for taking control of your exam is using the process of elimination wisely. It's standard test-taking wisdom that you should always read all the answer choices before choosing your answer. This helps you find the right answer by eliminating wrong answer choices.

And, sure enough, that standard wisdom applies to your exam, too.

Choosing the Right Answer by Process of Elimination

As you read a question, you may find it helpful to underline important information or to make some notes about what you're reading. When you get to the heart of the question, circle it and make sure you understand what it is asking. If you're not sure of what's being asked, you'll never know whether you've chosen the right answer. What you do next depends on the type of question you're answering.

Take a quick look at the answer choices for some clues. Sometimes this helps to put the question in a new perspective and makes it easier to answer. Then make a plan of attack to solve the problem.

Otherwise, follow this simple process-of-elimination plan to manage your testing time as efficiently as possible: Read each answer choice and make a quick decision about what to do with it, marking your test book accordingly. If:

- . . . the answer seems reasonable, keep it. Put a ✓ next to the answer.

- . . . the answer seems awful, get rid of it. Put an ✗ next to the answer.

- . . . you can't make up your mind about the answer, or you don't understand it, keep it for now. Put a **?** next to it.

Whatever you do, don't waste time with any one answer choice. If you can't figure out what an answer choice means, don't worry about it. If it's the right answer, you may be able to eliminate the other choices. And if it's the wrong answer, another answer will probably strike you more obviously as the right answer.

If you haven't eliminated any answers at all, skip the question temporarily, but don't forget to mark the question so you can come back to it later, if you have time. Since the ParaPro Assessment has no penalty for wrong answers, if you're certain that you could never answer this question in a million years, guess an answer, mark it, and move on!

If you've eliminated all but one answer, just reread the circled part of the question to make sure you're answering exactly what's asked. Mark your answer sheet and move on to the next question.

Here's what to do when you've eliminated some, but not all of the answer choices. Compare the remaining answers looking for similarities and differences, reasoning your way through these choices. Try to eliminate those choices that don't seem as strong to you. But *don't* eliminate an answer just because you don't understand it. You may even be able to use relevant information from other parts of the test. If you've narrowed it down to a single answer, check it against the part of the question you've circled, to be sure you've answered exactly what the question is asking. Then mark your answer sheet and move on. If you're down to only two or three answer choices, you've improved your odds of getting the question right. Make an educated guess and move on. However, if you think you can do better with more time, mark the question as one to return to later.

Guess on Every Question

Remember: you will *not* be penalized for getting a wrong answer on the ParaPro Assessment. This is very good news. That means you should absolutely answer every single question on the test. If you're hopelessly lost on a question and can't even cross off one answer choice, make sure that you don't leave it blank. Even if you only have 30 seconds left and 10 questions still to answer, you should just guess on all of those last questions.

Of course, if you can eliminate even one of the choices, you improve your odds of guessing correctly. If you can identify *two* of the choices as definitely wrong, you have a one-in-two chance of answering the

question correctly. Either way, be sure to answer every question.

If You Finish Early . . .

Use any time you have left to do the following:

- Go back to questions you marked to return to later, and try them again.
- Check your work on all the other questions. If you have a good reason for thinking an answer is wrong, change it.
- Review your answer sheet if you are taking the paper-and-pencil version of the test. Make sure you've put the answers in the right places and that you've marked only one answer for each question. (Most tests are scored in such a way that questions with more than one answer are marked wrong.)
- If you've erased an answer, make sure you've done a good job of it.
- Check for stray marks on your answer sheet that could distort your score.

Whatever you do, don't waste time when you've finished a test section. Make every second count by checking your work over and over again until time is called.

Try using your powers of elimination on the questions in the worksheet on pages 20–21 called "Using the Process of Elimination." The answer explanations that follow show one possible way you might use the process to arrive at the right answer.

The process of elimination is your tool for the next step: knowing when to guess.

Use the process of elimination to answer the following questions.

1. Ilsa is as old as Meghan will be in five years. The difference between Ed's age and Meghan's age is twice the difference between Ilsa's age and Meghan's age. Ed is 29. How old is Ilsa?
   a. 4
   b. 10
   c. 19
   d. 24

2. "All drivers of commercial vehicles must carry a valid commercial driver's license whenever operating a commercial vehicle." According to this sentence, which of the following people need NOT carry a commercial driver's license?
   a. a truck driver idling his engine while waiting to be directed to a loading dock
   b. a bus operator backing her bus out of the way of another bus in the bus lot
   c. a taxi driver driving his personal car to the grocery store
   d. a limousine driver taking the limousine to her home after dropping off her last passenger of the evening

3. Smoking tobacco has been linked to
   a. increased risk of stroke and heart attack.
   b. all forms of respiratory disease.
   c. increasing mortality rates over the past ten years.
   d. juvenile delinquency.

4. Which of the following words is spelled correctly?
   a. incorrigible
   b. outragous
   c. domestickated
   d. understandible

Answers

Here are the answers, as well as some suggestions as to how you might have used the process of elimination to find them.

1. d. You should have eliminated choice **a** off the bat. Ilsa can't be four years old if Meghan is going to be Ilsa's age in five years. The best way to eliminate other answer choices is to try plugging them in to the information given in the problem. For instance, for choice **b**, if Ilsa is 10, then Meghan must be 5. The difference in their ages is 5. The difference between Ed's age, 29, and Meghan's age, 5, is 24. Is 24 two times 5? No. Then choice **b** is wrong. You could eliminate choice **c** in the same way and be left with choice **d**.

2. c. Note the word *not* in the question, and go through the answers one by one. Is the truck driver in choice **a** "operating a commercial vehicle"? Yes, idling counts as "operating," so he needs to have a commercial driver's license. Likewise, the bus operator in choice **b** is operating a commercial vehicle; the question doesn't say the operator has to be on the street. The limo driver in choice **d** is operating a commercial vehicle, even if it doesn't have a passenger in it. However, the cabbie in choice **c** is *not* operating a commercial vehicle, but his own private car.

3. a. You could eliminate choice **b** simply because of the presence of the word *all*. Such absolutes hardly ever appear in correct answer choices. Choice **c** looks attractive until you think a little about what you know—aren't fewer people smoking these days, rather than more? So how could smoking be responsible for a higher mortality rate? (If you didn't know that mortality rate means the rate at which people die, you might keep this choice as a possibility, but you would still be able to eliminate two answers and have only two to choose from.) And choice **d** is not logical, so you could eliminate that one, too. You are left with the correct answer, choice **a.**

4. a. How you used the process of elimination here depends on which words you recognized as being spelled incorrectly. If you knew that the correct spellings were *outrageous*, *domesticated*, and *understandable*, then you were home free. Surely you knew that at least one of those words was wrong.

Step 6: Know When to Guess

Time to complete: 20 minutes

Activity: Complete worksheet on your guessing ability

Armed with the process of elimination, you're ready to take control of one of the big questions in test-taking: Should I guess? In the Praxis II: ParaPro Assessment, the number of questions you answer correctly yields your raw score. So you have nothing to lose and everything to gain by guessing.

The more complicated answer to the question, "Should I guess?" depends on you, your personality, and your "guessing intuition." There are two things you need to know about yourself before you go into the exam:

1. Are you a risk-taker?
2. Are you a good guesser?

To find out if you're a good guesser, complete the worksheet called "Your Guessing Ability" that begins on page 22. Frankly, even if you're a play-it-safe person with terrible intuition, you're still safe in guessing every time because the exam has no guessing penalty. The best thing would be if you could overcome your anxieties and go ahead and mark an answer. But you may want to have a sense of how good your intuition is before you go into the exam.

Step 7: Reach Your Peak Performance Zone

Time to complete: 10 minutes to read; weeks to complete!

Activity: Complete the Physical Preparation Checklist

To get ready for a challenge like a big exam, you have to take control of your physical, as well as your mental, state. Exercise, proper diet, and rest will ensure that your body works with, rather than against, your mind on test day, as well as during your preparation.

Exercise

If you don't already have a regular exercise program going, the time during which you're preparing for an exam is actually an excellent time to start one. If you're already keeping fit—or trying to get that way—don't let the pressure of preparing for an exam fool you into quitting now. Exercise helps reduce stress by pumping wonderful, good-feeling hormones called "endor-

The following are ten really hard questions. You are not supposed to know the answers. Rather, this is an assessment of your ability to guess when you don't have a clue. Read each question carefully, just as if you did expect to answer it. If you have any knowledge at all of the subject of the question, use that knowledge to help you eliminate wrong answer choices.

1. September 7 is Independence Day in
   a. India.
   b. Costa Rica.
   c. Brazil.
   d. Australia.

2. Which of the following is the formula for determining the momentum of an object?
   a. $p = mv$
   b. $F = ma$
   c. $P = IV$
   d. $E = mc^2$

3. Because of the expansion of the universe, the stars and other celestial bodies are all moving away from each other. This phenomenon is known as
   a. Newton's first law.
   b. the big bang.
   c. gravitational collapse.
   d. Hubble flow.

4. American author Gertrude Stein was born in
   a. 1713.
   b. 1830.
   c. 1874.
   d. 1901.

5. Which of the following is NOT one of the Five Classics attributed to Confucius?
   a. the *I Ching*
   b. the *Book of Holiness*
   c. the *Spring and Autumn Annals*
   d. the *Book of History*

6. The religious and philosophical doctrine that holds that the universe is constantly in a struggle between good and evil is known as
   a. Pelagianism.
   b. Manichaeanism.
   c. neo-Hegelianism.
   d. Epicureanism.

7. The third Chief Justice of the U.S. Supreme Court was
   a. John Blair.
   b. William Cushing.
   c. James Wilson.
   d. John Jay.

8. Which of the following is the poisonous portion of a daffodil?
   a. the bulb
   b. the leaves
   c. the stem
   d. the flowers

9. The winner of the Masters golf tournament in 1953 was
   a. Sam Snead.
   b. Cary Middlecoff.
   c. Arnold Palmer.
   d. Ben Hogan.

10. The state with the highest per capita personal income in 1980 was
    a. Alaska.
    b. Connecticut.
    c. New York.
    d. Texas.

Answers

Check your answers against the following correct answers.

1. c.
2. a.
3. d.
4. c.
5. b.
6. b.
7. b.
8. a.
9. d.
10. a.

How Did You Do?

You may have simply gotten lucky and actually known the answer to one or two questions. In addition, your guessing was more successful if you were able to use the process of elimination on any of the questions. Maybe you didn't know who the third Chief Justice was (question 7), but you knew that John Jay was the first. In that case, you would have eliminated choice **d** and therefore improved your odds of guessing right from one in four to one in three.

You should get two and a half answers correct, out of ten, so getting either two or three right would be average. If you got four or more right, you may be a really terrific guesser. If you got one or none right, you may have decided not to guess. Remember not to leave any question blank, no matter how hard it may seem!

You should continue to keep track of your guessing ability as you work through the sample questions in this book. Circle the numbers of questions you guess; or, if you don't have time during the practice tests, go back afterward and try to remember which answers you guessed. Remember, on a test with four answer choices, your chances of getting a right answer is one in four. So keep a separate "guessing" score for each exam. How many questions did you guess on? How many did you get right? If the number you got right is at least one-fourth of the number of questions you guessed, you are at least an average guesser—and you should always go ahead and guess on the real exam if you don't know the answer.

phins" into your system. It also increases the oxygen supply throughout your body and your brain, so you'll be at peak performance on test day.

Half an hour of vigorous activity—enough to break a sweat—every day should be your aim. If you're really pressed for time, every other day is OK. Choose an activity you like, and get out there and do it. Jogging with a friend always makes the time go faster, as does listening to music.

But don't overdo it. You don't want to exhaust yourself. Moderation is the key.

Diet

First of all, cut out the junk. Go easy on caffeine and nicotine, and eliminate alcohol and any other drugs from your system at least two weeks before the exam. Promise yourself a special treat the night after the exam, if need be.

What your body needs for peak performance is simply a balanced diet. Eat plenty of fruits and vegetables, along with protein complex and carbohydrates. Foods that are high in lecithin (an amino acid), such as fish and beans, are especially good "brain foods."

Rest

You probably know how much sleep you need every night to be at your best, even if you don't always get it. Make sure you do get that much sleep, though, for at least a week before the exam. Moderation is important here, too. Extra sleep will just make you groggy.

If you're not a morning person and your exam will be given in the morning, you should reset your internal clock so that your body doesn't think you're taking an exam at 3 A.M. You have to start this process well before the exam. The way it works is to get up half an hour earlier each morning, and then go to bed half an hour earlier that night. Don't try it the other way around; you'll just toss and turn if you go to bed early without getting up early. The next morning, get up another half an hour earlier, and so on. How long you will have to do this depends on how late you're used to getting up. Use the "Physical Preparation Checklist" on page 25 to make sure you're in tip-top form.

Step 8: Get Your Act Together

Time to complete: 10 minutes to read; time to complete will vary
Activity: Complete Final Preparations worksheet
Once you feel in control of your mind and body, you're in charge of test anxiety, test preparation, and test-taking strategies. Now it's time to make charts and gather the materials you need to take to the exam.

Gather Your Materials

The night before the exam, lay out the clothes you will wear and the materials you have to bring with you to the exam. Plan on dressing in layers because you won't have any control over the temperature of the exam room. Have a sweater or jacket you can take off if it's warm. Use the checklist on the worksheet entitled "Final Preparations" on page 26 to help you pull together what you'll need.

Follow Your Routine

If you usually have coffee and toast every morning, then you should have coffee and toast before the test. If you don't usually eat breakfast, don't start changing your habits on exam morning. Do whatever you normally do so that your body will be used to it. If you're not used to it, a cup of coffee can really disrupt your stomach. Doughnuts or other sweet foods can give you a stomachache, too. When deciding what to have for breakfast, remember that a sugar high will leave you with a sugar low in the middle of the exam. A mix of protein and carbohydrates is best: Cereal with milk or eggs with toast will do your body a world of good.

Step 9: Do It!

Time to complete: 10 minutes, plus test-taking time
Activity: Ace your test!
Fast-forward to exam day. You're ready. You made a study plan and followed through. You practiced your test-taking strategies while working through this book. You're in control of your physical, mental, and emotional state. You know when and where to show up and what to bring with you. In other words, you're better prepared than most of the other people taking the test with you. You're psyched!

Just one more thing. When you're done with the exam, you will have earned a reward. Plan a night out. Call your friends and plan a party, or have a nice dinner for two—whatever your heart desires. Give yourself something to look forward to.

And then do it. Go into the exam, full of confidence, armed with test-taking strategies you've practiced until they're second nature. You're in control of yourself, your environment, and your performance on exam day. You're ready to succeed. So do it. Go in there and ace the ParaPro Assessment! And then, look forward to your new career.

Physical Preparation Checklist

For the week before the test, write down what physical exercise you engaged in, the length of time you exercised, and what you ate for each meal. Remember, you're trying for at least half an hour of exercise every other day (preferably every day) and a balanced diet that's light on junk food.

Exam minus 7 days

Exercise: _____ for _____ minutes

Breakfast: _____

Lunch: _____

Dinner: _____

Snacks: _____

Exam minus 6 days

Exercise: _____ for _____ minutes

Breakfast: _____

Lunch: _____

Dinner: _____

Snacks: _____

Exam minus 5 days

Exercise: _____ for _____ minutes

Breakfast: _____

Lunch: _____

Dinner: _____

Snacks: _____

Exam minus 4 days

Exercise: _____ for _____ minutes

Breakfast: _____

Lunch: _____

Dinner: _____

Snacks: _____

Exam minus 3 days

Exercise: _____ for _____ minutes

Breakfast: _____

Lunch: _____

Dinner: _____

Snacks: _____

Exam minus 2 days

Exercise: _____ for _____ minutes

Breakfast: _____

Lunch: _____

Dinner: _____

Snacks: _____

Exam minus 1 day

Exercise: _____ for _____ minutes

Breakfast: _____

Lunch: _____

Dinner: _____

Snacks: _____

Final Preparations

Getting to the Exam Site

Location of exam: _____

Date of exam: _____

Time of exam: _____

Do I know how to get to the exam site?

   Yes _____ No _____

If no, make a trial run.

Time it will take to get to exam site: _____

Things to Lay Out the Night Before

Clothes I will wear   _____

Sweater/jacket   _____

Watch   _____

Photo ID   _____

No. 2 pencils   _____

Admission card   _____

4 no. 2 pencils   _____

CHAPTER

3  DIAGNOSTIC TEST

This diagnostic test should be taken before you begin reviewing the topics in Chapters 4 through 6. The diagnostic test will provide valuable feedback that can be utilized not only to identify your strengths and weaknesses, but also to direct your efforts in preparing for the ParaPro Assessment.

Diagnostic Test

Reading	Mathematics	Writing

Reading

1. ⓐ ⓑ ⓒ ⓓ
2. ⓐ ⓑ ⓒ ⓓ
3. ⓐ ⓑ ⓒ ⓓ
4. ⓐ ⓑ ⓒ ⓓ
5. ⓐ ⓑ ⓒ ⓓ
6. ⓐ ⓑ ⓒ ⓓ
7. ⓐ ⓑ ⓒ ⓓ
8. ⓐ ⓑ ⓒ ⓓ
9. ⓐ ⓑ ⓒ ⓓ
10. ⓐ ⓑ ⓒ ⓓ
11. ⓐ ⓑ ⓒ ⓓ
12. ⓐ ⓑ ⓒ ⓓ
13. ⓐ ⓑ ⓒ ⓓ
14. ⓐ ⓑ ⓒ ⓓ
15. ⓐ ⓑ ⓒ ⓓ
16. ⓐ ⓑ ⓒ ⓓ
17. ⓐ ⓑ ⓒ ⓓ
18. ⓐ ⓑ ⓒ ⓓ
19. ⓐ ⓑ ⓒ ⓓ
20. ⓐ ⓑ ⓒ ⓓ
21. ⓐ ⓑ ⓒ ⓓ
22. ⓐ ⓑ ⓒ ⓓ
23. ⓐ ⓑ ⓒ ⓓ
24. ⓐ ⓑ ⓒ ⓓ
25. ⓐ ⓑ ⓒ ⓓ
26. ⓐ ⓑ ⓒ ⓓ
27. ⓐ ⓑ ⓒ ⓓ
28. ⓐ ⓑ ⓒ ⓓ
29. ⓐ ⓑ ⓒ ⓓ
30. ⓐ ⓑ ⓒ ⓓ

Mathematics

31. ⓐ ⓑ ⓒ ⓓ
32. ⓐ ⓑ ⓒ ⓓ
33. ⓐ ⓑ ⓒ ⓓ
34. ⓐ ⓑ ⓒ ⓓ
35. ⓐ ⓑ ⓒ ⓓ
36. ⓐ ⓑ ⓒ ⓓ
37. ⓐ ⓑ ⓒ ⓓ
38. ⓐ ⓑ ⓒ ⓓ
39. ⓐ ⓑ ⓒ ⓓ
40. ⓐ ⓑ ⓒ ⓓ
41. ⓐ ⓑ ⓒ ⓓ
42. ⓐ ⓑ ⓒ ⓓ
43. ⓐ ⓑ ⓒ ⓓ
44. ⓐ ⓑ ⓒ ⓓ
45. ⓐ ⓑ ⓒ ⓓ
46. ⓐ ⓑ ⓒ ⓓ
47. ⓐ ⓑ ⓒ ⓓ
48. ⓐ ⓑ ⓒ ⓓ
49. ⓐ ⓑ ⓒ ⓓ
50. ⓐ ⓑ ⓒ ⓓ
51. ⓐ ⓑ ⓒ ⓓ
52. ⓐ ⓑ ⓒ ⓓ
53. ⓐ ⓑ ⓒ ⓓ
54. ⓐ ⓑ ⓒ ⓓ
55. ⓐ ⓑ ⓒ ⓓ
56. ⓐ ⓑ ⓒ ⓓ
57. ⓐ ⓑ ⓒ ⓓ
58. ⓐ ⓑ ⓒ ⓓ
59. ⓐ ⓑ ⓒ ⓓ
60. ⓐ ⓑ ⓒ ⓓ

Writing

61. ⓐ ⓑ ⓒ ⓓ
62. ⓐ ⓑ ⓒ ⓓ
63. ⓐ ⓑ ⓒ ⓓ
64. ⓐ ⓑ ⓒ ⓓ
65. ⓐ ⓑ ⓒ ⓓ
66. ⓐ ⓑ ⓒ ⓓ
67. ⓐ ⓑ ⓒ ⓓ
68. ⓐ ⓑ ⓒ ⓓ
69. ⓐ ⓑ ⓒ ⓓ
70. ⓐ ⓑ ⓒ ⓓ
71. ⓐ ⓑ ⓒ ⓓ
72. ⓐ ⓑ ⓒ ⓓ
73. ⓐ ⓑ ⓒ ⓓ
74. ⓐ ⓑ ⓒ ⓓ
75. ⓐ ⓑ ⓒ ⓓ
76. ⓐ ⓑ ⓒ ⓓ
77. ⓐ ⓑ ⓒ ⓓ
78. ⓐ ⓑ ⓒ ⓓ
79. ⓐ ⓑ ⓒ ⓓ
80. ⓐ ⓑ ⓒ ⓓ
81. ⓐ ⓑ ⓒ ⓓ
82. ⓐ ⓑ ⓒ ⓓ
83. ⓐ ⓑ ⓒ ⓓ
84. ⓐ ⓑ ⓒ ⓓ
85. ⓐ ⓑ ⓒ ⓓ
86. ⓐ ⓑ ⓒ ⓓ
87. ⓐ ⓑ ⓒ ⓓ
88. ⓐ ⓑ ⓒ ⓓ
89. ⓐ ⓑ ⓒ ⓓ
90. ⓐ ⓑ ⓒ ⓓ

Reading

Directions: Each of the following questions is followed by four answer choices. Choose the best answer choice by filling in the corresponding answer choice on your answer sheet.

Answer questions 1–2 based on the following passage.

Man first stepped on the Moon on July 21, 1969, when Neil Armstrong put his left boot on the surface of the satellite. In the four years that followed, 11 more people walked on the Moon. But since 1972, human beings have not returned.

Given all the advancements in technology since 1972, it might seem unusual that mankind has not attempted another Moon landing. The truth is, however, that trips to the Moon are extraordinarily expensive. The Apollo program, responsible for sending all 12 men to the Moon, cost nearly $150 billion in today's dollars. In contrast, NASA's 2009 budget was $17.2 billion. When the United States entered a recession in the 1970s, it became impossible to justify the exorbitant public costs to return to the Moon.

1. The purpose of the first paragraph is to
   a. describe the danger and thrill of going to the Moon.
   b. tell about the events of the Apollo 13 mission.
   c. provide a short account of the brief history of walks on the Moon.
   d. present an alternative use of public funding than space travel.

2. What is the primary reason that the United States has not sent astronauts to the Moon since 1972?
   a. The cost of the mission would be too expensive.
   b. Astronauts are not trained properly for such a mission.
   c. There is no new scientific knowledge to be gained from the trip.
   d. NASA no longer has the proper technology.

3. What conclusion can you draw from the bar graph shown below?

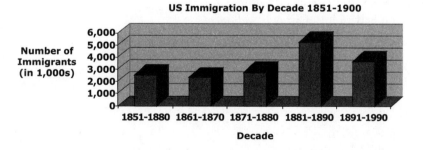

US Immigration By Decade 1851-1900

Number of Immigrants (in 1,000s) / Decade: 1851-1880, 1861-1870, 1871-1880, 1881-1890, 1891-1990

   a. The decade from 1881–1890 had a greater number of immigrants than in any decade in America's history.
   b. About half as many immigrants came to the United States during the 1850s than during the 1880s.
   c. People came to the United States during the second half of the 20th century to find work and avoid persecution.
   d. Most immigrants came to the United States during the 1800s from Germany, England, and Ireland.

Answer questions 4–5 based on the following passage.

Of all the birds in the sky, none is more stunning than the legendary California condor. As a type of vulture, the condor's head is mostly bald, but its body is covered in beautiful black feathers. If you are lucky enough to see one, you will be stunned by its size and speed. The length of its wingspan can be nearly 10 feet across, and they can fly at speeds of up to 55 miles per hour! The condor's bald head can also change colors to match the mood of the animal. The California condor nearly went extinct during the 1980s when there were only 23 left in the world. But thanks to the success of a captive breeding program, the condor is making a comeback. There are now more than 350 California condors roaming the skies of the American west.

4. The passage mentions all of the following about the California condor EXCEPT its
   a. size.
   b. speed.
   c. physical appearance.
   d. diet.

5. Which of the following sentences from the passage is an example of an opinion?
   a. "Of all the birds . . . California condor."
   b. "As a type of vulture . . . black feathers."
   c. "The length of its wingspan . . . miles per hour!"
   d. "There are now more than . . . American west."

6. Perhaps the most famous home run in baseball history was hit off the bat of the New York Giants' Bobby Thompson in a 1951 playoff game against the Brooklyn Dodgers. The home run won the game for the Giants, and sent them to the World Series to face the New York Yankees. The big hit became known as "the shot heard 'round the world." The home run earned this nickname because many American soldiers fighting in Korea had been listening to the game on their radios.

The primary purpose of this passage is to
   a. tell about the most incredible home runs in baseball history.
   b. explain how a local sporting event had an international audience.
   c. describe the events of the 1951 World Series.
   d. provide a historical account of the U.S. involvement in the Korean War.

Answer questions 7–9 based on the passage below.

(1) During any military operation it is critical to keep communications secret. (2) Soldiers sometimes try to translate their messages into a complicated code so that the enemy cannot understand them. (3) At the beginning of World War II, a veteran had a terrific idea: Use the Navajo language used by some Native Americans for top-secret communications.

(4) The Navajo language is one of the most complicated languages on the planet. (5) It uses grammar and tones that are unlike other known languages. (6) There are also dialects within the language that make it even more difficult for non-speakers to understand. (7) In fact, the language was once so unusual that very few people outside of the Navajo lands knew how to speak or understand it. (8) Because of these qualities, it was a perfect code to use overseas in wartime. (9) Whereas coding machines could take a half an hour to turn an English message into a secret code, the Navajo speakers could do it in less than a minute. (10) The people who used the Navajo language for the U.S. military were called the Navajo "code talkers." (11) The code talkers were involved in every battle involving the U.S. Marines in the Pacific from 1942 until the war's end in 1945.

7. The author mentions that every Marine battle in the Pacific from 1942–1945 involved the Navajo code talkers for which likely reason?
   a. to show the importance of the Navajo language during World War II
   b. to describe the U.S. dominance during the mid-twentieth century
   c. to explain the difficulties in learning the Navajo language
   d. to show how hard it was to translate a secret message using a machine

8. The Navajo language was used by the U.S. military to send secret messages for all of the following reasons EXCEPT
   a. it was not spoken by many people.
   b. it uses unusual grammar.
   c. it was important to keep the language alive.
   d. its speakers could translate a code faster than a machine.

9. The meaning of the word *turn* in sentence 9, in context of the passage, most likely means
   a. rotate.
   b. flip.
   c. translate.
   d. refuse.

A Biography of Ronald Reagan

TABLE OF CONTENTS

Answer questions 10–11 based on the following table of contents.

10. The chapters in the book are organized by
 a. time.
 b. area.
 c. importance.
 d. interest.

11. If a reader wanted to learn about the jobs that Ronald Reagan had in the 1950s, in which chapter should he or she look?
 a. Chapter 1
 b. Chapter 2
 c. Chapter 3
 d. Chapter 4

Answer questions 12–13 based on the following passage.

Jessica and I sat under the shade of an oak tree in the middle of a large, green field. Jessica seemed bored, unsure what to do with herself. "What do you want to do?" she asked.

"This," I said, smiling slightly but still facing up toward the bright sky. "If you watch the clouds for a while, you can see some amazing stuff."

"I don't see anything," said Jessica, impatiently.

"Just wait and watch," I told her.

A few moments later, Jessica pointed to a small, fluffy cloud floating low over the horizon. "Doesn't that look like a lobster?" she asked.

I nodded. "And it looks like it's running away from that bear," I told her, pointing to a darker tower of clouds floating toward the lobster. Jessica laughed and looked for more patterns in the clouds.

12. The narrator in the story thinks that watching clouds is
   a. boring.
   b. scary.
   c. tiring.
   d. entertaining.

13. The passage talks about two children who are
   a. unsure of what to do with themselves.
   b. playing sports on a big field.
   c. getting ready to prepare a gigantic meal.
   d. amusing themselves using their imaginations.

Answer questions 14–15 based on the following passage.

There are about 40,000 different species of spiders in the world, living on every continent but Antarctica. Scientists have been studying spiders for many years, but a recent discovery has changed a common perception about the eight-legged creatures. A species of spider, named *Bagheera kiplingi,* was the first spider observed to have a mostly vegetarian diet. This tropical spider, native to Mexico and Costa Rica, hops onto plants and eats their buds.

14. The passage suggests that most spiders
   a. are dangerous creatures.
   b. are meat-eaters.
   c. live in Antarctica.
   d. eat the buds of plants.

15. The author of the passage was likely interested in
  a. describing an unusual scientific discovery.
  b. telling how all spiders are the same.
  c. describing the beauty of Mexico and Costa Rica.
  d. scaring readers with creepy stories about spiders.

Answer questions 16–18 based on the following passage.

There is one organism that you will find in almost any lake, pond, sea, or ocean: plankton. Plankton generally drift in the water and move only when the currents carry them. Although some plankton can be big, such as jellyfish, most types of plankton are tiny. Many are even too small to see with the naked eye, and must be seen through a microscope.

Though they may be small, plankton play a hugely important role in underwater ecosystems. Newborn fish rely on plankton for food. Shellfish, such as oysters, also feed on plankton. Larger fish then eat the animals that eat the plankton. In fact, some whales, among the largest animals on earth, eat nothing but krill—a certain type of plankton.

16. How is the second paragraph organized?
  a. The events are told in the order in which they happened.
  b. A fact is presented and then followed by several opinions.
  c. Each side of a scientific argument is provided.
  d. A broad statement is offered and then backed up with details.

17. The passage says all of the following facts about plankton EXCEPT that
  a. jellyfish are a type of plankton.
  b. many animals use plankton for food.
  c. an oyster is a type of plankton.
  d. plankton are usually very small.

18. Which conclusion can be most likely inferred from the passage?
  a. Plankton are poisonous to human beings.
  b. Some plankton can grow as large as a building.
  c. There is a lot of plankton in the seas and oceans.
  d. Plankton can live for many years in the ocean.

Answer questions 19–22 based on the following passage.

(1) It may come as a surprise to learn that one of the most useful inventions of the twentieth century was the result of an accident. (2) It's true: Two scientists created a tube in the 1940s that created microwave energy—but the original purpose of this invention was to help spot enemy aircraft during World War II. (3) It was not until the microwave energy from the tube melted a chocolate bar in an inventor's pocket that the cooking uses became noticeable. (4) As a result, the idea for the microwave developed. The first commercial microwave oven became available shortly thereafter in 1947.

19. A paraprofessional asks the students in a class to tell about the main idea of the passage. Which sentence from a student's answer shows that he or she understands the passage's main idea?
   a. The invention of the microwave was an accident.
   b. Microwaves can cook food quickly.
   c. Microwave energy can be used to spot aircraft.
   d. It is dangerous to keep a chocolate bar in your pocket in front of a microwave oven.

20. Which question can a paraprofessional ask his or her students to find out whether they recognize the discovery that led to the microwave oven?
   a. What kinds of food can you put in a microwave oven?
   b. What happened to the chocolate bar in the inventor's pocket?
   c. In which year was the first commercial microwave oven produced?
   d. Do you have a microwave oven in your kitchen?

21. Students in a classroom are learning about words that begin with blended consonant sounds, such as the words *brother* or *flat*. Which word from the passage also has a beginning sound with blended consonants?
   a. learn
   b. tube
   c. help
   d. spot

22. A student in a classroom does not understand the word *noticeable* from sentence 3. Which approach by a paraprofessional would be most effective to help the student comprehend its meaning?
   a. Using a microwave oven, demonstrate how many objects can be heated or melted.
   b. Tell the student to define what he or she thinks the word *noticeable* means.
   c. Writing out the parts of the word, explain that after the chocolate bar melted, the inventor was "able" to "notice" the microwave's other uses.
   d. Using letter flashcards, have the student spell out the word *noticeable* and then explain what patterns he or she sees in it.

23. A student reads the following sentence in a book:

"Though ten strands together are not even as thick as a normal human hair, the *fine* silky webs of a spider are strong enough to stop and trap large flying insects—and, occasionally, birds."

fine (adjective). 1. pure or clean; 2. thin; 3. superior or excellent; 4. very well.

Which dictionary definition should the student use to understand the meaning of the word *fine* in context?
a. dictionary definition 1
b. dictionary definition 2
c. dictionary definition 3
d. dictionary definition 4

Answer questions 24–26 based on the following passage from a book students are reading.

Juan's Visit to London
Chapter 1: Getting Set

Juan woke up an hour before his alarm clock went off. He had trouble sleeping all night, and now he sat up in his bed in the dark. He was excited for an adventure, but he was also scared to go on an airplane. He had never flown before. He wasn't sure if he could do it.

One by one, the other members of Juan's family woke up. By the time the sun began to rise, they were all together at the kitchen table. Juan could hardly eat.

"What's the matter?" asked Juan's mom.

Juan was quiet for a few moments and then blurted out, "I don't think I can get on an airplane!"

Juan's mother smiled. "Come over here," she said as she walked into the living room. She opened up a book. "Look at this," she said.

Juan's mother flipped the book open to a page showing a castle. There were some funny-looking guards in front of the castle wearing giant black hats. "That's Buckingham Palace, where the Queen of England lives."

She flipped to another page with a picture of a gigantic Ferris wheel, bigger than any he'd ever seen. "That's the London Eye," she said.

Juan's mom then turned to another page. On it was the coolest bridge he'd ever seen. "Is that the London Bridge?" he asked.

His mom nodded. Juan could feel his heart racing. He imagined himself in the places from the book. He wasn't even thinking about the airplane anymore.

Just then Juan's father honked the horn in the car. "Are we ready to go?" he hollered.

24. The following list includes events from the story:
I. Juan's family sat at the kitchen table.
II. Juan's father honked the horn.
III. Juan sat up in his bed.
IV. Juan's mother showed him pictures of London.

A student in the class must put the events in the order that they happened in the story. Which shows the correct order?
a. II, IV, I, III
b. III, IV, I, II
c. I, III, IV, II
d. III, I, IV, II

25. A student can demonstrate his or her comprehension of a story by predicting an event that will happen next. The student can use clues from the story, as well as any other given information, such as the title or author. Which prediction from a student should a paraprofessional use to verify comprehension?
a. Juan will go back to bed.
b. Juan will stay home while his family goes to England.
c. Juan will get in his father's car and get on the plane.
d. Juan will go to the park and play sports.

26. It is important that students can recognize compound words. Which word from the excerpt is an example of a compound word?
a. airplane
b. gigantic
c. hardly
d. imagined

27. The students in a class are working on a lesson about synonyms. Four groups of students write two words that they think are synonyms. Which words are synonyms?
a. two and too
b. tiny and huge
c. rule and ruler
d. student and pupil

Answer questions 28–30 based on the following teacher-created lesson plan.

Prefix Lesson Plan

Objective: Students will apply their knowledge of other words with identical prefixes to determine the likely meaning of an unfamiliar vocabulary word.

Explanation: I will describe the meaning of a prefix, the letter, or group of letters at the beginning of a word that can help to define the word's meaning. The paraprofessional will hand out index cards with different words that include prefixes, including *copilot, replay, extraordinary, bicycle, submarine,* and *unfinished.* Students will then try to define the meaning of each word and determine its prefix, with the aid of the paraprofessional. Once students have correctly separated the prefix from the word, they will work in groups to try to come up with other words that share the same prefix. Groups will then share their results with the class. Students from other groups will also have an opportunity to share other words that share the same prefix. The paraprofessional will then collect all of the index cards from the students and organize them alphabetically.

28. The only action that the paraprofessional will NOT be expected to do is
    a. collect all of the index cards from the students at the end of class.
    b. come up with words with the same prefix as the word on the card.
    c. help students find the prefix of the words on the index cards.
    d. assist students with the definitions of the words on the index cards.

29. One group of students comes up with four words that they think share the same prefix as *bicycle.* Which word best shows that the students comprehend the meaning and use of a prefix?
    a. tricycle
    b. bite
    c. scooter
    d. binocular

30. The students in a class come up with the words *repay, rerun, redo,* and *reuse.* Which list shows these words in alphabetical order?
    a. repay, rerun, redo, reuse
    b. redo, rerun, repay, reuse
    c. redo, repay, rerun, reuse
    d. reuse, repay, redo, rerun

Mathematics

Directions: Each of the following questions is followed by four answer choices. Choose the best answer choice by filling in the corresponding answer choice on your answer sheet. You will NOT be allowed to use a calculator.

31. What is the value of m if $8m = 40$?
 a. 5
 b. 32
 c. 48
 d. 320

DISTANCES SOME STUDENTS LIVE FROM SCHOOL	
Student	**Distance from School (in miles)**
Ray	two-thirds
Maria	two-fifths
Owen	three-eights
Nadine	four-sixths
Zachary	three-tenths

32. The table above shows the distances that five students live from school. How many students listed in the table live less than one-half mile from school?
 a. two
 b. three
 c. four
 d. five

33. $244.66 + 5.25 =$
 a. 239.41
 b. 249.81
 c. 249.91
 d. 769.91

34. Which is equal to two tenths of a percent?
 a. 0.02%
 b. 0.2%
 c. 2%
 d. 200%

35. Which is the best estimate for the product of 497.81 × 2.08?

  a. 500

  b. 1,000

  c. 2,000

  d. 10,000

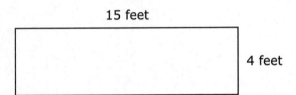

36. The students in a class are working on a rectangular banner for the school play, with dimensions as shown in the diagram above. What is the perimeter of the students' banner?

  a. 19 feet

  b. 28 feet

  c. 38 feet

  d. 60 feet

37. A student is having a hard time understanding how to find the value of 5^3. What is the best way to explain to the student how to solve it?

  a. Multiply 5 by 3, and then multiply the answer by 5 again.

  b. Multiply 3 by itself, and then multiply the answer by 5.

  c. Multiply 3 by 3, and then multiply the answer by 5.

  d. Multiply 5 by itself, and then multiply the answer by 5 again.

38. Between which two numbers would the fraction $\frac{5}{2}$ appear on the number line above?

  a. 0 and 1

  b. 1 and 2

  c. 2 and 3

  d. 4 and 5

39. A student gives a wrong answer to the following problem:

$10 - 5 + (2 + 3) + 4 \times 6$

Which operation should the student do first to get the correct answer?
a. $10 - 5$
b. $(2 + 3)$
c. $3 + 4$
d. 4×6

40. $28 \times 14 =$
a. 216
b. 332
c. 402
d. 432

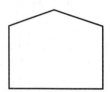

41. Baseball players use a home plate in the shape shown above. What is the name of this shape?
a. Triangle
b. Quadrilateral
c. Pentagon
d. Hexagon

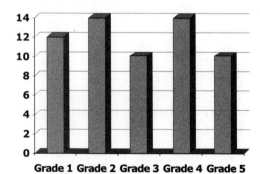

42. The graph above shows the number of girls in each grade of an elementary school. How many girls attend the elementary school in total?
a. 60
b. 58
c. 50
d. 14

43. Which inequality is correct?

    a. $7 - 8 > 0$

    b. $5 - 7 < 0$

    c. $-4 + -6 > -9$

    d. $4 + 5 < 9$

44. The students in a class are working with base-ten blocks to understand the place value system. The teacher has 150 hundreds cubes to distribute to 25 students. How many hundreds cubes can each student get if each student gets the same number of hundreds cubes?

    a. 4

    b. 6

    c. 60

    d. 125

45. There are two fish tanks in a sixth-grade classroom. The tank for the goldfish holds 12 gallons and 1 quart of water. The tank for the tadpoles holds 8 gallons and 2 quarts of water. How much more water does the tank for the goldfish hold?

    a. 3 gallons and 3 quarts

    b. 3 gallons and 9 quarts

    c. 4 gallons and 3 quarts

    d. 20 gallons and 3 quarts

HEIGHT OF A SKYSCRAPER DURING CONSTRUCTION	
Week #	Height (in yards)
1	2.5
2	5
3	7.5
4	10
5	12.5

46. The table above shows the height of a skyscraper after the first five weeks of its construction. If the rate of the construction grows at the same rate, what will the height of the skyscraper be after eight weeks?

    a. 15 yards

    b. 17.5 yards

    c. 19 yards

    d. 20 yards

47. $18 \times 28 =$

A student solves the equation above and gets an answer of 504. How can a paraprofessional suggest that the student check that his or her answer is correct?

a. Divide 28 by 18 and see if the quotient matches the student's original answer, 504.

b. Add 18 and 28 and see whether the student can also find the sum of the two numbers.

c. Divide 504 by 18 and see if the quotient matches the other factor in the problem, 28.

d. Multiply 18 by 504 and also 28 by 504 and then determine the difference between the products.

48. Which set of numbers is in order from greatest to least?

a. $\frac{7}{8}, \frac{2}{5}, \frac{3}{10}$

b. $\frac{2}{5}, \frac{7}{8}, \frac{3}{10}$

c. $\frac{7}{8}, \frac{3}{10}, \frac{2}{5}$

d. $\frac{3}{10}, \frac{2}{5}, \frac{7}{8}$

49. On a short quiz in class, $\frac{1}{3}$ of the students in a class received an A on a quiz. On the same quiz, $\frac{1}{2}$ of the students received a B. What fraction of the students in the class received either an A or a B on the quiz?

a. $\frac{1}{6}$

b. $\frac{2}{6}$

c. $\frac{2}{5}$

d. $\frac{5}{6}$

50. There are two fourth-grade classes in a school. One class has 20 students, and the other class has 24 students. What is the mean (average) number of students in the school's fourth-grade classes?

a. 4

b. 22

c. 24

d. 44

51. A family goes out to dinner together. The total cost of the bill is $60, including tax. The family wants to leave an additional 15% tip on top of the total cost. Which expression can the family use to determine the total amount that should be paid, including the tip?

a. $60 + 60 \times 0.15$

b. 60×0.15

c. $60 + 15$

d. $60 \times 60 \times 0.15$

June	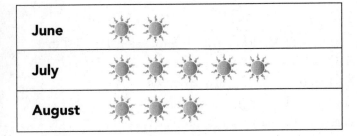
July	
August	

 = **4 sunny days**

52. The graph above shows how many sunny days there were in a town for each of the summer months. How many sunny days were there in July and August?

a. 8

b. 20

c. 28

d. 32

53. 1, 2, 4, 8, 16 . . .

The series of numbers above show the first five terms of a pattern. If the pattern continues, the seventh number in the pattern will be

a. 28.

b. 32.

c. 48.

d. 64.

54. 148.67

Which digit is in the tenths place of the number above?

a. 4

b. 6

c. 7

d. 8

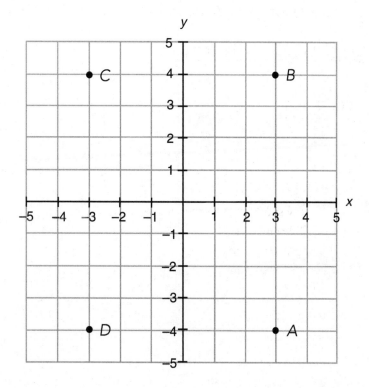

55. Which point on the *xy*-plane above has the ordered pair (3, 4)?
 a. point *A*
 b. point *B*
 c. point *C*
 d. point *D*

56. A student is having a difficult time understanding how to convert a fraction into its decimal value. What direction should a teacher provide to explain how to find the fraction's decimal value?
 a. Divide the numerator of the fraction by its denominator.
 b. Find the common denominator of the fraction.
 c. Divide the denominator of the fraction by its numerator.
 d. Multiply the denominator of the fraction by its numerator.

57. On one autumn day, 20 students wore jackets to school. If there are 25 students in the class, what percentage of the students wore a jacket to school that day?
 a. 1.25%
 b. 20%
 c. 75%
 d. 80%

58. Which of the following groups of coins does NOT equal $1?

a.

b.

c.

d.

59. $\frac{3}{4} \div \frac{1}{2}$

    a. $\frac{3}{8}$

    b. $\frac{3}{6}$

    c. $\frac{3}{2}$

    d. $\frac{6}{4}$

60. Which of the following is equal to 8?

    a. 2^3

    b. 4^2

    c. 1^8

    d. 2^4

Writing

Directions: Questions 61–68 each include a sentence with four parts underlined. One of the four underlined parts will contain an error in grammar, punctuation, or word usage. Each sentence will have exactly one error. Select the letter of the answer choice that corresponds to that error.

61. Mt. Vesuvius, the only <u>active</u> volcano on mainland Europe, last <u>erupts</u> in 1944 but <u>is</u> better known for
               a   **b**   **c**   **d**
destroying Pompeii in 79 A.D.

62. Although the 19th Amendment <u>granted</u> American women the right <u>to vote</u> in 1920<u>;</u> women in New
                                a   **b**   **c**
Zealand <u>had been voting</u> legally since 1893.
        d

63. All of the students <u>in the class</u> <u>works</u> together <u>to create</u> an <u>extraordinarily</u> beautiful collage.
                 a   **b**   **c**   **d**

64. Some large <u>state's</u>, such as Alaska or Montana, <u>do</u> not have as many residents as smaller,
              a   **b**
<u>more densely populated</u> states, <u>such as</u> New Jersey or Massachusetts.
        c   **d**

65. <u>Each of</u> New York's three largest daily newspapers <u>experienced</u> a dramatic <u>decrease</u> in <u>their</u> circulations
     a   **b**   **c**   **d**
between April 2008 and October 2008.

66. Although slow-moving manatees <u>are</u> most <u>frequent</u> seen in the warm waters of Florida, <u>they</u> <u>have been</u>
                             a   **b**   **c**   **d**
spotted as far north as Cape Cod.

67. The <u>majestic</u> American <u>eagle,</u> once an endangered species in the continental United States, <u>are</u> now
      a   **b**   **c**
thriving <u>in many areas</u> of the country.
        d

68. The manager of the grocery store <u>unloaded</u> the produce from the truck, carried the crates <u>into</u> the store,
                              a   **b**
and <u>than</u> stocked the <u>market's</u> shelves.
    c   **d**

Directions: Answer questions 69–90 by selecting the answer choice that best answers the given question or completes the statement. Fill in the corresponding answer choice on your answer sheet.

69. The ceiling of the Sistine Chapel, painted by Michelangelo during a four-year period in the 1500s, is both expansive and <u>exquisitely</u> detailed.

The underlined word in the sentence above is an example of
a. an adverb.
b. an adjective.
c. a noun.
d. a verb.

70. For many years thought of as a food for the underprivileged, lobster is now considered a delicacy.

What is the subject of the sentence above?
a. years
b. food
c. lobster
d. delicacy

71. Before it became America's 49th state, the territory of Alaska was purchased from Russian empire <u>for</u> the paltry sum of $7.2 million.

The underlined word in the sentence above is an example of
a. a preposition.
b. a verb.
c. an adverb.
d. an adjective.

72. Leaner and higher in iron, buffalo meat is considered by many diners to be a healthier alternative to beef.

What is the subject of the sentence above?
a. iron
b. buffalo meat
c. diners
d. beef

73. Many professional hockey players wore them before then, but helmets were not mandatory in the NHL until 1979.

Which word from the sentence above is a pronoun?
a. many
b. them
c. were
d. until

74. While the enemy's army slept on Christmas Eve, 1776, George Washington's army planned a successful surprise Christmas battle.

Which word from the sentence above is the simple predicate?
a. slept
b. planned
c. surprise
d. battle

75. Which of the following words is NOT spelled properly?
a. rustle
b. banter
c. rambel
d. jacket

76. Which of the following words is NOT spelled properly?
a. magazine
b. tornado
c. sincere
d. presedent

77. Which of the following words is NOT spelled properly?
a. arogant
b. laundry
c. confident
d. accurate

78. Which of the following words is NOT spelled properly?
a. rench
b. unique
c. nuclear
d. vinegar

79. A student is trying to understand the rule for creating contractions, such as *it's*. Which is a true statement about contractions?

   a. The apostrophe should always come before the letter *S*.

   b. Contractions should only be used when there is more than one of something.

   c. Contractions stand for a noun or a noun phrase.

   d. The apostrophe stands for a missing letter or letters.

Answer questions 80–81 based on the following passage, which is a rough draft written by a fourth-grade student.

Cats Are Better Than Dogs
by Lewis, 4th Grade
(1) Cats do not smell badly like some dogs I know. (2) They actually clean themselves. (3) My friend Danielle has a dog and she has to walk it every morning. (4) You do not need to walk a cat. (5) Cats are very easy to take care of. (6) You only need to feed cats. (7) You also need to change their water and clean their litter often. (7) They will give you a lot of love in return.

80. Lewis wants to add a sentence to the beginning of his essay that will help explain the main idea of his argument. Which would be the best sentence for Lewis to add?

   a. My cat's name is Jibboo.

   b. Some people like dogs more than cats, but I think cats are better.

   c. There are lots of different types of pets that people can have.

   d. Cats are really funny and can make you laugh.

81. Which sentence could Lewis add to his draft to make his argument stronger?

   a. Cats keep you warm during the winter when they curl up in your lap.

   b. Sometimes cats can destroy furniture because they like to use their claws.

   c. Dogs are amazing how they can catch Frisbees in their mouths.

   d. Unfortunately, a lot of people are allergic to cats.

82. How could Lewis combine sentences 6 and 7 from his draft so that he makes a new sentence which conveys the same information, and is clear and correct?

   a. You need to feed cats, change their water, and clean their litter.

   b. You not only need to feed cats, you also need to change their water and clean their litter often.

   c. The only things you need to do for cats are feed them and change their water.

   d. You need to feed cats, and change their water, and also clean their litter.

Answer questions 83–84 based on the following outline, written by a sixth-grade student. The student will use the outline to write a school paper about Antarctica.

Antarctica

I. Basic Facts

    A. Geography

        1. Location at South Pole

    B. Weather

        1. Considered a desert

        2. Coldest continent

II. History

    A. Geology

        1. More than 170 million years ago

        2. _____

        3. Modern day

    B. Discovery

        1. First sighting in 1820

        2. Nimrod Expedition in 1907

        3. First to South Pole in 1911

    C. Politics

        1. Belongs to no country

        2. Antarctic Treaty in 1959

III. Animals

    A. Penguins

        1. Emperor penguin

        2. King penguin

        3. Chinstrap penguin

    B. Seals

        1. Weddell seal

        2. Antarctic fur seal

IV. Environment

    A. Ice Mass

        1. Covered with ice 1 mile thick

        2. Has 70% of Earth's freshwater

    B. Climate Change

        1. Temperatures increasing

        2. Ice shelf collapses

83. The student wants to add information about the whales that live in the oceans around Antarctica. In which section of her outline should she add it?

a. I. Basic Facts

b. II. History

c. III. Animals

d. IV. Environment

84. The student accidentally left out some information in section II. What information should go on the blank space in that section?

a. The future of Antarctica

b. Who the pilot was on the first airplane to land on Antarctica

c. Other birds that live on and around the Australian continent

d. The geological history of Antarctica between 170 million years ago and now

Answer questions 85–87 based on the following set of directions, written by a fifth-grade student.

How to Plant a Tree
by Tameka, 5th Grade

(1) The first thing to do before planting a tree is to figure out where and when to plant it. (2) In general, you don't want to plant a tree in the summer. (3) You should also choose a location that makes sense for the type of tree you're going to plant. (4) Once you have found a good time and a good spot, dig a hole that is a good size for the tree. (5) Be very gentle placing the tree into the hole, tree roots are very fragile. (6) Add fertilizer or compost if the soil needs it. (7) Once the plant is in the ground, give it some water. (8) Put mulch on top of the soil to keep weeds away. (9) Water it again. (10) Finally, enjoy watching your tree grow tall and beautiful.

85. Tameka thinks that her set of instructions would be easier to understand if she split it into two paragraphs. Before which sentence should she break her directions into a new paragraph?
   a. sentence 3
   b. sentence 4
   c. sentence 6
   d. sentence 7

86. Tameka wants to add transitions to her set of directions to make it easier to understand. Which transition word or words would improve sentence 5 before the word *tree*?
   a. therefore
   b. in other words
   c. however
   d. because

87. The people who will be reading Tameka's directions will not know much about gardening. As a result, how could she improve her set of directions for her audience?
   a. Define the words *mulch* and *compost*
   b. Remove several of the steps
   c. Describe in detail why each step is so important
   d. Separate the set of directions into many paragraphs

Answer questions 88–89 based on the following passage, which has examples from different types of reading materials.

Students in a classroom are learning how different types of writing may have different purposes. The list below shows a sentence from four different reading materials in the classroom.

1. Step 3: Rub your hands with soap for 20 seconds before rinsing them with warm water.
2. Billy the Beaver ran to his friend Bob the Bear and said he needed help with his dam.
3. Theodore Roosevelt was born on October 27, 1858, in Manhattan, New York City.
4. We strongly believe that a longer recess will improve students' attitudes and behaviors during the day.

88. Which sentence looks as if its purpose is to persuade the reader of something?
   a. sentence 1
   b. sentence 2
   c. sentence 3
   d. sentence 4

89. Which sentence seems to have been taken from a book whose purpose is to tell an entertaining story?
   a. sentence 1
   b. sentence 2
   c. sentence 3
   d. sentence 4

90. A student wants to learn about the habitat of loggerhead turtles. Which would be the best resource for the student to use to get this information?
   a. a tale about a talking turtle
   b. the dictionary entry for *loggerhead* and *turtle*
   c. an encyclopedia article about loggerhead turtles
   d. a picture book of underwater animals

Answers and Explanations

Question Number	Correct Answer	Content Category
1	c	Reading Skills: Main idea/primary purpose
2	a	Reading Skills: Main idea/primary purpose
3	b	Reading Skills: Interpreting graphic text
4	d	Reading Skills: Supporting ideas
5	a	Reading Skills: Fact/opinion
6	b	Reading Skills: Main idea/primary purpose
7	a	Reading Skills: Organization
8	c	Reading Skills: Supporting ideas
9	c	Reading Skills: Vocabulary in context
10	a	Reading Skills: Interpreting graphic text
11	b	Reading Skills: Interpreting graphic text
12	d	Reading Skills: Inferences
13	d	Reading Skills: Main idea/primary purpose
14	b	Reading Skills: Inferences
15	a	Reading Skills: Main idea/primary purpose
16	d	Reading Skills: Organization
17	c	Reading Skills: Supporting ideas
18	c	Reading Skills: Inferences
19	a	Reading Application: Making accurate observations
20	b	Reading Application: Asking questions
21	d	Reading Application: Sounding out words
22	c	Reading Application: Decoding words using context clues
23	b	Reading Application: Using a dictionary
24	d	Reading Application: Making accurate observations
25	c	Reading Application: Making predictions

Question Number	Correct Answer	Content Category (continued)
26	a	Reading Application: Breaking down words into parts
27	d	Reading Application: Synonyms, antonyms, and homonyms
28	b	Reading Application: Interpreting directions
29	d	Reading Application: Breaking down words into parts
30	c	Reading Application: Alphabetizing words
31	a	Math Skills: Number sense and basic algebra
32	b	Math Skills: Number sense and basic algebra
33	c	Math Skills: Number sense and basic algebra
34	b	Math Skills: Number sense and basic algebra
35	b	Math Skills: Number sense and basic algebra
36	c	Math Application: Geometry and measurement
37	d	Math Application: Number sense and basic algebra
38	c	Math Skills: Number sense and basic algebra
39	b	Math Application: Number sense and basic algebra
40	d	Math Skills: Number sense and basic algebra
41	c	Math Skills: Geometry and measurement
42	a	Math Application: Number sense and basic algebra
43	b	Math Skills: Number sense and basic algebra
44	b	Math Application: Number sense and basic algebra
45	a	Math Application: Geometry and measurement
46	d	Math Skills: Data analysis
47	c	Math Application: Number sense and basic algebra
48	a	Math Skills: Number sense and basic algebra
49	d	Math Application: Number sense and basic algebra
50	b	Math Application: Data analysis
51	a	Math Skills: Number sense and basic algebra
52	d	Math Skills: Number sense and basic algebra

Question Number	Correct Answer	Content Category (continued)
53	d	Math Skills: Number sense and basic algebra
54	b	Math Skills: Number sense and basic algebra
55	b	Math Skills: Geometry and measurement
56	a	Math Application: Number sense and basic algebra
57	d	Math Application: Number sense and basic algebra
58	c	Math Skills: Geometry and measurement
59	d	Math Skills: Number sense and basic algebra
60	a	Math Skills: Number sense and basic algebra
61	c	Writing Skills: Grammatical errors
62	c	Writing Skills: Errors in punctuation
63	b	Writing Skills: Grammatical errors
64	a	Writing Skills: Errors in punctuation
65	d	Writing Skills: Grammatical errors
66	b	Writing Skills: Grammatical errors
67	c	Writing Skills: Grammatical errors
68	c	Writing Skills: Error in word usage
69	a	Writing Skills: Parts of speech
70	c	Writing Skills: Parts of a sentence
71	a	Writing Skills: Parts of speech
72	b	Writing Skills: Parts of a sentence
73	b	Writing Skills: Parts of speech
74	b	Writing Skills: Parts of a sentence
75	c	Writing Skills: Spelling
76	d	Writing Skills: Spelling
77	a	Writing Skills: Spelling
78	a	Writing Skills: Spelling
79	d	Writing Application: Editing written documents

Question Number	Correct Answer	Content Category (continued)
80	b	Writing Application: Drafting and revising
81	a	Writing Application: Writing in different modes and forms
82	a	Writing Application: Editing written documents
83	c	Writing Application: Prewriting
84	d	Writing Application: Prewriting
85	b	Writing Application: Drafting and revising
86	d	Writing Application: Editing written documents
87	a	Writing Application: Writing for different purposes and audiences
88	d	Writing Application: Writing in different modes and forms
89	b	Writing Application: Writing in different modes and forms
90	c	Writing Application: Reference materials

1. c. The paragraph tells when the first man landed on the Moon, how many men have been to the Moon, and when the last person went to the Moon. It does not talk about the danger of going to the Moon, choice **a**, nor does it tell anything specifically about Apollo 13, choice **b**. The costs of space travel are not mentioned until the second paragraph. The first paragraph is a summary of our walks on the Moon, choice **c**.

2. a. The passage mentions how expensive a trip to the Moon is, choice **a**. It does not provide any information about the explanations in choices **b**, **c**, or **d**.

3. b. Although 1881–1890 shows a greater number of immigrants than in any decade on the chart, the chart does not show every decade in America's history—so you do not know if choice **a** is correct. The graph does not tell from where the immigrants came, or why, so choices **c** and **d** are not possible. You can compare the heights of the bars in the graph to tell that about half as many immigrants came to the United States during the 1850s than during the 1880s, choice **b**.

4. d. The passage mentions the size (very large), speed (very fast), and physical appearance (bald and black) of the California condor—but it does not mention the condor's diet, choice **d**.

5. a. An opinion is a statement that cannot be proven. The sentences in choices **b**, **c**, and **d** are all facts. The sentence in choice **a**, saying the condor is the most "stunning bird," cannot be proven.

6. b. The passage is only about one home run, so choice **a** is not correct. Because the call of the home run was listened to by soldiers all over the world, it had an international audience, choice **b**. The game was not a part of the 1951 World Series, choice **c**. While the passage mentions the U.S. involvement in Korea, choice **d**, it only does so by explaining how soldiers were listening to a baseball game in New York.

7. a. Because every Marine battle in the Pacific from 1942–1945 involved the Navajo code talkers, the Navajo language must have been important, as in choice **a**. While the statements made in choices **b**, **c**, and **d** may be true, the fact that the code talkers were very involved from 1942–1945 does not prove those facts.

8. c. The passage mentions all of the reasons in choices **a**, **b**, and **d** to explain why the Navajo language was used by the U.S. military, but it does not say that it was important to keep the language alive, choice **c**.

9. c. If you replace the words *rotate*, *flip*, *translate*, and *refuse* with the word *turn* from the passage, the only word that makes sense is *translate*, choice **c**.

10. a. Each chapter lists the years that the events take place, so the chapters in the book are in order by time, choice **a**.

11. b. Because the book is organized in chronological order, an event that happened in the 1950s should appear in Chapter 2, choice **b**, which covers the time from 1932 to 1965.

12. d. Maybe Jessica thinks that watching clouds is boring, choice **a**, or tiring, choice **c**, but the narrator in the story is entertained by watching the clouds, choice **d**.

13. d. The passage is about two children who are pretending to see animals in the clouds. They are not playing sports, choice **b**, or preparing a meal, choice **c**. Jessica is initially unsure of what do, but then she learns to amuse herself, along with the narrator, using her imagination, choice **d**.

14. b. Since the passage tells about the only known vegetarian spider, you can infer that all other spiders are meat-eaters, choice **b**.

15. a. The passage is about an unusual spider, so the author is definitely not saying all the spiders are the same, choice **b**, or that spiders are creepy, choice **d**. The author does not focus on Mexico and Costa Rica, choice **c**. The author most likely wanted to share an interesting discovery, choice **a**.

16. d. The first sentence of the second paragraph says that plankton are very important. The rest of the paragraph goes on to explain why. That sums up the organization of the paragraph provided in choice **d**.

17. c. The passage lists jellyfish as a type of plankton, says that animals eat plankton, and that plankton are usually tiny. It mentions oysters as an example of animals that eat plankton, so choice **c** is not a fact about plankton.

18. c. The passage says that many animals eat plankton, including whales. That must mean there is a lot of plankton! The statements in choices **a**, **b**, and **d** are not supported by the passage at all, making **c** the correct answer.

19. a. The main idea of the passage is that the microwave was invented by accident. If a student provided the main idea listed in choice **a**, then he or she has a good idea of what the passage is about.

20. b. It was the melting of a chocolate bar in the inventor's pocket which let to the discovery of the microwave oven. The paraprofessional should ask his or her students about this event to find out whether or not they recognize the important discovery.

21. d. The only word in the answer choices that begins with blended consonants is *spot*, choice **d**, because it starts with a *sp-* sound.

22. c. It would be most helpful for a student to see how a long word like *noticeable* can be broken down into smaller parts that are more easily understood. The only approach that does this is listed in choice **c**.

23. b. The word *fine*, as it is used in the sentence, is not intended to mean *pure*, **a**, *excellent*, choice **c**, or *well*, choice **d**. Because the passage tells about how thin the web is, dictionary definition 2, choice **b**, should be used.

24. d. The first thing that happened in the story is that Juan sat up on his bed. That eliminates choices **a** and **c** and leaves the order of events listed in choices **b** and **d**. Because Juan's family then sat at the kitchen table before his mother showed him pictures of London, the order in choice **d** must be correct.

25. c. Students should recognize that Juan is excited and not worried about getting on the plane by the end of the story. Therefore, the most likely prediction of the choices given would be that Juan will get on the plane, choice **c**.

26. a. A compound word can be split into two words. The only word listed in the choices that can be split into two words is airplane, choice **a**, which can be split into *air* and *plane*.

27. d. Synonyms are words that mean the same thing. The words in choice **a** are homonyms (which means they sound the same) and the words in choice **b** are antonyms (which have opposite meanings). The words in choice **d** mean approximately the same thing, so they are synonyms.

28. b. Carefully read the lesson plan and get rid of any actions that the paraprofessional is expected to do. The parapro must collect all the index cards, help students find the prefixes, and come up with definitions of the words. The paraprofessional is *not* expected to come up with words with the same prefix as the words on the card—that is the students' job—so choice **b** is correct.

29. d. A prefix is the first part of a word. So, for another word to share the same prefix as *bicycle*, it must also start with the letters *bi-*, which means "two." While the word *bite* also starts with *bi-*, that is not a prefix because it

does not mean "two." The word *binocular*, choice **d**, shares the same prefix.

30. c. Students who organized the words in the order listed in **c**. will have put the words in alphabetical order.

31. a. If a number and a variable are joined together like 8*m*, it means they are multiplied together. You need to find the value for *m*, that, when multiplied by 8, is equal to 40. You can divide both sides of the equation by 8 to find the answer. $40 \div 8 = 5$, so choice **a** is the correct answer.

32. b. The students who live less than one-half mile from school are Maria (two-fifths), Owen (three-eights), and Zachary (three-tenths). So there are three students in total, choice **b**.

33. c. When adding or subtracting decimals, be sure to align the numbers by place value first. If you got choice **b**, you forgot to regroup the 10 hundredths into one tenth for the final sum. If you align the numbers and regroup properly, you will get 249.91, choice **c**.

34. b. Two-tenths of a percent is equivalent to 0.2%.

35. b. To find an estimate for 497.81×2.08, round the factors to numbers that are easy to multiply, such as 500×2. The best estimate is 1,000, choice **b**.

36. c. The perimeter is the distance around a figure. In the case of a rectangle, it is the sum of the two lengths and the two widths. The given figure provides the length and the width of the rectangle. To find the complete perimeter, each side needs to be counted twice. 15 feet + 15 feet + 4 feet + 4 feet = 38 feet, choice **c**.

37. d. To solve an exponent, multiply the base number by itself the number of times of the power. In the case of 5^3, 5 is the base number and 3 is the power. To solve it, 5 should be multiplied by itself 3 times, or $5 \times 5 \times 5$, choice **d**.

38. c. The improper fraction $\frac{5}{2}$ is equivalent to 2.5. Therefore, it should be between the numbers 2 and 3 on the number line.

39. b. The first step to solving any expression or equation is to perform any operation within a set of parentheses. In this expression for this problem, $(2 + 3)$, choice **b**, should be solved first.

40. d. If you chose **a**, you misread the symbol as addition. If you chose **b**, you forgot to include a zero as a placeholder during the multiplication algorithm. If you chose **c**, you made a regrouping error. The correct product of 28 and 14 is 392, choice **d**.

41. c. A polygon with five sides is called a pentagon, choice **c**. A quadrilateral, choice **b**, has four sides and a hexagon, choice **d**, has six sides.

42. a. Each bar represents the number of girls in each grade of an elementary school. To find the total number of girls in the school in total, you must add the numbers from each grade. Based on the data from the graph, that should be $12 + 14 + 10 + 14 + 10 = 60$, choice **a**.

43. b. Remember that the sign in an inequality points to the smaller number. Because negative numbers are smaller than zero, choice **a** is not correct. The inequalities in choices **c** and **d** are also incorrect. $5 - 7 = -2$, so $-2 < 0$; thus choice **b** is correct.

44. b. To solve this problem, divide 150 cubes by the 25 students. The quotient is 6, choice **b**, so that each student will get 6 hundreds cubes.

45. a. This question asks for the difference between the volumes of the two fish tanks. The larger tank is 12 gallons and 1 quart; the smaller tank is 8 gallons and 2 quarts. There are 4

quarts in 1 gallon, so you can regroup 12 gallons and 1 quart to 11 gallons and 5 quarts. Then it will be easier to subtract 8 gallons and 2 quarts and see that the answer is 3 gallons and 3 quarts, choice **a**.

46. d. The skyscraper is growing at a rate of 2.5 yards per week. That means that after eight weeks, it will be 2.5×8, or 20 yards tall (choice **d**). You can continue the table if it is easier to solve that way.

47. c. Multiplication and division are inverse operations. Therefore, division can be used to check the answer to a multiplication problem and vice versa. The scenario provided in choice **c** is the best way for a student to check that his or her answer is correct.

48. a. The most surefire way to compare or order fractions is to give them like denominators. Then all you have to do is compare the numerators (the numbers on the top). $\frac{7}{8} = \frac{(7 \times 5)}{(8 \times 5)} = \frac{35}{40}$, $\frac{2}{5} = \frac{(2 \times 8)}{(5 \times 8)} = \frac{16}{40}$, $\frac{3}{10} = \frac{(3 \times 4)}{(10 \times 4)} = \frac{12}{40}$. Because $35 > 16 > 12$, $\frac{7}{8} > \frac{2}{5} > \frac{3}{10}$. This order matches the sequence listed in choice **a**.

49. d. To find the total fraction of students who received either an A or a B on the quiz, the fractions representing each grade must be added. To add fractions, they must have the same denominator. Then you can simply add the numerators, keeping the denominator the same. $\frac{1}{3} + \frac{1}{2} = \frac{2}{6} + \frac{3}{6} = \frac{5}{6}$, choice **d**.

50. b. To find the mean (average) of any set of numbers, add all of the numbers together and then divide the sum by the number of values added. In this case, 20 and 24 are added together to get 44. Because there are two values, 44 must be divided by 2 to find the mean. The answer is 22, choice **c**.

51. a. To convert a number into a percentage, multiply the number by the decimal equivalent of the percent. So, to find a 15% tip on a $60 bill, multiply 60 by 0.15. But because the problem is asking for the *total* amount to be paid, the original $60 must also be included. That means $60 + (60 \times 0.15)$, choice **a**.

52. d. Each sun icon in the pictograph represents four sunny days. To find out the number of sunny days in July and August, count the sun icons in July and August, and then multiply the sum by 4. $(5 + 3) = 8; 8 \times 4 = 32$, choice **d**. If you chose **a**, you probably did not notice the key that says each sun represents four days. Always check to see if there's a key providing additional information.

53. d. Each term in the pattern is twice as large as the previous term. The fifth term is 16, so the sixth term will be 32. The seventh term will then be twice as large as the sixth term, or 64, choice **d**.

54. b. The tenths place is the first place value directly to the right of the decimal point. Be careful not to confuse tens and tenths; if you see the place value end in *-ths*, it is asking about a place to the right of the decimal point.

55. b. An ordered pair will always list the *x*-coordinate first, and the *y*-coordinate second. In this problem, you are looking for a point that is three units to the right of 0, and four units up. That is point *B*, choice **b**.

56. a. A fraction is simply another way to show division. For students who do not know how to translate a fraction into a decimal, showing them how to divide the numerator by the denominator (choice **a**) will show them how fractions and decimals are related.

57. d. Twenty students out of 25 is equal $20 \div 25$, or 0.80. To translate a decimal into a percent, move the decimal point two places to the right and add a percent symbol. That will result in the percent 80%, choice **d**.

58. c. The only combination of coins that does not add up to exactly one dollar is choice **c**: 3 quarters ($0.75), 2 dimes ($0.20), and 3

nickels ($0.15). If you regroup properly, you will find that the sum of those coins is $1.10.

59. d. To divide a fraction by a fraction, change the symbol to a multiplication symbol and then flip the second fraction upside-down. Therefore, $\frac{3}{4} \div \frac{1}{2}$ is equal to $\frac{3}{4} \times \frac{2}{1}$. Then you can simply multiply across: $\frac{3}{4} \times \frac{2}{1} = \frac{(3 \times 2)}{(4 \times 1)} = \frac{6}{4}$, choice **d**.

60. a. 2^3 is equivalent to $2 \times 2 \times 2$, which is 8, so choice **a** is correct. 4^2 is equal to 4×4, which is 16. 1^8 is equal to $1 \times 1 \times 1 \times 1 \times 1 \times 1 \times 1 \times 1$, which is 1. 2^4 is equal to $2 \times 2 \times 2 \times 2$, which is 16.

61. c. The event from the sentence occurred completely in the past, so the verb should also be in the past tense; *erupts* should be *erupted* (choice **c**).

62. c. A semicolon should be used to separate an independent thought; a comma would be more appropriate in this instance.

63. b. The subject of the sentence (*students*) is plural, so the verb should match the subject. In the given sentence, *works* is singular and incorrect; it should be *work* instead. A student works; students work.

64. a. Pluralized words do not need apostrophes. In this sentence, the plural word *states* should not have an apostrophe, so choice **a** is the correct answer.

65. d. Be careful with pronouns. The pronoun *their* is used for plural items. However, the subject of this sentence is actually the word *each*, which is singular.

66. b. The word *frequent* is being used to describe how often manatees are seen. Because it describes the verb, it is an adverb—and therefore should be written as *frequently* instead of *frequent*.

67. c. This sentence is about the American eagle, a single entity. As such, the corresponding verb, *are*, should be singular as well: *is*.

68. c. The difference between *then* and *than* can be very confusing. However, the word *then* is always used to show a change in time or a sequence.

69. a. Almost any word that ends in *-ly* will be an adverb. Because the underlined word (*exquisitely*) is being used to describe how detailed the ceiling was (and it is telling about an adjective), it is indeed an adverb, choice **a**.

70. c. Even though the word does not appear until the 12th word in the sentence, *lobster* (choice c) is the subject of the sentence; the first part of the sentence is being used to describe lobsters.

71. a. Words like *of*, *for*, or *to* are all prepositions. The phrases *for the paltry sum* and *of $7.2 million* from the sentence are both examples of prepositional phrases, so the underlined word *for* (choice **a**) is the correct answer.

72. b. The first part of the sentence, including the mention of iron, is referring to buffalo meat; *diners* and *beef* are parts of prepositional phrases. The subject is the buffalo meat, choice **b**.

73. b. A pronoun is a word used in place of a thing or a group. In this case, the word *them* (choice **b**) stands for the phrase *professional hockey players*. Pronouns are used to avoid repetitiveness within a sentence.

74. b. The subject of the sentence is Washington's army. The major action, or simple predicate, in this sentence is that the army *planned* a successful battle, choice **b**.

75. c. Like the word *rustle*, the word *ramble* should also be spelled with the letter *L* before the letter *E* at the end of the word.

76. d. A president *presides* over something, like the United States President presides over the country. There needs to be a letter *I* in the word.

77. a. There should be two *R*s in the word *arrogant*, just as the word *accurate* from choice **d** has two *C*s.

78. a. A wrench, a common hardware tool, has a silent *W* at the beginning of the word.

79. d. Every contraction uses an apostrophe in place of a letter or letters, such as the apostrophe in *you're* replacing the letter *A* from *you are*. In the case of *you're*, the statements in choices **a**, **b**, and **c** are disproved.

80. b. The main idea of Lewis's argument is that cats are better than dogs. Therefore, it only makes sense that he should begin his essay with a statement that sums up that argument. The sentence in choice **b** does the best job of doing that.

81. a. The main argument is that cats are good pets. The statement in choice **a** gives another reason that cats are good. The statement in choice **b** would weaken the argument, because it provides a reason why cats are *not* good pets. The statements in choices **c** and **d** do not provide additional reasons why cats are good pets.

82. a. Sentences 6 and 7 tell of all the things you need to do to take care of a cat. The best way to combine them is to provide a simple list separated by commas. Remember, however, that the items should be in a parallel format—and that the new sentence must maintain the same information as the original two sentences. Only the sentence in choice **a** provides the information in a clear and concise way that also provides all the necessary information.

83. c. The student wants to add information about an animal, so it makes the most sense that it should be added to section III, "Animals" (choice **c**).

84. d. If you look at the information above and below the blank space, you will see that they form part of a timeline. The line before the blank mentions more than 170 million years ago. The line after the blank is about Antarctica today. It would make sense, then, that the blank line in the middle would be about the time periods after 170 million years ago and today. That is represented by the title in choice **d**.

85. b. The first three sentences of the original paragraph are about figuring out where and when to plant a tree. The rest of the paragraph talks about all the steps involved for successfully planting the tree in that spot. If the paragraph were split into two, it would make the most sense after the third sentence—and before the fourth sentence, choice **b**.

86. d. You can plug each word into the sentence to see which one fits the best. The reason why one should be gentle placing the tree in the hole is *because* tree roots are very fragile (choice **d**). That causal word is the only one that makes sense in the context of the sentence.

87. a. It is always important to consider your audience with any type of writing. If the audience for this passage does not know much about gardening, there is a good chance that they do not know the meaning of the terms *mulch* or *compost*, as in choice **a**. Fewer steps, choice **b**, may not help an amateur gardener, and the changes listed in choices **c** and **d** will not be helpful either.

88. d. Persuasive writing is intended to convince the reader of something. In sentence 4, choice **d**, it seems as if the writer wants to convince the reader that the school day needs a longer recess. Its purpose is to persuade.

89. b. While any of these sentences *could* have been taken from an entertaining story, the word *story* is often associated with fiction. Sentence 2 (*Billy the Beaver ran to his friend Bob the Bear and said he needed help with his dam*) is clearly from a fiction book because it includes a talking beaver. It is therefore the best choice taken from a book whose purpose was to entertain.

90. c. Encyclopedias, choice **c**, are terrific resources for specific information. A tale about a talking turtle, choice **a**, might not give factual information about loggerhead turtles. A dictionary, choice **b**, would only tell what those words mean—not about the habits of the animals. While a picture book of underwater animals, choice **d**, might include some pictures of loggerhead turtles, it is not the best resource to use to learn about loggerheads specifically.

4 ▶ READING SKILLS AND KNOWLEDGE

CHAPTER SUMMARY
The Reading Skills and Knowledge section of the ParaPro Assessment includes 30 questions, makes up one-third of the entire test, and will always appear first on the test.

Because the Reading Skills and Knowledge section is one-third of the test, you should expect to spend about one-third of the available time on it. That means you will have about 50 minutes to answer the 30 questions. You can spend more time on one section of the test than on another section. However, if you decide to spend more time on this section, be aware that you will have less time to answer the questions in a later section. For example, you may choose to spend more time reading the passages carefully—but then you will have a bit less time to solve the math or writing problems in the following sections.

Of the 30 questions on the reading section, you can expect that about the first 18 will test your reading skills. That means those problems may ask you to read a passage and identify its main idea or supporting details, or they may ask you to identify a fact from the passage. The last 12 questions or so on the reading section will test your ability to apply reading skills to classroom use. That means those problems may ask you to identify the best way to help a struggling reading student or help a teacher perform a reading lesson.

About the Reading Skills and Knowledge Section

Every question on the reading section of the ParaPro Assessment is multiple-choice with four answer choices. The answer choices will always be **a**, **b**, **c**, and **d**.

Most questions on the Reading Skills and Knowledge section of the ParaPro Assessment are based on a short reading passage, book excerpt, or lesson plan. Fortunately, most of the passages on the ParaPro will be relatively short—one or two paragraphs. Each passage will then include anywhere from one to four questions. There will be a few "stand-alone" questions in between passages that are not related to any particular passage.

Most problems on the reading section of the ParaPro Assessment will ask a specific question, such as the following problem:

1. Which pair of words are antonyms?
    a. high and far
    b. big and large
    c. find and lose
    d. there and their

Even though this book calls them "questions," some of the problems on the ParaPro Assessment do not include a question mark. Those questions will ask you to complete a sentence, such as the following problem:

2. The main idea of the passage is
    a. building the ancient pyramids was a very difficult job.
    b. Egypt is the best place to see pyramids.
    c. it can be very hot if you visit Egypt in the middle of the summer.
    d. there are pyramids in several different countries in the world.

A few questions on the reading section will ask you to find the answer choice that is NOT true. These types of questions can be very tricky! Fortunately, the makers of the test will capitalize the word that tells you that you are looking for the answer that is NOT true.

3. The passage says all of the following facts about snakes EXCEPT that they
    a. live in almost every part of the world.
    b. are all poisonous.
    c. have two lungs.
    d. are a type of reptile.

For this type of question, you would need to get rid of any answer choice that presents a true fact, based on the information in the passage. The one statement that is NOT supported by the passage will be the correct choice.

Test-Taking Tips for Reading Skills and Knowledge Questions

Below are a handful of specific tips for the reading section of the ParaPro Assessment.

Always Consider the Main Idea

The ParaPro Assessment will include several questions about the main idea of a passage. In fact, about half of the passages you will read in the section will include some type of main idea question. (It may use the term *central idea*, *primary purpose*, or a similar term which still means the same thing.) Therefore, always consider the main idea of a passage as you begin to read it.

As you start reading a passage on the test, look for its main idea right away. This will save you time and energy later on if you see a question about the main idea. Even if there is no question about the main idea, understanding the purpose of the passage can help you identify other important information—such as supporting details. Therefore, always consider what the main idea of a passage is while you're reading it— rather than having to go back later and figure it out.

Use Any Information before the Passages

It may be tempting to skip the directions before a passage and just start reading. After all, the ParaPro Assessment is a timed test! However, the sentence or two that precedes the passage and its questions may contain some important information. That is why those words will be in italics. For example, the italicized words before the passage may tell you about the author or how students will be using the passage. Or it may tell you that the passage you are about to read is only an excerpt, suggesting that there is a lot more to the story that isn't necessarily given in your test. That may be useful to know when answering a question, so be sure to spend the few extra moments to read the directions text in bold.

Peek at the Questions

For tests that have really long passages with many questions, it isn't advisable to look at the questions first. (You probably wouldn't remember all of the questions by the time you finished the passage!) But the passages on the ParaPro Assessment are very short—usually only one or two paragraphs. And there are usually only two or three questions per passage. Therefore, it is absolutely to your advantage to take a peek at the questions before reading the passage.

For example, if you look over at the questions and see that one asks for the organization of the passage, you can then read the passage with its organization in the back of your mind. You may not have paid too much attention to the organization of the passage if you were

reading it on your own. But by peeking at the questions before you read, you can get a head start on figuring out the answer. And now you might not have to waste precious time by reading the passage twice.

Important Reading Vocabulary

The reading section of the ParaPro Assessment will test your knowledge of important literary terms. You will be expected to know the bolded words in the following paragraphs. Make sure you are familiar with every one of these terms before taking the test.

An **antonym** is a word that has an opposite meaning. For example, *tall* is an antonym of *short*. It may help to remember the meaning of this word if you consider that *ant-* is a prefix that means *opposite*, just as *Antarctica* means the *opposite of the Arctic*.

The **author** of a story is the person who wrote it.

A **compound** word is a word that is created by putting two words together, such as *extraordinary*, *teacup*, or *butterfly*.

The **context** of a word, or a **context clue,** is the area around the word or phrase that helps to determine its meaning. For example, the context clue that helps define *frigid* in the following sentence is that Jack needed to wear his heavy coat: *Because it was so frigid, Jack needed to wear his heavy coat.* (*Frigid* means *very cold*.)

A **consonant** is a letter of the alphabet that is not a vowel. The consonants are *b, c, d, f, g, h, j, k, l, m, n, p, q, r, s, t, v, w, x, z,* and *y* in words like *yes* or *beyond*.

A **dictionary** is resource that provides the meaning, or definition, of words.

A **fact** is a statement that can be proven. For example, the sentence *Barack Obama was an Illinois senator before he became U.S. President* is a fact.

First-person point of view expresses the writer's personal feelings and experiences directly to the reader using these pronouns: *I, me, mine; we, our, us.* The first person creates a sense of intimacy between the reader and writer because it expresses a *subjective* point of view.

A **homonym** is a word that sounds like another word but has a different meaning. For example, *two* and *to* are homonyms.

An **inference** is a conclusion that can be made from given information.

The **narrator** in a story is the person who is telling the story. Many stories do not have a narrator. If the passage includes a speaker speaking in the first person (using words like *I* or *me*), then that speaker is the narrator.

An **opinion** is a statement that cannot be proven. For example, *Fuji apples are the most delicious types of apples* is an opinion.

A **paragraph** is a group of related sentences together in a story. Some of the passages on the ParaPro Assessment will only have one paragraph. Most will have one or two paragraphs.

A **prefix** is the beginning part of the word that helps identify its meaning. For example, the prefix in the word *tripod* is *tri-*, meaning "three." Many words do not have a prefix.

The **root** of a word is the main part of a word that conveys the word's meaning, without any prefixes or suffixes. For example, the root of *disinterested* is *interest*.

Second-person point of view is another personal perspective in which the writer speaks directly to the reader, addressing the reader as *you*. Writers use the second person to give directions or to make the reader feel directly involved with the argument or action of their message.

A **suffix** is the ending part of the word that helps identify its meaning. For example, the suffix in the word *dogs* is *-s*, meaning that there is more than one dog. Many words do not have a suffix.

A **syllable** is one sound of a word. For example, the word *baseball* has two syllables: *base-* and *-ball*. Some words with only one sound only have one syllable, such as the words *talk* and *peace*.

A **synonym** is a word that has the same meaning as another word. For example, *use* and *utilize* mean essentially the same thing, and are synonyms.

Third-person point of view expresses an impersonal point of view by presenting the perspective of an outsider (a third person) who is not directly involved with the action.

A **vowel** is a letter of the alphabet that is not a consonant. The vowels are *a, e, i, o, u,* and *y* in words like *hymn* or *my*. A **short vowel** sound has a shorter vowel sound like *ah, eh, ih* or *uh* in the words *lab, egg, big, top,* or *fun*. A **long vowel** sound has a longer vowel sound like *ay, ee, eye,* or *oh* in the words *hay, me, bye,* or *no*.

Reading Skills and Knowledge Review

ETS, the maker of the ParaPro Assessment, says that there are seven key skills to know for the reading section of the test. The key skills are as follows:

1. understand the main idea or primary purpose
2. understand supporting ideas
3. understand the organization of a passage
4. understand vocabulary in context
5. draw inferences or implications from directly stated content
6. distinguish between fact and opinion
7. interpret graphic text

The next seven sections explain each type of skill, with examples that show how you might see the concept tested on the ParaPro Assessment.

Main Idea or Primary Purpose

For this question type, you need to be able to identify the main idea or primary purpose of the passage or a specific paragraph in the passage.

When standardized reading tests ask you to find the main idea of a passage, they are asking you to determine an overall feeling or thought that a writer wants to convey about his or her subject. To find the main idea, think about a **general statement** that brings together all of the ideas in a paragraph or passage. Look out for statements that are too specific—a main idea must be broad enough to contain all of the concepts presented in a passage. Test takers often confuse the main idea of a passage with its main topic. The topic is the *subject*— what the passage is about. The main idea is what the author wants to express *about* the subject.

Textbook writing and the passages on the Para-Pro Assessment often follow a basic pattern of **general idea → specific idea**. In other words, a writer states his or her main idea (makes a general claim about the subject) and then provides evidence for it through specific details and facts. Do you always find main ideas in the first sentence of the passage? The answer is no; although a first sentence may contain the main idea, an author may decide to build up to the main point. In that case, you may find the main idea in the last sentence of an introductory paragraph, or even in the last paragraph of the passage.

Here are some examples of ways that main idea may be tested on the ParaPro Assessment:

- The passage is primarily concerned with . . .
- What is the author's main purpose in this passage?
- Which of the following would be the best title for this passage?

Read the following paragraph and answer the practice question that follows.

Experts say that if you feel drowsy during the day, even during boring activities, you haven't had enough sleep. If you routinely fall asleep within five minutes of lying down, you may have severe sleep deprivation. *Microsleep*, or a very brief episode of sleep in an otherwise awake person, is another mark of sleep deprivation. In many cases, people are not aware that they are experiencing microsleeps. The widespread practice of "burning the candle at both ends" in many societies has created so much sleep deprivation that what is really abnormal sleepiness is now almost the norm.

1. What is the main point of this passage?
   a. If you fall asleep within five minutes every time you lie down, you are sleep deprived.
   b. If you experience enough microsleeps, you can attain the sleep you need to function.
   c. Sleep deprivation is a pervasive problem in many cultures.
   d. If trends in sleep deprivation continue, our society will experience grave consequences.

Choice **a** is a true statement, but too specific to be a main idea. Choice **b** is a false statement. Choice **d** is a speculative statement that is not implied in the passage. Only choice **c** represents a general or umbrella statement that covers all of the information in the paragraph.

Notice that in the sample passage, the author does not present the main idea in the first sentence, but rather builds up to the main point, which is expressed in the last sentence of the paragraph.

Supporting Ideas

Some of the questions on the reading section of the ParaPro Assessment will ask you identify a detail from a passage. You will need to be able to locate specific information in the passage, such as a fact, figure, or name. How can you distinguish a main idea from a supporting idea? Unlike main ideas, supporting ideas present facts or **specific information**. They often answer the questions *what? when? why?* or *how?*

> Here are some examples of questions that test supporting details on the ParaPro Assessent:
>
> - According to the passage, how many people in the United States have Type II diabetes?
> - The passage states that a lunar eclipse occurs when . . .
> - Which of the following is NOT mentioned as one of the reasons for the Cuban Missile Crisis?

How can you locate a supporting detail in a passage that is 200 words long? One thing you *don't* have to do is memorize the passage. This test does not require that you have perfect recall. Instead, it measures your ability to read carefully and know where to look for specific information. Here are some tips for finding supporting details.

- **Look for language clues.** Writers often use transitional words or phrases to signal that they are introducing a fact or supporting idea. As you read, keep your eye out for these common phrases:

for example	for instance	in particular
in addition	furthermore	some
other	specifically	such as

■ **Focus on key words from the question.** Questions often contain two or three important words that signal what information to look for in the passage. For example, a question following a passage about the American car industry reads, "The passage states that hybrid automobiles work best if . . ." The key words are *hybrid automobiles* and *best.* They tell you to look for a sentence that contains the phrase *hybrid automobiles* and describes an optimal situation. Instead of rereading the passage, *skim* through the paragraphs looking for the key words. Keep in mind that the passage may use a slightly different wording than the key words. As you scan, look for words that address the same idea.

■ **Pay attention to the structure of the passage.** Take note of how the passage is organized as you read. Does the author begin with or build to the main point? Is information presented chronologically? Where does the author offer evidence to back up the main point? Understanding how a passage is structured can help you locate the information you need. Read on for more about common organizational models.

Read the following paragraph, focusing on its main idea and the details that support the main idea. Then, answer the practice questions that follow.

(1) The history of microbiology begins with a Dutch haberdasher named Antonie van Leeuwenhoek, a man with no formal scientific education. (2) In the late 1600s, Leeuwenhoek, inspired by the magnifying lenses used to examine cloth, assembled some of the first microscopes. (3) He developed a technique for grinding and polishing tiny lenses, some of which could magnify an object up to 270 times. (4) After scraping some plaque from between his teeth and examining it under a lens, Leeuwenhoek found tiny squirming creatures, which he called "animalcules." (5) His observations, which he reported to the Royal Society of London, are among the first descriptions of living bacteria.

2. What inspired Leeuwenhoek's invention of the microscope?
   a. his training in science
   b. the great microbiologists of his era
   c. the lenses used by the practitioners of his profession
   d. the desire to observe bacteria

3. In which sentence does the author give Leeuwenhoek's description of living bacteria?
   a. sentence 1
   b. sentence 2
   c. sentence 4
   d. sentence 5

Answers

2. c. The first paragraph provides the supporting detail to answer this question. Leeuwenhoek, a haberdasher, was *inspired by the magnifying lenses used to examine cloth.* One of the key words from the question—*inspired*—leads you to the location of the detail in the passage. Choice **a** is refuted by a detail presented in the line: *a man of no formal scientific education.* Choice **b** is untrue, because the first sentence of the passage states that *the history of microbiology begins with* Leeuwenhoek. Choice **d** is also incorrect, because Leeuwenhoek did not know *what* he would discover under his microscope.

3. c. You can find Leeuwenhoek's description of bacteria in sentence 4: *tiny squirming creatures, which he called "animalcules."* You may have been tricked into selecting choice **d** because of its repetition of the phrase *descriptions of living bacteria,* from sentence 5. Be sure to always refer back to the passage when answering a question—do not rely on your memory. Choice **d** is incorrect because it does not refer to Leeuwenhoek's own description, but rather the significance of his observation. This question highlights the importance of taking note of where crucial details are located in a passage. Again, do not try to memorize or learn facts or details, but have an idea about where to find them.

Organization

Organization questions in the reading section of the ParaPro Assessment ask you to identify how a passage is structured. You need to be able to recognize organizational patterns, common transitional phrases, and how ideas relate within a passage. Understanding the structure of a passage can also help you locate concepts and information, such as the main idea or supporting details.

> Here are some examples of ways in which organization may be tested on the ParaPro Assessment:
>
> - Which of the following best describes the organization of the passage?
> - This passage is most likely taken from a . . . (newspaper column, textbook, etc.)?
> - The phrase *the contrast in meaning and tone* refers to the contrast between . . . ?
> - Why is the word *indescribably* used in sentence 4?

To organize their ideas effectively, writers rely on one of several basic organizational patterns. The four most common strategies are:

1. chronological order
2. order of importance
3. comparison and contrast
4. cause and effect

Chronological order arranges events by the order in which they happened, from beginning to end. Textbooks, instructions and procedures, essays about personal experiences, and magazine feature articles may use this organizing principle. Passages organized by chronology offer language cues—in the form of transitional words or phrases—to signal the passage of time and link one idea or event to the next. Here are some of the most common chronological transitions:

first, second, third, etc.	before	after	next	now
then	when	as soon as	immediately	suddenly
soon	during	while	meanwhile	later
in the meantime	at last	eventually	finally	afterward

Order of importance organizes ideas by thematic significance instead of by time. Instead of describing what happened next, this pattern presents what is most, or least, important. The structure can work two ways: Writers can organize their ideas either by increasing importance (least important idea to most important idea) or by decreasing importance (most important idea to least important idea).

Newspaper articles follow the principle of decreasing importance; they cover the most important information in the first sentence or paragraph (the *who*, *what*, *when*, *where*, and *why* about an event). As a result, readers can get the most important facts of an event without reading the entire article. Writing that is trying to persuade its readers or make an argument often uses the opposite pattern of increasing importance, saving the most important details for the end of the piece. By using this structure, a writer creates a snowball effect, building and building upon the original idea. "Saving the best for last" can create suspense for the reader and leave a lasting impression of the writer's main point. Just as a chronological arrangement uses transitions, so does the order of importance principle. Keep your eye out for the following common transitional words and phrases:

first and foremost	most important	more important	moreover
above all	first, second, third, etc.	last but not least	finally

Comparison and contrast arranges two things or ideas side by side to show the ways in which they are similar or different. This organizational model allows a writer to analyze two things and ideas and determine how they measure up to one another. For example, this description of the artists Pablo Picasso and Henri Matisse uses comparison and contrast:

> The grand old lions of modernist innovation, Picasso and Matisse, originated many of the most significant developments of twentieth-century art [comparison]. However, although they worked in the same tradition, they each had a different relationship to painting [contrast]. For example, Picasso explored signs and symbols in his paintings, whereas Matisse insisted that the things represented in his paintings were merely things: The oranges on the table of a still life were simply oranges on the table [contrast].

Writers use two basic methods to compare and contrast ideas. In the **point-by-point** method, each aspect of idea A is followed by a comparable aspect of idea B, so that a paragraph resembles this pattern: ABABABAB. In the **block** method, a writer presents several aspects of idea A, followed by several aspects of idea B. The pattern of the block method looks like this: AAAABBBB. Again, transitions can signal whether a writer is using the organizing principle of comparison and contrast. Watch for these common transitions:

Transitions Showing Similarity

similarly	in the same way	likewise
like	in a like manner	just as
and	also	both

Transitions Showing Difference

but	on the other hand	yet
however	on the contrary	in contrast
conversely	whereas	unlike

Cause and effect arranges ideas to explain why an event took place (cause) and what happened as a result (effect). Sometimes one cause has several effects, or an effect may have several causes. For example, a historian writing about World War I might investigate several causes of the war (assassination of the heir to the Austro-Hungarian throne, European conflicts over territory, and economic power), and describe the various effects of the war (ten million soldiers killed, weakened European powers, and enormous financial debt).

Key words offer clues that a writer is describing cause and effect. Pay attention to these words as you read:

Words Indicating Cause

because	created by
since	caused by

Words Indicating Effect

therefore	so
hence	consequently
as a result	

A writer might also describe a **contributing** cause, which is a factor that *helps* to make something happen but can't make that thing happen by itself. On the opposite end of the spectrum is a **sufficient** cause, which is an event that, by itself, is strong enough to make the event happen. Often, an author will offer an opinion about the cause or effect of an event. In that case, readers must judge the validity of the author's analysis. Are the author's ideas logical? Does the author properly support the conclusions?

Read the following excerpt and answer the practice question.

When Rosa Parks refused to give up her seat to a white person in Montgomery, Alabama, in December 1955, she set off a train of events that generated a momentum the Civil Rights movement had never before experienced. Local Civil Rights leaders were hoping for such an opportunity to test the city's segregation laws. Deciding to boycott the buses, the African-American community soon formed a new organization to supervise the boycott, the Montgomery Improvement Association (MIA). The young pastor of the Dexter Avenue Baptist Church, Reverend Martin Luther King, Jr., was chosen as the first MIA leader. The boycott, more successful than anyone hoped, led to a 1956 Supreme Court decision banning segregated buses.

Source: Excerpt from the Library of Congress exhibition The African American Odyssey: A Quest for Full Citizenship.

4. The author implies that the action of Rosa Parks directly resulted in
   a. the 1956 Supreme Court decision banning segregated buses.
   b. Martin Luther King, Jr.'s ascendancy as a Civil Rights leader.
   c. the formation of the Civil Rights movement in Montgomery, Alabama.
   d. the bus boycott in Montgomery, Alabama.

The correct answer is choice **d**. According to the passage, Rosa Parks's action directly inspired local Civil Rights leaders to institute the Montgomery bus boycott. Although Rosa Parks's action may have been a *contributing* factor to King's emergence as a Civil Rights leader (choice **b**) and the Supreme Court's later decision to ban segregated buses (choice **a**), it was not the

direct cause of these events, according to the passage. Choice **c** is incorrect because the passage makes clear that a local Civil Rights movement already existed and was not the result of Rosa Parks's refusal to give up her bus seat. Rosa Parks may have furthered the national Civil Rights movement, but she was not its direct cause.

Vocabulary

This question type asks you to determine the meaning of a word as it is used in the passage. If you encounter an unfamiliar word when you are reading, you may likely grab a dictionary or go online and look it up. During the ParaPro Assessment, however, you can't use a dictionary to check the meaning of new words—and you can't use a computer. Fortunately, you can use a number of strategies to figure out what a word means.

Vocabulary questions measure your word power, but they also evaluate an essential reading comprehension skill, which is your ability to determine the meaning of a word from its **context**. The sentences that surround the word offer important clues about its meaning. For example, see if you can figure out the meaning of the word *incessant* from this context: *The incessant demands of the job are too much for me. The responsibilities are endless!*

5. The word *incessant* most likely means
   a. inaccessible.
   b. difficult.
   c. unceasing.
   d. compatible.

The best answer is choice **c**. The second sentence, *The responsibilities are endless*, restates the phrase in the first sentence, *incessant demands*. This restatement, or elaboration, suggests the meaning of *incessant*: continuing or following without interruption.

If the context of an unfamiliar word does not restate its meaning, try these two steps to figure out what the word means:

1. **Is the word positive or negative?** Using the context of the passage, determine whether the unfamiliar word is a positive or negative term. If a word is used in a positive context, you can eliminate the answer choices that are negative. In the preceding example, you can guess that the word *incessant* is used negatively. The phrase *too much for me*, suggests that the demands of the job are overwhelming and negative. Thus, you can eliminate the answer choice **d** because it represents positive terms.

2. **Replace the vocabulary word** with the remaining answer choices, one at a time. Does the answer choice make sense when you read the sentence? If not, eliminate the answer choice. In the previous example, choice **a**, *inaccessible*, simply does not make sense in the sentence. Choice **b**, *difficult*, is too general to be a likely synonym. Only choice **c**, *unceasing*, makes sense in the context.

Here are some examples of ways that vocabulary may be tested on the ParaPro Assessment:

- As the word is used in the passage, *flag* most likely means . . .
- Which of the following is the best meaning of the word *experience* as it is used in the passage?
- The word *protest* in the passage could be replaced by . . .
- Which of the following words, if substituted for the word *indelible* in the passage, would introduce the least change in the meaning of the senctence?

Inferences

Inference questions on the ParaPro Assessment test will ask you to make an inference, or draw a logical conclusion, about what you read. Sometimes a writer does not explicitly state the main idea or offer a conclusion. The reader must infer the writer's meaning. To make an inference, you need to look for clues in the context of the passage.

The trick to making inferences on passages on the ParaPro Assessment is finding the answer choice that is supported. The exact answer will not be spelled out exactly, but the author's position should be clear.

Inference questions may ask you to identify the author's assumptions and attitudes and evaluate the weaknesses and strengths of the author's argument or logic. To determine a writer's underlying assumptions or attitude, you need to look for clues in the context of the passage. One revealing clue to the writer's meaning is word choice.

Word choice, also called **diction**, is the specific language the writer uses to describe people, places, and things. Word choice includes these elements:

- particular words or phrases a writer uses
- the way words are arranged in a sentence
- repetition of words or phrases
- inclusion of particular details

Writers can reveal their attitude toward a subject through the use of positive or negative expressions. Additionally, an author's style can alert you to his or her underlying message. **Style** is the distinctive way in which a writer uses language to inform or promote an idea. Lastly, writers who want to persuade a reader of something may rely on emotional language. **Emotional language** targets a reader's emotions—fears, beliefs, values, prejudices—instead of appealing to a reader's reason or critical thinking. Just as advertising often uses emotional language to sell a product, writers use emotional appeals to sell an idea.

> Here are some examples of ways that inferences may be tested on the ParaPro Assessment:
>
> - This passage suggests that Greek tragedies are still so powerful because . . .
> - It can be inferred from the passage that the art of Picasso and Matisse differ in all of the following ways EXCEPT . . .
> - The author would be LEAST likely to agree with which of the following statements?

Try the following inference question, based on a passage about Jane Austen.

Jane Austen died in 1817, leaving behind six novels that have since become English classics. Most Austen biographers accept the image of Jane Austen as a sheltered spinster who knew little of life beyond the drawing rooms of her Hampshire village. They accept the claim of Austen's brother, Henry: "My dear sister's life was not a life of events."

Biographer Claire Tomalin takes this view to task. She shows that Jane's short life was indeed tumultuous. Not only did Austen experience romantic love (briefly, with an Irishman), but her many visits to London and her relationships with her brothers (who served in the Napoleonic wars) widened her knowledge beyond her rural county, and even beyond England. Tomalin also argues that Austen's unmarried status benefited her ability to focus on her writing. I believe that Jane herself may have viewed it that way. Although her family destroyed most of her letters, one relative recalled that "some of her [Jane's] letters, triumphing over married women of her acquaintance, and rejoicing in her freedom, were most amusing."

6. The passage suggests that Jane Austen
   a. never left the comfort of her Hampshire village.
   b. may have enjoyed being unmarried.
   c. did not get along with her brothers.
   d. wished that she married the Irishman.

To solve this inference problem, you need to choose the answer choice that is most supported by the passage itself. Because the passage mentions that Jane Austen had "many visits to London," it is not true that she never left her village, eliminating choice **a**. There is nothing in the passage to support the idea that she did not get along with her brothers, choice **b**. The relative mentions at the end of the passage that Austen wrote letters "triumphing over married women" and "rejoicing in her freedom." You can infer from those statements that she may have enjoyed being unmarried, choice **b**—and that she did not wish to marry the Irishman, eliminating choice **d**.

Fact and Opinion

Just because something is in print does not mean that it is fact. Most writing contains some form of *bias*—the personal judgment of a writer. Sometimes a writer's beliefs unknowingly affect how he or she writes about a topic. In other cases, a writer deliberately attempts to shape the reader's reaction and position. For example, a writer may present only one perspective about a subject or include only facts that support his or her point of view.

Questions on the ParaPro Assessment will ask you to distinguish between fact and opinion. To separate fact from opinion, consider these differences:

- A **fact** is a statement that can be verified by a reliable source.
- An **opinion** is a statement about the beliefs or feelings of a person or group.

When determining whether a statement is factual, consider whether a source gives researched, accurate information. The following is an example of a factual statement—it can be supported by the recent national census:

The U.S. population is growing older—in fact, adults over age 85 are the fastest-growing segment of today's population.

Opinions, on the other hand, reflect judgments that may or may not be true. Opinions include speculation or predictions of the future that cannot be proven at the present time. The following statement represents an opinion—it offers a belief about the future. Others may disagree with the prediction:

Many believe that the population boom among elderly Americans will create a future healthcare crisis.

Language clues can alert you to a statement that reflects an opinion. Look for these common words that introduce opinions:

likely	should/could say	charge
possibly	think	attest
probably	believe	

Exhibit A: Evidence

Most writing presents *reasonable opinions*, based on fact: A writer asserts an opinion and supports it with facts or other evidence. A writer can use different types of evidence to build an argument—some forms of proof are more reliable than other types. When you read, look for the forms of evidence listed here and consider how accurate each might be:

observations	experiments
interviews	personal experience
surveys and questionaires	expert opinions

Here are some examples of ways that facts may be tested on the ParaPro Assessment:

- Which sentence from the passage presents an example of an opinion rather than a fact?
- Which sentence from the passage presents an example of a fact rather than an opinion?

Read the following excerpt and answer the practice question.

In the long history of soccer, no single player has changed the game as much as Pelé. Born in Brazil in 1940, Pelé's played professional soccer for 20 years—including a season in an America soccer league at the end of his career. Pelé's 1,281 goals are recognized as the most goals by any professional soccer player. In fact, Pelé's athletic skills were so impressive that he earned the title "Athlete of the Century" by the International Olympic Committee.

7. Which sentence from the passage presents an example of an opinion rather than a fact?
   a. "In the long . . . as Pelé."
   b. "Born in Brazil . . . of his career."
   c. "Pelé's 1,281 goals . . . soccer player."
   d. "In fact, Pelé's . . . Olympic Committee."

The correct answer is choice **a**. It cannot be proven that one player changed the game of soccer more than any other player. The other three choices provide statements that *can* be verified, such as the year and place of his birth (choice **b**), the number of goals he scored (choice **c**), or that he was given a title from a large institution (choice **d**).

Graphic Text

The reading section of the ParaPro Assessment will include several questions about a graphic text, such as a table of contents, chart, table, or index. These questions will make sure that you know how to interpret the information from these graphics. The graphic texts that are part of a book, such as a table of contents or an index, will likely have at least two questions associated with them.

It may help to review how a table of contents and an index are organized. Most textbooks will have these graphics; the table of contents will be at the beginning of the book, and the index should be at the end. Whereas the table of contents will be organized in the order of the book, the index will be arranged alphabetically. Both graphic texts serve to help readers find information quickly and effectively. They also show how the information is organized throughout the resource.

The graphs that appear on the ParaPro Assessment include line graphs, bar graphs, circle graphs, and tables. Each type of graph serves a different purpose. A line graph is generally used to show how data changes over time. A bar graph shows how different amounts are related. A circle graph compares parts to a whole.

Be sure to use the title and the labels for the axes when interpreting the data in one of these types of graphs. These parts of the graph provide critical information to understanding what the graphic is showing. The graph may also include a legend, which is a key that shows what different aspects of the graph means. (For example, a double-bar graph may show the population for two different cities; the legend will explain what each bar stands for.)

Here are some examples of ways that graphic text may be tested on the ParaPro Assessment:

- What conclusion can be dawn from the graph shown?
- On which page would a reader find information about the population of Peru?
- In which section of the book does information about the Earth's core belong?

A question on the ParaPro Assessment may ask you to find a particular piece of information in the graphic text. It may also ask you to identify the organizational structure of the graphic. Try your hand at the following problem:

8. On which page would you most likely find information about Woodrow Wilson's decision to enter World War I?

  a. 24

  b. 35

  c. 47

  d. 49

This question is asking you where you would find not just information about Woodrow Wilson, but specific information about World War I. You can look through the list of subheadings under the main topic, Woodrow Wilson. The subheading that corresponds to WWI is "military involvement." Because the index says that information is on page 47, choice **c** is the correct answer.

Application of Reading Skills and Knowledge to Classroom Instruction

The last 12 questions on the reading section of the ParaPro Assessment will test your ability to apply reading skills and knowledge to the classroom. That may mean, for example, that you will be asked to show how you would aid students in their reading comprehension. You may also be asked to choose the best method for classroom instruction in your role as a paraprofessional, such as demonstrating how you would help students improve their ability to decipher the meanings of words.

Reading Application questions on the ParaPro Assessment test both the foundations of reading and the tools of the reading process. The ability to break words apart to decipher their meaning is an example of a foundation of reading. Reading strategies like skimming and asking questions are both examples of the tools of the reading process. The following review section includes all of the major elements of both the foundations of reading and the tools of the reading process.

Foundations of Reading

The foundations of reading questions on the reading section of the ParaPro Assessment assess the test taker's ability to help students with the following skills:

- alphabetize words
- recognize antonyms, homonyms, and synonyms
- use context clues to determine the meaning of a word or phrase
- recognize the parts of a word, such as its prefix, suffix, or root
- identify the sounds that can be used to construct words

For example, the following question shows how the ParaPro Assessment may test your ability to alphabetize words.

9. Four students work together in a reading group. Each student's name begins with the letter *D*. Which of the following shows the names in alphabetical order?
   a. Dina, Devon, Deanna, Dave
   b. Dave, Devon, Deanna, Dina
   c. Dave, Deanna, Dina, Devon
   d. Dave, Deanna, Devon, Dina

To solve this problem, you need to order the names alphabetically. The first letter of each name is *D*, so you need to look at the second letters of each name. The second letter of Dave is *A*, so it should come first. The second letters of Deanna and Devon are *E* and the second letter of Dina is *I*. So Dina should go last. To order Deanna and Devon, you need to look at the third letter. The third letter of Deanna is *A* and the third letter of Devon is *V*, so Deanna should come before

Devon. The proper order should be Dave, Deanna, Devon, Dina—which is answer choice **d**.

Tools of the Reading Process

The tools of the reading process questions on the reading section of the ParaPro Assessment assess the test taker's ability to help students with the following skills:

- using reading strategies, such as predicting what will come next in a story
- recognizing the parts of a word, such as its prefix, suffix, or root
- using a dictionary

You will also be expected to ask questions which help students interpret a text, as well as help you understand their ability to comprehend its meaning. As an assistant to the classroom teacher, you will also be expected to follow his or her written directions.

For example, the following question shows how the ParaPro Assessment may test your ability to help students recognize the parts of a word.

10. A student in a class is trying to understand the meaning of the word *hopped*. Which word has the same suffix?
    a. topping
    b. holy
    c. reasoned
    d. jump

The suffix is the part at the end of the word that helps tell what it means. In the case of *hopped*, the suffix is *-ed*, which means that the verb is in the past tense. The only word in the answer choices with the same suffix is *reasoned*, which means choice **c** is correct.

Reading Practice

Directions: Each of the following questions is followed by four answer choices. Choose the best answer choice by filling in the corresponding answer choice on your answer sheet.

Answer questions 1–2 based on the following passage.

(1) Though some of the world's largest creatures may be scary, such as the great white shark or the boa constrictor, some of the smallest creatures pose the greatest threat. (2) The poison dart frog, for example, may seem adorable with its minute size, but the level of its toxicity is no joking matter. (3) The adults of some species never grow larger than one inch in length, but they still contain enough poison to kill 10 adult humans. (4) It may be hard to imagine that a creature that weighs only 2 grams can have such deadly capabilities. (5) However, it is important to remember that size does not matter when comparing the dangers of Earth's creatures.

1. The main idea of the passage is that
   a. large animals like great white sharks are the scariest.
   b. some adult frogs don't grow to be more than one inch in length.
   c. sometimes small animals can be deceptively dangerous.
   d. the poison dart frog seems adorable.

2. The word *minute* in sentence 2 most closely means
   a. a period of time.
   b. modern.
   c. unimportant.
   d. tiny.

Answer questions 3–4 based on the following passage.

The Brooklyn Bridge has many admirers for its historical and cultural significance. Built in 1883, the bridge was the longest suspension bridge in the world—by far—until the early twentieth century. In fact, when it was built, the towers that hold the bridge's cables were the tallest structures in the western hemisphere. The bridge connected the New York City boroughs of Manhattan and Brooklyn, even though Brooklyn was its own city until 1898. The ancient bridge, an icon of New York City, became a national historic landmark in 1964. Despite all of these reasons to admire the Brooklyn Bridge, I just like it because it's beautiful.

3. The author states all of the following reasons to appreciate the Brooklyn Bridge EXCEPT its
   a. size.
   b. cost.
   c. age.
   d. beauty.

4. The passage suggests that the Brooklyn Bridge
   a. is not the longest suspension bridge in the world.
   b. is one of the most highly trafficked bridges in the world.
   c. inspired Brooklyn to become part of New York City.
   d. is the oldest suspension bridge in the world.

Answer questions 5–6 based on the following section of an index from an astronomy textbook.

Magnetic Fields, 314–317
Mars
    Geology of, 214
    Discovery of, 210–212
    Moons of, 213
    Orbit and rotation, 215–217
Mercury (planet)
    Geology of, 198–199
    Discovery of, 197
    Orbit and rotation, 200–203
Mercury (NASA program), 257–260
Messier, Charles, 443–444
Meteors
    Meteor showers, 355–357
    Origins of, 352–354
Microquasar, 508

5. On which page would a reader most likely find information about the types of rocks that make up the planet Mars?
   a. 199
   b. 213
   c. 214
   d. 215

6. The first American astronauts to reach space were a part of the Mercury missions. On which page might a person learn about these early astronauts?
   a. 197
   b. 257
   c. 443
   d. 508

Answer questions 7–8 based on the following excerpt from a short story about a group of children at a park.

The neighborhood kids gathered at Anderson Park on Saturday morning, as they had for as long as any of them could remember. Owen brought the football, and he and his friend Yuri met to begin the usual process of picking teams. This time, however, something was on Owen's mind.

"The last time we picked teams, Ollie was upset that he was picked last," Owen said to Yuri.

"That's true," Yuri agreed. "But how can we pick fair teams for a football game if we don't pick in order of who we want first?"

Owen thought for a moment. Then he suggested, "We could pick our teams in private. Then we could just tell everyone which team they're on."

Yuri smiled and nodded. "No one will know who was selected first or last!" he said in agreement. The two boys walked away from the crowd and began to plan their teams in private.

7. The primary purpose of this story is to tell about
   a. two children's unique solution to a sensitive problem.
   b. the outcome of a neighborhood pickup football game.
   c. how children can be mean when they play sports.
   d. the growing friendship between two boys.

8. What inspired Owen to change the system in which he and Yuri picked teams?
   a. Owen did not want Ollie on his team again.
   b. It isn't fair for the same people to make the teams each Saturday.
   c. The teams that were selected were not evenly matched.
   d. Ollie's feelings were hurt the last time they picked teams.

Answer question 9 based on the following graph.

Hickory Hills Farm 2006–2009

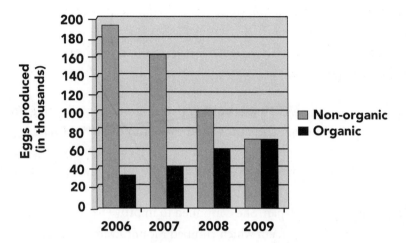

9. Which conclusion is supported by the information in the double-bar graph?
   a. The year in which Hickory Hills Farm produced the most eggs was 2006.
   b. Hickory Hills Farm makes more money selling organic eggs.
   c. More customers are buying organic produce than ever before.
   d. The first year that Hickory Hills Farm produced more organic eggs than non-organic eggs was 2010.

Answer questions 10–11 based on the following passage.

(1) While Hawaii is famous for its beaches and surfing, it is the north shore of the Hawaiian island of O'ahu that is truly the greatest surfing spot in the world. (2) With storms in the North Atlantic driving swells south to Hawaii, the waves at the north shore can be gigantic. (3) When the weather conditions are right, waves can grow to be 35 feet tall—or higher. (4) These waves are simply terrifying to behold. Yet it is these very same waves that draw the best surfers to the north shore. (5) In fact, there are several world-class surfing competitions held on its beaches. (6) One of them actually requires that the waves are at least 20 feet tall. (7) The men and women who surfboard professionally risk injury and death for the conquest of these monstrous waves. (8) In no place can they achieve as much glory as at O'ahu's north shore.

10. Which of the following sentences from the passage is an example of a fact rather than an opinion?
    a. "While Hawaii is famous . . . spot in the world."
    b. "When the weather conditions are right . . . or higher."
    c. "These waves . . . terrifying to behold."
    d. "In no place . . . O'ahu's north shore"

11. What is the best meaning of the word *draw* from the passage in sentence 4?
   a. bring
   b. sketch
   c. create
   d. infer

Answer questions 12–14 based on the following passage.

Junko Tabei was born in 1939 in Japan. When she was 10 years old, she went mountain climbing on a school trip with a teacher. She was so small that other students would make fun of her and call her names. But when she was on the mountain, her small size did not matter. In fact, she enjoyed that she did not have to compete with other people on the mountain. As an adult, she only grew to be 4 feet, 9 inches tall.

In 1969 Tabei formed the Ladies' Climbing Club: Japan. She continued to improve her mountain climbing skills. By 1975, she was part of an all-woman team which climbed Mount Everest, the tallest mountain in the world. An avalanche knocked her unconscious and buried her in snow, but she did not give up on her goal. On May 16, 1975, she became the first woman to reach the peak of Mount Everest. After that, she continued to add to her impressive climbing experience by reaching the highest peak of each of the seven continents on the planet. She was also the first woman to achieve this feat, completing the last of the "Seven Summits" at the age of 59. Now in her 70s, Tabei does not climb as many mountains, but she is still involved with improving the mountain climbing experience. She is the director of the Himalayan Adventure Trust of Japan, where she works to protect mountains for climbers.

12. In what way is the passage organized?
   a. A series of facts are presented in an increasing order of importance.
   b. A broad statement is offered and then backed up with details.
   c. The reasons for a climber's obsession are provided with several causes.
   d. The events are told in the order in which they happened.

13. It can be inferred from the passage that
   a. Junko Tabei was the first woman to climb Mount McKinley, the tallest mountain in North America.
   b. Junko Tabei's height was an advantage when climbing mountains.
   c. Junko Tabei has climbed Mount Vinson, the highest peak in Antarctica.
   d. Junko Tabei was the oldest person to climb Mount Everest.

14. Mountain climbing was appealing to Junko Tabei because
   a. she wanted to be the first woman to climb the tallest mountains.
   b. she was not scared by avalanches and other dangers of the mountain.
   c. she was able to go at her own pace without having to race others.
   d. there were not enough female mountain climbers before her.

Answer question 15 based on the following passage.

Airline pilots need to complete rigorous instruction before they can fly in the cockpit. Pilots need to be trained at a good flight school to earn their private license. They need a college degree, preferably one relating to aviation. They also need to be certified to fly a particular aircraft, as well as pass a medical check. Before they can be pilots—and for the rest of their careers—they take many tests, both written and oral. They also perform checkrides, which are tests performed on an aircraft to show that the pilot has the necessary flying skills. However, none of these credentials are as important to good flying as one critical qualification: experience.

15. The author of the passage is mostly concerned with
   a. the different types of aircraft that a pilot can fly.
   b. the importance of flying experience for a pilot.
   c. the glamorous lifestyle of a professional pilot.
   d. the different kinds of tests that a pilot must pass.

Answer questions 16–18 based on the following passage.

Two of the most famous and popular children's book authors are Eric Carle and Theodor Seuss Geisel, who is most commonly known as Dr. Seuss. Each author has published more than 60 books, many of which have been translated into multiple languages. Not only have Seuss and Carle written dozens of famous books, but they have illustrated them as well. Both authors were born in the northeastern United States, raised by parents of German descent.

Carle uses a unique collage process to illustrate his books, including his most famous book, *The Very Hungry Caterpillar*. To create the collages, he cuts brightly painted paper and uses the pieces to form recognizable shapes. Seuss, on the other hand, created most of the illustrations for his books, such as the legendary *The Cat in the Hat,* by drawing cartoons by hand. Regardless of the process used to illustrate their books, the end result was the same for Seuss and Carle's creations: Millions of children loved the stories and were inspired to read.

16. Why does the author mention the heritage of the two children's book authors?
   a. to show that the best children's authors always come from Germany
   b. to explain the ways in which Eric Carle created his illustrations
   c. to demonstrate the importance of a strong family life
   d. to show another way in which the two writers were alike

17. The passage mentions that both Eric Carle and Dr. Seuss have both done all of the following EXCEPT
   a. written and illustrated children's books.
   b. lived in the northeastern part of the United States.
   c. drawn the illustrations for their books by hand.
   d. inspired millions of children with their books.

18. The author most likely mentions Eric Carle's collage process in order to
   a. show students an easy and fun way to create beautiful artwork.
   b. give an example of Eric Carle's level of brilliance as an artist.
   c. show the reasons for the wild success of *The Very Hungry Caterpillar*.
   d. demonstrate the difference between the illustration styles of Carle and Seuss.

Answer questions 19–21 based on the following passage, which is being read by a student in class.

It was a completely ordinary evening. I was walking down the beach after dinner, which I do every night to clear my head. The cloudless night revealed a thin crescent moon and a countless array of stars sparkling like jewels. I walked a few steps toward the ocean, admiring the reflection of the lights on the surface of the water. Just then, I noticed a new light develop in the mirror reflection. I looked up to see a fireball screaming down from the heavens. A meteor lit up the night as it slashed a burning streak through the sky. A moment later, the light was gone and the sky returned to normal. No one else was on the beach. I began to wonder if anyone else had seen the unusual event.

19. Students are learning about how writers use comparisons to tell a story. The students are asked to find an object from the story that is described using a comparison. Which of the following is compared to something else in the passage?
   a. the stars
   b. the ocean
   c. the meteor
   d. the moon

20. Students are learning how some letters can have different sounds. They are beginning to understand that the letter *C* can sound like the letter *S* in words like *snake* or *sad*. Which word from the passage would be a good model to show how the letter *C* can have this sound?
   a. completely
   b. ocean
   c. clear
   d. noticed

21. Students are learning about compound words, and they have each written down a word from the story that they believe is a compound word. Which student's answer is a compound word?
   a. ordinary
   b. fireball
   c. screaming
   d. unusual

Answer questions 22–25 based on the following excerpt from a book which is being read by a student in class.

Maximilian's Year
Chapter 1: The Surprise Party

(1) Maximilian awoke on the morning of his thirteenth birthday with a smile. (2) He got out of bed and looked in the mirror, staring for the first time at the reflection of himself as a teenager. (3) He walked downstairs to the kitchen, expecting his parents and his sister to shower him with birthday wishes on the Sunday morning.

(4) "Good morning, Max," said his father, not taking his eyes off the television in the living room. (5) No one else even looked at Max.

(6) "Hi, everyone!" shouted Max, assuming that they would remember that today was the big day. (7) Max's mother looked up from the newspaper. (8) His sister kept working on her homework at the desk.

(9) Max couldn't believe it. (10) No one remembered his birthday! (11) He plopped down on the couch by himself, dejected. (12) He slumped back in misery.

(13) "The stove is acting up," said Max's mom. (14) "I thought we would go out for brunch this morning."

(15) Max's dad and sister both casually said "sure," but Max was too depressed to even answer.

(16) Max's family members started to get ready for the brunch. (17) Max peeled himself off the couch and figured maybe a good meal would cheer him up.

22. A student does not understand the meaning of the word *dejected* from sentence 11. What could a paraprofessional do to help the student best understand the meaning of the word?
    a. Ask the student to recognize the prefix of the word and then use that information to determine its meaning.
    b. Recommend that the student read the sentence with the word and the sentence after it to determine the tone of the word.
    c. Tell the student to ignore the word if they do not know a word or are unsure of its meaning.
    d. Explain to the student that the day in the story is also Maximilian's thirteenth birthday.

23. Students are beginning to use the elements of a book—including its title, chapter heading, and even the parts of the story—to help make predictions about what will happen. A paraprofessional asks the students in a class what they think will probably happen next. Which answer best shows that the student understands how to use the elements of the book to make an accurate prediction?
    a. Max's family will make breakfast in the kitchen.
    b. Max's family will take him to a surprise birthday party.
    c. Max will not get anything to eat.
    d. Max will have a terrible day because no one remembers his birthday.

24. The events from the excerpt are mixed up in the following list.

I. Max's family got ready to go out.

II. Max looked in the mirror.

III. Max sat on the couch.

IV. Max walked to the kitchen.

A student in the class must put the events in the order that they happened in the excerpt. Which of the following shows the correct order?

a. II, IV, I, III

b. I, IV, III, II

c. IV, II, III, I

d. II, IV, III, I

25. What could a paraprofessional ask a student to find out if they understand the causes of Max's attitude near the end of this excerpt?

a. How does Max react when he thinks no one remembers his birthday?

b. How do you think Max feels now that he is a teenager?

c. Why does Max decide to go out to brunch with his family?

d. What is Max's sister doing when he comes downstairs?

26. Students in a class are working on a lesson about antonyms. Four groups of students write two words that they think are antonyms. Which words are antonyms?

a. Serious and silly

b. Whale and wail

c. Undress and unless

d. Amazing and incredible

27. A student reads the following sentence in a book:

"Squirrels prepare for the winter by assembling a *store* of nuts, which helps provide them with nutrients throughout the cold months."

store (noun). 1. A business where goods are sold; 2. a grocery; 3. a supply or stock; 4. a building or room for a business.

Which dictionary definition should the student use to understand the meaning of the word *store* in context?

a. dictionary definition 1

b. dictionary definition 2

c. dictionary definition 3

d. dictionary definition 4

Answer questions 28-30 based on the following lesson plan.

Lesson Plan for Homonyms

Objective: Students will use the context of homonyms in sentences to recognize that words that have identical sounds may have very different meanings.

Explanation: The teacher will prepare a series of index cards with a homonym on one side and a sentence that uses the homonym on the other side. Each homonym will have at least one other homonym with the same sound on another index card. The paraprofessional will supply each student with one homonym index card, making sure to create pairs or groups of students with matching homonym sounds. Students in each group will read the sentences on their index cards and compare the sounds and meanings of the homonyms. The students will then be asked to create their own sentences with the homonyms. The paraprofessional and the teacher will both walk around the room and ensure that students are using each word correctly. Once the students have demonstrated that they understand the meaning of the homonyms, the paraprofessional will collect the index cards, alphabetizing the words in each group.

28. Which direction will the paraprofessional NOT be expected to follow during the completion of this lesson plan?
   a. provide each student in the class with one homonym index card
   b. come up with sentences that use different homonyms correctly
   c. create groups of students with homonym cards with the same sounds
   d. collect the index cards from the students

29. One group of homonyms contains four different words. Which list shows the words listed in alphabetical order?
   a. caret, carat, carrot, karat
   b. carat, karat, caret, carrot
   c. karat, carat, caret, carrot
   d. carat, caret, carrot, karat

30. Four students write a sentence using a pair of homonyms. Which sentence demonstrates that the student needs additional help understanding the use of homonyms?
   a. Nadine sent a postcard with 28 one-cent stamps.
   b. Sebastian went to meet the butcher to buy some meat.
   c. Bella needs to do her homework before it is dew.
   d. Justin bought a pear and a pair of apples at the market.

Answers and Explanations

Question Number	Correct Answer	Content Category
1	c	Reading Skills: Main idea/primary purpose
2	d	Reading Skills: Vocabulary in context
3	b	Reading Skills: Supporting ideas
4	a	Reading Skills: Inferences
5	c	Reading Skills: Interpreting graphic text
6	b	Reading Skills: Interpreting graphic text
7	a	Reading Skills: Main idea/primary purpose
8	d	Reading Skills: Supporting ideas
9	a	Reading Skills: Interpreting graphic text
10	b	Reading Skills: Fact/opinion
11	a	Reading Skills: Vocabulary in context
12	d	Reading Skills: Organization
13	c	Reading Skills: Inferences
14	c	Reading Skills: Supporting ideas
15	b	Reading Skills: Main idea/primary purpose
16	d	Reading Skills: Organization
17	c	Reading Skills: Supporting ideas
18	d	Reading Skills: Organization
19	a	Reading Application: Making accurate observations
20	d	Reading Application: Sounding out words
21	b	Reading Application: Breaking down words into parts
22	b	Reading Application: Decoding words using context clues
23	b	Reading Application: Making predictions
24	d	Reading Application: Making accurate observations
25	a	Reading Application: Asking questions
26	a	Reading Application: Synonyms, antonyms, and homonyms

Question Number	Correct Answer	Content Category
27	**c**	Reading Application: Using a dictionary
28	**b**	Reading Application: Interpreting directions
29	**d**	Reading Application: Alphabetizing words
30	**c**	Reading Application: Synonyms, antonyms, and homonyms

1. c. The passage says that large animals can be scary, choice **a**, but that is not the main idea. The rest of the passage is about how small animals can also be deadly. While it is true that the poison dart frog may look adorable, choice **d**, or not grow to be more than one inch in length, choice **b**, the main point is that they—like other small animals—can be very dangerous. This is summed up in choice **c**.

2. d. The word *minute* is often used to describe a period of time, choice **a**, but the meaning in the context of this passage is different. The sentence refers to the *minute size* of the poison dart frog, which you can use to determine the intended meaning of the word *minute*, which is small or tiny, choice **d**.

3. b. This question asks for an attribute of the Brooklyn Bridge which the passage does NOT mention as a reason to admire it. The passage mentions the impressive size, choice **a**, and its historic age, choice **c**. The author likes the bridge for its beauty. The only that attribute of the bridge that is never mentioned is its cost, choice **b**.

4. a. To answer this question requires an inference, which means that the information will not be stated directly. The passage says that the Brooklyn Bridge was the longest suspension bridge when it was built, but only "until the twentieth century." That means that another bridge must have been built that was longer than the Brooklyn Bridge, making choice **a** the correct answer. There is no evidence in the passage to suggest that answer choice **b** or **c** is correct. While the Brooklyn Bridge is very old, the passage does not say that it is the oldest suspension bridge in the world.

5. c. The index lists different aspects of the planet Mars. Geology is the study of rocks, so the geology of Mars will tell a reader about the different rocks that make up the planet. The index says that can be found on page 214, choice **c**. Page 199, choice **a**, would tell a reader about the types of rocks that make up the planet Mercury.

6. b. There are entries in the index for the planet Mercury and for the NASA program Mercury. The astronauts were part of the NASA program, which is listed in the index on pages 257–260. A person might learn about the astronauts on page 257, choice **b**.

7. a. Yuri and Owen are the captains of a pickup football game and get to decide which players they want on their teams. But Owen remembers that the last time they picked teams, they hurt another boy's feelings by picking him last. The story is about how they figure out a way to solve this problem, choice **a**. The outcome of the game, choice **b**, is never mentioned. Owen and Yuri are actually trying to be kind to the children, so they are not mean, choice **c**. The story is not mainly about their friendship, so choice **d** is not correct either.

8. d. Ollie may not be the best football player, but the passage does not say that Owen doesn't want him on his team—or that he was ever on Owen's team—so choice **a** is not supported. Likewise, there is nothing in the passage to support the statements in choices **b** or **c**. Owen is concerned that Ollie was upset the last time they picked teams. That is why Owen and Yuri decide to pick teams in private, making choice **d** correct.

9. a. The graph shows that each year from 2006 to 2009, Hickory Hills Farm produced more organic eggs and fewer non-organic eggs. However, the number of non-organic eggs being produced each year is declining very steeply. The number of organic eggs produced goes up by only a little each year. Therefore, the year in which the farm produced the most eggs was 2006, choice **a**. The conclusion in choice **d** may be correct based on the trend of the data in the graph, but it cannot be known for certain. The conclusions in choices **b** and **c** may also be correct, but are not supported by the data in the graph.

10. b. A fact is a statement that can be proven to be true. Saying that the north shore is the "greatest surfing spot," choice **a**, cannot be proven to be true because it is the writer's opinion. The height of a wave *can* be proven, so the sentence in choice **b** is a fact. The statements in choices **c** and **d** are also opinions, and cannot be proven to be true, so they are not correct.

11. a. While the word *draw* is often used to mean *draw a picture*, the word has other meanings. In the context of the sentence from the passage, it means *bring*, choice **a**. If you were not sure how to solve this, you can substitute each word in the answer choices to replace the word from the passage to see which makes the most sense.

12. d. The first sentence of the passage tells the year that Junko Tabei was born in 1939. The passage then goes on to talk about Tabei's childhood, her early achievements, and then the mountains she climbed when she was older. Therefore, the passage is structured in the order in which the events happened, choice **d**.

13. c. Remember that the answers to inference questions are never stated directly in the passage. The passage says that Junko Tabei was the first woman to climb all seven peaks—but be careful, it does not say that she was the first to climb Mount McKinley, choice **a**. The passage mentions Tabei's short height, but does not say whether it was an advantage or a disadvantage in climbing, so choice **b** cannot be inferred. If Tabei was the first woman to climb the tallest mountain on every continent, then she must have climbed Mount Vinson, the tallest peak in Antarctica, choice **c**. Choice **d** is also tricky: Tabei was the first woman to climb Mount Everest, but she was not the *oldest*.

14. c. The passage does not mention that Junko Tabei wanted to be the first woman to climb the tallest mountains (choice **a**), only that she ended up achieving this. Tabei may not have been scared of the dangers of the mountain, but it was not the reason Tabei enjoyed the sport. Likewise, the passage does not suggest that Junko Tabei became a mountain climber because there were not enough female climbers, choice **d**. The passage says that she enjoyed not having to compete with other people on the mountain, so the correct answer is choice **c**.

15. b. The passage mentions all of the many qualifications necessary to be an airline pilot. But the most important qualification is saved for the last sentence: the experience, choice **b**. While the author mentions that a pilot must pass many tests, choice **d**, that is not the main focus of the passage. The statements in choices **a** and **c** are not supported by the passage.

16. d. The first paragraph mentions many similarities between two of the most popular children's book authors. The author includes the fact that their families were German to show another way that they were alike, choice **d**. Be careful of extreme answers, like choice **a**, which say that the best children's authors *always* come from Germany; those types of statements are rarely correct.

17. c. This question asks for the one attribute of Seuss and Carle that is NOT mentioned in the passage as a similarity between the two writers. The passage says that both men wrote and illustrated children's books, choice **a**, were born in the northeastern United States, choice **b**, and inspired children to read with their stories, choice **d**. Only Dr. Seuss drew his illustrations by hand; Eric Carle uses pieces of colored paper to create collages for his illustrations. Therefore, choice **c** is correct.

18. d. The second paragraph of the passage talks about Eric Carle's collage process. The author does this primarily to contrast with the process that Dr. Seuss uses to create his illustrations, choice **d**. The explanation of the collage process may show students a way to create artwork, choice **a**, or see another way that Carle was very talented, choice **b**, but those are not the most likely reasons why the author mentioned the collage process.

19. a. The author compares the stars in the sky to jewels, so choice **a** is correct. The ocean and the moon are not compared to anything else, so choices **b** and **d** are not correct. The author uses some descriptive language, including personification, to tell about the

meteor, choice **c**, but does not use a comparison.

20. d. Each of the words in the answer choices contains a letter *C*. However, only one word contains a letter *C* that makes an *s* sound like *snake* or *sad*. That word is *noticed*, choice **d**.

21. b. A compound word can be split into two other words. The only word in the answer choices that can be split into two words is *fireball*, which can be split into the words *fire* and *ball*. Therefore, choice **b** is correct.

22. b. A student may not know the meaning of the word *dejected*. But if a student reads the sentence with that word and the sentence after it, it should be clear that Max is not happy. That should help provide a student with the tone for the word and help him or her understand that the word has a negative meaning. Choice **b** is therefore the best option. The suggestions in choices **a**, **c**, and **d**. will not help a student understand the meaning of the unknown word.

23. b. The name of the chapter is "The Surprise Party". Therefore, it should be clear that although Max's family has not said anything about his birthday, they are likely planning a party for him. The most likely prediction is therefore choice **b**. While it looks like Max is going to have a terrible day, choice **d**, the title of the chapter implies that he will have a party for his birthday, so choice **d** is not correct. The family is heading to brunch, so choices **a** and **c** are not correct either.

24. d. The passage begins with Max waking up and looking at himself in the mirror, so step II should come first. He then walked to the kitchen to greet his family, so step IV should come next. Choices **a** and **d** both start with steps II and then IV, but only choice **d** continues the proper order, which is that he sat on the couch (III) before his family got ready to go out (I).

25. a. Max is feeling depressed toward the end of the excerpt. To determine whether students understand the causes, a paraprofessional should ask students about Max's birthday—and the fact that no one seems to remember it. Therefore, the question in choice **a** would be the most appropriate to ask.

26. a. Antonyms are words that have opposite meanings. The words *serious* and *silly* have opposite meanings, so choice **a** is correct. The words in choice **b** are homonyms. The words in choice **c** share the same prefix. The words in choice **d** are synonyms.

27. c. Students may be familiar with the word *store* as a place to go to buy goods, but the word is used with a different meaning in the given sentence. According to the sentence, the squirrels create a stock of nuts to help them get through the winter. Dictionary definition 3, choice **c**, should be used.

28. b. According to the explanation of the lesson plan, the paraprofessional will be expected to provide each student with an index card, group the students who have cards with homonyms containing the same sounds, and then collect the index cards at the end of the lesson. It is the students who are being asked in the lesson to come up with sentences using the different homonyms. Therefore, choice **b** is correct.

29. d. The four different words—*carat*, *caret*, *carrot*, and *karat*—have the same sound but different spellings. The words are listed in alphabetical order in answer choice **d**.

30. c. Each sentence uses a pair of homonyms with the same sound. However, one sentence uses a homonym incorrectly. The word *dew* means *water*, or *moisture*. The sentence in answer choice **c** uses the word *dew* when the word *due* would have been appropriate. Therefore, choice **c** is correct.

5 ▶ MATH SKILLS AND KNOWLEDGE

CHAPTER SUMMARY

The Math Skills and Knowledge section of the ParaPro Assessment includes 30 questions, and makes up one-third of the entire test. The math section will always appear second on the test, after the reading section and before the writing section.

Because the Math Skills and Knowledge section is one-third of the test, you should expect to spend about one-third of the available time on it. That means you will have about 50 minutes to answer the 30 questions. You can spend more time on one section of the test than on another section—however, if you decide to spend more time on this section, be aware that you will have less time to answer the questions in a later section. For example, you may choose to spend more time solving the math problems carefully—but then you will have a bit less time to solve the writing problems in the following section.

Of the 30 questions on the math section, you can expect that the first 18 or so will test your ability to solve math problems in real-life and conceptual contexts. The problem may set up a situation, or ask for the answer to a straightforward computation problem such as 14×25. The last 12 questions or so on the math section will test your ability to apply your math skills to classroom use. Those problems may ask you to identify the best way to help a struggling student with a math problem, or help a teacher complete a mathematics task in the classroom.

You will NOT be allowed to have a calculator on the ParaPro Assessment.

About the Math Skills and Knowledge Section

Every question on the Math Skills and Knowledge section of the ParaPro Assessment is multiple-choice, with four answer choices. The answer choices will always be **a**, **b**, **c**, and **d**.

Each question in this section is independent of one another. That means that there will not be more than one question for a scenario or a piece of art. About one-third of the questions will include a piece of art, such as a number line, coordinate plane, or polygon.

Most problems on the reading section of the ParaPro Assessment will ask a specific question, such as the following problem:

1. Which inequality is correct?
   a. $4 + 8 > 15 - 4$
   b. $15 - 6 < 4 + 4$
   c. $5 + 5 > 12 - 2$
   d. $11 - 1 < 9 + 1$

Even though this book calls them "questions," some of the problems on the ParaPro Assessment do not include a question mark. Those questions will ask you to complete a sentence or equation, such as the following problem:

2. $14 \times 25 =$
   a. 39
   b. 250
   c. 260
   d. 350

A few questions on the reading section will ask you to find the answer choice that is NOT true. These types of questions can be very tricky! Fortunately, the makers of the test will capitalize the word that tells you that you are looking for the answer that is NOT true.

3. Which of the following expressions is NOT equal to 100?
   a. 2×50
   b. $300 \div 3$
   c. $400 - 300$
   d. $20 + 5$

For this question, you would need to get rid of any answer choice that is equal to 100. The one expression that is NOT equal to 100 is the correct choice.

Test-Taking Tips for Math Skills and Knowledge Questions

Below are a handful of specific tips for the math section of the ParaPro Assessment.

Use the Answer Choices

Some math problems on the ParaPro Assessment can be very time-intensive—especially if you are not accustomed to solving those types of problems. However, every question on the test will have four answer choices. That means that the correct answer is right there, directly below each question. You can sometimes use that information to take a shortcut and save yourself some time. For example, look at the following algebra problem:

4. If $45 - z = 36$, the value of z must be
  a. 7
  b. 9
  c. 11
  d. 81

Maybe you've forgotten the steps needed to solve for a variable (z) in an equation. But you know, based on the given answer choices, that the value of z must be 7, 9, 11, or 81. It may be easier for you to simply plug the values for z from the answer choices into the equation and see which one fits. The number that makes the equation true is the correct answer choice. In this case, only 9 would fit the equation: $45 - 9 = 36$ is true, so choice **b** would be correct.

Recognize the Order of the Answer Choices

Chapter 3 of this book covered the usefulness of the process of elimination. That can be used on any multiple-choice standardized test. However, the answer choices on the math section of the ParaPro Assessment, when they are in numeric form, will always be in order. Sometimes they will be in order from smallest to largest; other times they will be in order from largest to smallest. Either way, you can use this quirk of the test design to your benefit. How? Look at the following question.

5. If $18 + k = 90$, $k =$
  a. 98
  b. 82
  c. 72
  d. 5

Notice that the numbers in the answer choices are listed from greatest to least. If you were unsure of how to solve this algebra problem, you could use this order to help save you time. In this case, you can start with the number in choice **b**. Using 82 for the value of k results in the following:

$$18 + 82 = 90$$
$$100 = 90$$

Using 82 for k gives you a value that is too high. The value of k must be lower than 82. Therefore, you don't even have to try choice **a**, 98, because it is higher than 82. You can skip right to the number in choice **c**, 72. You were able to eliminate choice **a** without even trying it. This can save you valuable time—especially since you will have to take a whole extra section of the test *after* the math section. The correct answer is indeed choice **c**, 72: $18 + 72 = 90$.

Rewrite the Problem

Many questions on the ParaPro Assessment will ask you to solve for the sum, difference, product, or quotient of whole numbers, decimals, or fractions. For example, a possible question on the test may look like this:

6. $32.13 + 5.8 =$
   a. 26.33
   b. 32.71
   c. 37.21
   d. 37.93

Do *not* try to solve this problem just by looking at it. It's much more difficult to solve a problem written horizontally like this. Rewrite the problem by stacking the numbers to be added, making sure to align them by the decimal value:

$$\begin{array}{r} 32.13 \\ +\ 5.8\ \ \ \\ \hline \end{array}$$

Now it's much easier to perform the addition. You can just add the numbers in each place value. You should get 37.93, the number listed in answer choice **d**.

Important Mathematics Vocabulary

The math section of the ParaPro Assessment will test your knowledge of important math terms. You will be expected to know the bolded words in the following paragraphs. Make sure you are familiar with every one of these terms before taking the test.

Area is the amount of space inside a two-dimensional shape.

The **average** (arithmetic mean) of a set of values is the number found when all the values are added together and divided by the number of values. For example, the average of 1, 2, and 6 is 3 because $1 + 2 + 6 = 9$ and $9 \div 3 = 3$.

A **bar graph** is a chart or graph that compares amounts for different categories.

A **circle** is a curved, two-dimensional figure where every point is the same distance from the center.

A **circle graph** is a diagram in the shape of a circle which shows the parts of a whole.

The **circumference** is the total distance around a circle.

A **composite number** is a number that has more than two factors. For example, the numbers 4, 9, and 100 are all composite numbers.

A **coordinate plane** is a grid created by a horizontal x-axis and a vertical y-axis.

The **denominator** is the bottom number of a fraction. For example, in the fraction $\frac{1}{2}$, the denominator is 2.

The **diameter** is a line that goes directly through the center of a circle—the longest line segment that can be drawn in a circle.

The **difference** is the solution to a subtraction problem.

A **digit** is a number from 0 through 9. For example, the number 123 has three digits: 1, 2, and 3.

An **equation** is a mathematical statement that states the equality of two expressions, and uses an equals sign, $=$. For example, $4 + 5 = 9$ is an equation.

An **equilateral** triangle is a triangle that has three sides with the same length.

An **expression** is a mathematical statement that does not use an equals sign, $=$, or inequality symbol, such as $<$ or $>$. For example, $3 + 1$ is an expression.

A **factor** of a number is any integer that divides evenly into another integer without a remainder. For example, the factors of 6 are –6, –3, –2, –1, 1, 2, 3, and 6.

A **fraction** is a part of a whole, represented with one number over another number. For example, $\frac{1}{2}$ and $\frac{6}{7}$ are fractions.

A **hexagon** is a polygon with six sides and six angles.

The **hundredths** digit is the digit two places to the right of the decimal point. For example, in the number 12.34, the digit 4 is in the hundredths place.

An **integer** is positive or negative whole number or 0. For example, the numbers –3, –1, 0, and 128 are all integers.

An **isosceles** triangle is a triangle that has two sides with the same length.

A **line graph** is a diagram that uses a line to show a change over time.

The **mean** of a data set is the average found by adding all of the numbers together and dividing by the quantity of numbers in the set. For example, the mean of 2, 4, 6, 8, and 10 is 6. ($2 + 4 + 6 + 8 + 10 = 30$; and $30 \div 5 = 6$.)

The **median** of a data set is the center number, if the values are in ascending or descending order. For example, the median of 3, 5, 7, 9, 11 is 7, because 7 is the digit in the middle of the set.

The **mode** of a data set is the number that appears the greatest number of times. For example, the mode of 3, 8, 3, 9, 16 is 3, because it appears the most out of the available numbers.

A **multiple** of a number is the product of an integer and another integer. For example, the numbers 3, 6, 9, and 12 are all multiples of 3.

The **numerator** is the top number of a fraction. In the fraction $\frac{1}{2}$, the numerator is 1.

An **octagon** is a polygon with eight sides and eight angles. It may help to remember the meaning of this polygon by seeing the prefix of the word, *oct–*, which means *eight* (like octopus).

A **pattern** is a series of figures of numbers that repeat in a predictable way.

A **percent** is a way to show a numerical fraction of 1 (whole), where 1 is equal to 100%.

The **perimeter** is the total distance around the edges of a polygon.

A **pictograph** is a diagram or chart that uses pictures, or graphics, to show the level of occurrence for different categories.

A **polygon** is a two-dimensional object with straight lines that create a closed figure.

A **prime number** is a number that is only evenly divisible by itself and the number 1. For example, 3, 7, and 29 are all prime numbers.

The **product** of two or more numbers is the result when they are multiplied together.

A **quadrilateral** is a polygon with four sides and four angles. It may help to remember the meaning of this polygon by seeing the prefix of the word, *quad–*, which means *four*.

The **quotient** is the solution to a division problem.

The **radius** is a line segment from the center of a circle to a point on the circle (half of the diameter).

A **rectangle** is a four-sided polygon with four right angles. All rectangles have two pairs of parallel sides.

A **right** triangle is a triangle that has one 90-degree (right) angle.

A **scalene** triangle is a triangle that has no sides that are the same length.

A **square** is a four-sided polygon with four right angles and four equal sides. All squares have two pairs of parallel sides.

The **sum** of two or more numbers is the result when they are added together.

The **tenths** digit is the digit one place to the right of the decimal point. For example, in the number 12.34, the digit 3 is in the tenths place.

The **thousandths** digit is the digit three places to the right of the decimal point. For example, in the number 12.345, the digit 5 is in the thousandths place.

A **triangle** is a polygon with three sides and three angles. It may help to remember the meaning of this polygon by seeing the prefix of the word, *tri–*, which means *three* (like *tripod*).

A **variable** is a letter that represents an unknown number.

Volume is the amount of space inside a three-dimensional shape.

A **whole number** is a positive number that is neither a decimal nor a fraction, or zero. The numbers 0, 3, 19, and 1,218 are all whole numbers.

Math Skills and Knowledge Review

ETS, the maker of the ParaPro Assessment, says that there are five different math subjects to know for the math section of the test. There will be about 18 questions on the math section that will test your knowledge of these subjects in a general way. The subjects are as follows, with bullet points to show how each subject will be tested on the ParaPro Assessment:

1. **Arithmetic**
   - add, subtract, multiply, and divide whole number, fractions, and decimals
   - understand the place-value system for both decimals and whole numbers
   - recognize the meaning of math terms and symbols, such as *product, quotient,* $\div$, $<$, or $>$
   - use percentages
   - understand that numbers can be expressed in different ways, such as one hundredth, 0.01, and 1%
   - identify the relative value of numbers, such as the fact that 2.5 is between 2 and 3
   - use estimation
   - demonstrate knowledge of the order of operations
2. **Algebra**
   - solve single-step linear equations with one variable, such as $x + 1 = 3$
   - identify a pattern and the numbers that follow
3. **Geometry**
   - recognize and name geometric shapes, such as triangles, quadrilaterals, or other polygons
   - find the perimeter, area, and volume for shapes
   - graph points and identify ordered pairs on a coordinate plane
4. **Measurement**
   - convert units within the same system, such as 2 feet to 24 inches or 200 centimeters to 2 meters
   - understand that information can be demonstrated in multiple ways, such as 1¢, $0.01, and 1 penny
5. **Data Organization and Interpretation**
   - create and interpret tables, graphs, or charts, and be able to identify trends
   - calculate the mean, median, and mode

The next five sections explain each type of skill with examples that show how you might see the subject tested on the ParaPro Assessment.

Arithmetic

This section covers the basics of mathematical operations and their sequence. It also reviews whole numbers, integers, fractions, decimals, percents, and estimation.

The Number Line

The number line is a graphical representation of the order of numbers. As you move to the right, the value increases. As you move to the left, the value decreases.

A number line can show the approximate values of certain numbers. For example, the following number line shows that −4.5 is halfway between −5 and −4 and that 2.2 is closer to 2 than it is to 3.

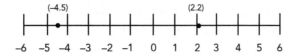

Comparison Symbols

The following table will illustrate some comparison symbols:

SYMBOL	MEANS	EXAMPLE
=	is equal to	5 = 5
≠	is not equal to	4 ≠ 3
>	is greater than	5 > 3
≥	is greater than or equal to	6 ≥ 5 or 6 ≥ 6
<	is less than	4 < 6
≤	is less than or equal to	5 ≤ 8 or 8 ≤ 8

Addition Symbols

In addition, the numbers being added are called **addends**. The result is called a **sum**. The symbol for addition is called a **plus** sign. In the following example, 4 and 5 are addends and 9 is the sum:

$$4 + 5 = 9$$

Subtraction Symbols

In subtraction, the number being subtracted is called the **subtrahend**. The number being subtracted *from* is called the **minuend**. The answer to a subtraction problem is called a **difference**. The symbol for subtraction is called a **minus** sign. In the following example, 15 is the minuend, 4 is the subtrahend, and 11 is the difference:

$$15 - 4 = 11$$

Multiplication Symbols

When two or more numbers are being multiplied, they are called **factors**. The answer that results is called the **product**. In the following example, 5 and 6 are factors and 30 is their product:

$$5 \times 6 = 30$$

There are several ways to represent multiplication in this mathematical statement.

A dot between factors indicates multiplication:

$5 \cdot 6 = 30$

Parentheses around any one or more factors indicate multiplication:

$(5)6 = 30$, $5(6) = 30$, and $(5)(6) = 30$.

Multiplication is also indicated when a number is placed next to a variable: $5a = 30$. In this equation, 5 is being multiplied by a.

Division Symbols

In division, the number being divided *by* is called the **divisor**. The number being divided *into* is called the **dividend**. The answer to a division problem is called the **quotient**.

There are a few different ways to represent division with symbols. In each of the following equivalent expressions, 3 is the divisor and 8 is the dividend:

$8 \div 3$, $\frac{8}{3}$, and $3\overline{)8}$

Prime and Composite Numbers

A positive integer that is greater than the number 1 is either prime or composite, but not both.

- A **prime number** is a number that has exactly two factors: 1 and itself. For example, 2, 3, 5, 7, 11, 13, 17, 19, and 23 are all prime numbers.
- A **composite number** is a number that has more than two factors. For example, 4, 6, 8, 9, 10, 12, 14, 15, and 16 are all composite numbers.
- The number 1 is neither prime nor composite since it has only one factor.

Whole Numbers

Whole numbers are the set of nonnegative numbers that are not expressed as a fraction or a decimal. For example, 0, 4, 39, and 3,318 are all whole numbers. For the ParaPro Assessment, you will be expected to know how to add, subtract, multiply, divide, compare, and order them.

Comparing and Ordering Whole Numbers

To compare and order whole numbers, it is essential that you are familiar with the place value system. The following table shows the place values for a very large number: 3,294,107.

Digit	3	2	9	4	1	0	7
Place Value	Millions	Hundred Thousands	Ten Thousands	Thousands	Hundreds	Tens	Ones

To compare or order whole numbers, you need to look at the digits in the largest place value of a number first.

Example
Compare 3,419 and 3,491.

Begin by comparing the two numbers in their largest place value. They both have the digit 3 in the thousands place. Therefore, you do not know which number is larger. Move to the smaller place values (to the right) of each number and continue comparing. The digit in the hundreds place for each number is 4. You still do not know which number is larger. However, when you compare the digits in the tens places, you see that the 9 is greater than the 1. That means 3,491 is greater than 3,419. This can be represented with the greater than symbol: 3,491 > 4,419.

Example
Put the following numbers in order from greatest to least: 307, 319, 139, 301.

To order these numbers, the digits in their place values must be compared. Three of the numbers have a 3 in the hundreds place, but one number has a 1 in the hundreds place. Therefore, 139 is the smallest number. Next the digits in the tens places must be compared with the remaining numbers. The tens digit in 319 is 1, and the tens digit in 307 and 301 is 0. Therefore, 319 is the largest number. To order 307 and 301, compare the digits in the ones place: 7 is greater than 1, so 307 is greater than 301.

The correct order of the numbers, from greatest to least, is 319, 307, 301, and 139.

Adding Whole Numbers

Addition is used when it is necessary to combine amounts. It is easiest to add when the addends are stacked in a column with the place values aligned. Work from right to left, starting with the ones column.

Example

Add 40 + 129 + 24.

1. Align the addends in the ones column. Because it is necessary to work from right to left, begin to add starting with the ones column. The ones column totals 13, and 13 equals 1 ten and 3 ones, so write the 3 in the ones column of the answer, and regroup, or "carry" the 1 ten to the next column as a 1 over the tens column, so that it gets added with the other tens:

$$
\begin{array}{r}
\overset{1}{}40 \\
129 \\
+\ 24 \\
\hline
3
\end{array}
$$

2. Add the tens column, including the regrouped 1.

$$
\begin{array}{r}
\overset{1}{}40 \\
129 \\
+\ 24 \\
\hline
93
\end{array}
$$

3. Then add the hundreds column. Because there is only one value, write the 1 in the answer.

$$
\begin{array}{r}
\overset{1}{}40 \\
129 \\
+\ 24 \\
\hline
193
\end{array}
$$

Subtracting Whole Numbers

Subtraction is used to find the difference between amounts. It is easiest to subtract when the minuend and subtrahend are in a column with the place values aligned. Again, just as in addition, work from right to left. It may be necessary to regroup.

Example

If Becky has 52 clients and Claire has 36, how many more clients does Becky have?

1. Find the difference between their client numbers by subtracting. Start with the ones column. Because 2 is less than the number being subtracted (6), regroup, or "borrow," a ten from the tens column. Add the regrouped amount to the ones column. Now subtract 12 – 6 in the ones column.

$$
\begin{array}{r}
{\scriptstyle 4\,1} \\
\cancel{5}2 \\
-\ 36 \\
\hline
6
\end{array}
$$

2. Regrouping 1 ten from the tens column left 4 tens. Subtract 4 – 3 and write the result in the tens column of the answer. Becky has 16 more clients than Claire. Check by addition: 16 + 36 = 52.

$$
\begin{array}{r}
{\scriptstyle 4\,1} \\
\cancel{5}2 \\
-\ 36 \\
\hline
16
\end{array}
$$

Multiplying Whole Numbers

In multiplication, the same amount is combined multiple times. For example, instead of adding 30 three times, 30 + 30 + 30, it is easier to simply multiply 30 by 3. If a problem asks for the product of two or more numbers, the numbers should be multiplied to arrive at the answer.

Example

A school auditorium contains 54 rows, each containing 34 seats. How many seats are there in total?

1. In order to solve this problem, you could add 34 to itself 54 times, but we can solve this problem more easily with multiplication. Line up the place values vertically, writing the problem in columns. Multiply the number in the ones place of the top factor (4) by the number in the ones place of the bottom factor (4): 4 × 4 = 16. Because 16 = 1 ten and 6 ones, write the 6 in the ones place in the first partial product.

$$
\begin{array}{r}
{\scriptstyle 1} \\
34 \\
\times\ 54 \\
\hline
6
\end{array}
$$

2. Multiply the number in the tens place in the top factor (3) by the number in the ones place of the bottom factor (4): $4 \times 3 = 12$. Then add the regrouped amount: $12 + 1 = 13$. Write the 3 in the tens column and the 1 in the hundreds column of the partial product.

$$
\begin{array}{r}
^1 \\
34 \\
\times\ 54 \\
\hline
136
\end{array}
$$

3. The last calculations to be done require multiplying by the tens place of the bottom factor. Multiply 5 (tens from bottom factor) by 4 (ones from top factor); $5 \times 4 = 20$, but because the 5 really represents a number of tens, the actual value of the answer is 200 ($50 \times 4 = 200$). Therefore, write the two zeros under the ones and tens columns of the second partial product and regroup or carry the 2 hundreds by writing a 2 above the tens place of the top factor.

$$
\begin{array}{r}
^2 \\
34 \\
\times\ 54 \\
\hline
136 \\
00
\end{array}
$$

4. Multiply 5 (tens from bottom factor) by 3 (tens from top factor); $5 \times 3 = 15$, but because the 5 and the 3 each represent a number of tens, the actual value of the answer is 1,500 ($50 \times 30 = 1,500$). Add the two additional hundreds carried over from the last multiplication: $15 + 2 = 17$ (hundreds). Write the 17 in front of the zeros in the second partial product.

$$
\begin{array}{r}
^2 \\
34 \\
\times\ 54 \\
\hline
136 \\
1,700
\end{array}
$$

5. Add the partial products to find the total product:

$$
\begin{array}{r}
^2 \\
34 \\
\times\ 54 \\
\hline
136 \\
+\ 1,700 \\
\hline
1,836
\end{array}
$$

Note: It is easier to perform multiplication if you write the factor with the greater number of digits in the top row. In this example, both factors have an equal number of digits, so it does not matter which is written on top.

Dividing Whole Numbers

In division, the same amount is subtracted multiple times. For example, instead of subtracting 5 from 25 as many times as possible, $25 - 5 - 5 - 5 - 5 - 5$, it is easier to simply divide, asking how many 5s are in 25: $25 \div 5$.

Example

At a road show, three artists sold their beads for a total of $54. If they share the money equally, how much money should each artist receive?

1. Divide the total amount ($54) by the number of ways the money is to be split (3). Work from left to right. How many times does 3 divide into 5? Write the answer, 1, directly above the 5 in the dividend, because both the 5 and the 1 represent a number of tens. Now multiply: since $1(\text{ten}) \div 3(\text{ones}) = 3(\text{tens})$, write the 3 under the 5, and subtract; $5(\text{tens}) - 3(\text{tens}) = 2(\text{tens})$.

$$
\begin{array}{r}
1 \\
3\overline{)54} \\
\underline{-3} \\
2
\end{array}
$$

2. Continue dividing. Bring down the 4 from the ones place in the dividend. How many times does 3 divide into 24? Write the answer, 8, directly above the 4 in the dividend. Because $3 \div 8 = 24$, write 24 below the other 24 and subtract $24 - 24 = 0$.

$$
\begin{array}{r}
18 \\
3\overline{)54} \\
\underline{-3} \\
24 \\
\underline{-24} \\
0
\end{array}
$$

Remainders

If you get a number other than zero after your last subtraction, this number is your remainder.

Example

What is 9 divided by 4?

$$
\begin{array}{r}
2 \\
4\overline{)9} \\
\underline{-8} \\
1
\end{array}
$$

1 is the remainder.

The answer is 2 R1. This answer can also be written as $2\frac{1}{4}$, because there was one part left over out of the four parts needed to make a whole.

Estimating with Whole Numbers

Some questions on the ParaPro Assessment will ask you for an estimate. That means you will not need to find the actual answer, but should instead find an answer that is *close* to the actual answer. One way to solve estimation problems with whole numbers is to use numbers that are easy to work with, and that are close to the actual numbers.

Example

A television set weighs 21 pounds. About how much will a case weigh if it carries 46 television sets?

The number 21 is close to 20, and 20 is much easier to work with than 21. The number 46 is close to 50, and 50 is much easier to work with than 46. To find the approximate weight of the 46 television sets, you can just multiply 20 by 50. A proper estimate would be 1,000 pounds.

Integers

An integer is a whole number or its opposite. Here are some rules for performing operations with integers:

Adding Integers

Adding numbers with the same sign results in a sum of the same sign:

(positive) + (positive) = positive
(negative) + (negative) = negative

When adding numbers of different signs, follow this two-step process:

1. Subtract the positive values of the numbers. Positive values are the values of the numbers without any signs.
2. Keep the sign of the number with the larger positive value.

Example

$-2 + 3 =$

1. Subtract the positive values of the numbers: $3 - 2 = 1$.
2. The number 3 is the larger of the two positive values. Its sign in the original example was positive, so the sign of the answer is positive. The answer is positive 1.

Example

$8 + -11 =$

1. Subtract the positive values of the numbers: $11 - 8 = 3$.
2. The number 11 is the larger of the two positive values. Its sign in the original example was negative, so the sign of the answer is negative. The answer is negative 3.

Subtracting Integers

When subtracting integers, change the subtraction sign to an addition sign, and change the sign of the number being subtracted to its opposite. Then follow the rules for addition.

Examples

$(+10) - (+12) = (+10) + (-12) = -2$

$(-5) - (-7) = (-5) + (+7) = +2$

Multiplying and Dividing Integers

A simple method for remembering the rules of multiplying and dividing is that if the signs are the same when multiplying or dividing two quantities, the answer will be positive. If the signs are different, the answer will be negative.

$(positive) \times (positive) = positive$

$$\frac{(positive)}{(positive)} = positive$$

$(positive) \times (negative) = negative$

$$\frac{(positive)}{(negative)} = negative$$

$(negative) \times (negative) = positive$

$$\frac{(negative)}{(negative)} = positive$$

Examples

$(10)(-12) = -120$

$-5 \times -7 = 35$

$12 \div -3 = -4$

$15 \div 3 = 5$

Exponents

An exponent indicates the number of times a base is used as a factor to attain a product.

Example

Evaluate 2^5.

In this example, 2 is the base and 5 is the exponent. Therefore, 2 should be used as a factor 5 times to attain a product:

$$2^5 = 2 \times 2 \times 2 \times 2 \times 2 = 32$$

Zero Exponent

Any nonzero number raised to the zero power equals 1.

Examples

$5^0 = 1$ 　　　　　 $70^0 = 1$ 　　　　 $29,874^0 = 1$

Perfect Squares

The number 5^2 is read "5 to the second power," or, more commonly, "5 squared." Perfect squares are numbers that are second powers of other numbers. Perfect squares are always zero or positive, because when you multiply a positive or a negative by itself, the result is always positive. The perfect squares are 0^2, 1^2, 2^2, 3^2 ... Therefore, the perfect squares are 0, 1, 4, 9, 16, 25, 36, 49, 64, 81, 100 ...

Perfect Cubes

The number 53 is read as "5 to the third power," or, more commonly, "5 cubed." (Powers higher than three have no special name.) Perfect cubes are numbers that are third powers of other numbers. Perfect cubes, unlike perfect squares, can be either positive or negative. This is because when a negative is multiplied by itself three times, the result is negative. The perfect cubes are 0^3, 1^3, 2^3, 3^3 ... Therefore, the perfect cubes are 0, 1, 8, 27, 64, 125 ...

The Order of Operations

There is an order in which a sequence of mathematical operations must be performed, known as PEMDAS:

P: *Parentheses/Grouping Symbols*. Perform all operations within parentheses first. If there is more than one set of parentheses, begin to work with the innermost set and work toward the outside. If more than one operation is present within the parentheses, use the remaining rules of order to determine which operation to perform first.

E: *Exponents*. Evaluate exponents.

M/D: *Multiply/Divide*. Work from left to right in the expression.

A/S: *Add/Subtract*. Work from left to right in the expression.

This order and the acronym PEMDAS, which can be remembered by using the first letter of each of the words in the phrase: **P**lease **E**xcuse **M**y **D**ear **A**unt **S**ally.

Example

$$\frac{(5+3)^2}{4} + 27$$

$$= \frac{8^2}{4} + 27$$

$$= \frac{64}{4} + 27$$

$$= 16 + 27$$

$$= 43$$

Properties of Arithmetic

While ETS says that the ParaPro Assessment will not test your knowledge of the properties of mathematics, they are very important to know.

Commutative Property: This property states that the result of an arithmetic operation is not affected by reversing the order of the numbers. Multiplication and addition are operations that satisfy the commutative property.

> *Examples*
> $5 \times 2 = 2 \times 5$
> $(5)a = a(5)$
> $b + 3 = 3 + b$

However, neither subtraction nor division is commutative, because reversing the order of the numbers does not yield the same result.

> *Examples*
> $5 - 2 \neq 2 - 5$
> $6 \div 3 \neq 3 \div 6$

Associative Property: If parentheses can be moved to group different numbers in an arithmetic problem without changing the result, then the operation is associative. Addition and multiplication are associative.

> *Examples*
> $2 + (3 + 4) = (2 + 3) + 4$
> $2(ab) = (2a)b$

Distributive Property: When a value is being multiplied by a sum or difference, multiply that value by each quantity within the parentheses. Then, take the sum or difference to yield an equivalent result.

> *Examples*
> $5(a + b) = 5a + 5b$
> $5(100 - 6) = (5 \times 100) - (5 \times 6)$

This second example can be proved by performing the calculations:

> $5(94) = 5(100 - 6)$
> $470 = 500 - 30$
> $470 = 470$

Additive and Multiplicative Identities and Inverses

The **additive identity** is the value that, when added to a number, does not change the number. For all integers, the additive identity is 0.

> ### Examples
> $5 + 0 = 5$
> $-3 + 0 = -3$
>
> Adding 0 does not change the values of 5 and −3, so 0 is the additive identity.

The **additive inverse** of a number is the number that, when added to the number, gives you the additive identity.

> ### Example
> What is the additive inverse of −3?
>
> This means, "What number can I add to −3 to give me the additive identity (0)?"
> $-3 + \underline{} = 0$
> $-3 + 3 = 0$
>
> The answer is 3.

The **multiplicative identity** is the value that, when multiplied by a number, does not change the number. For all integers, the multiplicative identity is 1.

> ### Examples
> $5 \times 1 = 5$
> $-3 \times 1 = -3$
>
> Multiplying by 1 does not change the values of 5 and −3, so 1 is the multiplicative identity.

The **multiplicative inverse** of a number is the number that, when multiplied by the number, gives you the multiplicative identity.

> ### Example
> What is the multiplicative inverse of 5?
>
> This means, "What number can I multiply 5 by to give me the multiplicative identity (1)?"
> $5 \times \underline{} = 1$
> $\frac{1}{5} \times 5 = 1$
>
> The answer is $\frac{1}{5}$.

There is an easy way to find the multiplicative inverse. It is the **reciprocal**, which is obtained by reversing the numerator and denominator of a fraction. In the preceding example, the answer is the reciprocal of 5; 5 can be written as $\frac{5}{1}$, so the reciprocal is $\frac{1}{5}$.

Note: Reciprocals do not change signs.

Note: The additive inverse of a number is the opposite of the number; the multiplicative inverse is the reciprocal.

Factors and Multiples

Factors are numbers that can be divided into a larger number without a remainder.

Example
$12 \div 3 = 4$

The number 3 is, therefore, a factor of the number 12. Other factors of 12 are 1, 2, 4, 6, and 12. The common factors of two numbers are the factors that both numbers have in common.

Examples
The factors of 24 = 1, 2, 3, 4, 6, 8, 12, and 24.
The factors of 18 = 1, 2, 3, 6, 9, and 18.

From the examples, you can see that the common factors of 24 and 18 are 1, 2, 3, and 6. From this list it can also be determined that the *greatest* common factor of 24 and 18 is 6. Determining the **greatest common factor** (GCF) is useful for simplifying fractions.

Example
Simplify $\frac{16}{20}$.

The factors of 16 are 1, 2, 4, 8, and 16. The factors of 20 are 1, 2, 4, 5, and 20. The common factors of 16 and 20 are 1, 2, and 4. The greatest of these, the GCF, is 4. Therefore, to simplify the fraction, both numerator and denominator should be divided by 4.

$$\frac{16}{20} = \frac{(16 \div 4)}{(20 \div 4)} = \frac{4}{5}$$

Multiples are numbers that can be obtained by multiplying a number x by a positive integer.

Example
$5 \times 7 = 35$

The number 35 is, therefore, a multiple of the number 5 and of the number 7. Other multiples of 5 are 5, 10, 15, 20, and so on. Other multiples of 7 are 7, 14, 21, 28, and so on.

The common multiples of two numbers are the multiples that both numbers share.

Example
Some multiples of 4 are: 4, 8, 12, 16, 20, 24, 28, 32, 36 . . .
Some multiples of 6 are: 6, 12, 18, 24, 30, 36, 42, 48 . . .

Some common multiples are 12, 24, and 36. From the above it can also be determined that the *least* common multiple of the numbers 4 and 6 is 12, since this number is the smallest number that appeared in both lists. The **least common multiple**, or LCM, is used when performing addition and subtraction of fractions to find the least common denominator.

Example (using denominators 4 and 6 and LCM of 12)

$$\frac{1}{4} + \frac{5}{6} = \frac{1(3)}{4(3)} + \frac{5(2)}{6(2)}$$
$$= \frac{3}{12} + \frac{10}{12}$$
$$= \frac{13}{12}$$
$$= 1\frac{1}{12}$$

Decimals

It is very important to remember the place values of a decimal. The first place value to the right of the decimal point is the tenths place. The place values from thousands to ten thousandths are as follows:

1	2	6	8	.	3	4	5	7
THOUSANDS	HUNDREDS	TENS	ONES	DECIMAL POINT	TENTHS	HUNDREDTHS	THOUSANDTHS	TEN THOUSANDTHS

In expanded form, this number can also be expressed as:

$1{,}268.3457 = (1 \times 1{,}000) + (2 \times 100) + (6 \times 10) + (8 \times 1) + (3 \times 0.1) + (4 \times 0.01) + (5 \times 0.001) + (7 \times 0.0001)$

Comparing and Ordering Decimals

To compare or order decimals, compare the digits in their place values. It's the same process as comparing or ordering whole numbers. You just need to pay careful attention to the decimal point.

Example
Compare 0.2 and 0.05.

Compare the numbers by the digits in their place values. Both decimals have a 0 in the ones place, so you need to look at the place value to the right. 0.2 has a 2 in the tenths place while 0.05 has a 0 in the tenths place. Because 2 is bigger than 0, 0.2 is bigger than 0.05. You can show this as 0.2 > 0.05.

Example
Order 2.32, 2.38, and 2.29 in order from greatest to least.

Again, look at the place values of the numbers. All three numbers have a 2 in the ones place, so you cannot order them yet. Looking at the next place value to the right, tenths, reveals that 2.29 has the number 2 in the tenths place whereas the other numbers have a 3. So 2.29 is the smallest number. To order 2.32 and 2.38 correctly, compare the digits in the hundredths place. 8 > 2, so 2.38 > 2.32. The correct order from greatest to least is 2.38, 2.32, and 2.29.

Rounding Decimals

It is often inconvenient to work with decimals. It is much easier to have an approximation value for a decimal. In this case, you can **round** decimals to a certain number of decimal places. The most common ways to round are as follows:

- To the nearest integer: zero digits to the right of the decimal point
- To the nearest tenth: one digit to the right of the decimal point (tenths unit)
- To the nearest hundredth: two digits to the right of the decimal point (hundredths unit)

In order to round, look at the digit to the immediate right of the digit you are rounding to. If the digit is less than 5, leave the digit you are rounding to alone, and omit all the digits to its right. If the digit is 5 or greater, increase the digit you are rounding by one, and omit all the digits to its right.

Example

Round 14.38 to the nearest whole number.

The digit to the right of the ones place is 3. Therefore, you can leave the digit you are rounding to alone, which is the 4 in the ones place. Omit all the digits to the right.

14.38 is 14 when rounded to the nearest whole number.

Example

Round 1.084 to the nearest tenth.

The digit to the right of the tenths place is 8. Therefore, you need to increase the digit you are rounding to by 1. That means the 0 in the tenths place becomes a 1. Then all of the digits to the right can be omitted.

1.084 is 1.1 to the nearest tenth.

Adding and Subtracting Decimals

Adding and subtracting decimals is very similar to adding and subtracting whole numbers. The most important thing to remember is to line up the numbers to be added or subtracted by their decimal points. Zeros may be filled in as placeholders when all numbers do not have the same number of decimal places.

Examples

What is the sum of 0.45, 0.8, and 1.36?

$$
\begin{array}{r}
{\scriptstyle 1\ 1} \\
0.45 \\
0.80 \\
+\ 1.36 \\
\hline
2.61
\end{array}
$$

Take away 0.35 from 1.06.

$$
\begin{array}{r}
{\scriptstyle 0\ 1} \\
\cancel{1}.06 \\
-\ 0.35 \\
\hline
0.71
\end{array}
$$

Multiplying Decimals

The process for multiplying decimals is exactly the same as multiplying whole numbers. Multiply the numbers, ignoring the decimal points in the factors. Then add the decimal point in the final product later.

Example

What is the product of 0.14 and 4.3?

First, multiply as usual (do not line up the decimal points):

$$
\begin{array}{r}
4.3 \\
\times\ 0.14 \\
\hline
172 \\
+\ 430 \\
\hline
602
\end{array}
$$

Now, to figure out where the decimal point goes in the product, count how many decimal places are in each factor. 4.3 has one decimal place and 0.14 has two decimal places. Add these in order to determine the total number of decimal places the answer must have to the right of the decimal point. In this problem, there are a total of three (1 + 2) decimal places. Therefore, the decimal point needs to be placed three decimal places from the right side of the answer. In this example, 602 turns into 0.602. If there are not enough digits in the answer, add zeros in front of the answer until there are enough.

Example

Multiply 0.03 × 0.2.

$$
\begin{array}{r}
0.03 \\
\times\ 0.2 \\
\hline
6
\end{array}
$$

There are three total decimal places in the two numbers being multiplied. Therefore, the answer must contain three decimal places. Starting to the right of 6 (because 6 is equal to 6.0), move left three places. The answer becomes 0.006.

Dividing Decimals

To divide decimals, you need to change the divisor so that it does not have any decimals in it. In order to do that, simply move the decimal place to the right as many places as necessary to make the divisor a whole number. The decimal point must also be moved in the dividend the same number of places to keep the answer the same as the original problem. Moving a decimal point in a division problem is equivalent to multiplying a numerator and denominator of a fraction by the same quantity, which is the reason the answer will remain the same.

If there are not enough decimal places in the dividend (the number being divided) to accommodate the required move, simply add zeros at the end of the number. Add zeros after the decimal point to continue the division until the decimal terminates, or until a repeating pattern is recognized. The decimal point in the quotient belongs directly above the decimal point in the dividend.

Example

What is $0.425\overline{)1.53}$?

To make 0.425 a whole number, move the decimal point three places to the right: 0.425 becomes 425. Now move the decimal point three places to the right for 1.53: You need to add a zero, but 1.53 becomes 1,530.

The problem is now a simple long division problem.

$$
\begin{array}{r}
3.6 \\
425\overline{)1{,}530.0} \\
-1{,}275 \downarrow \\
\hline
2{,}550 \\
-2{,}550 \\
\hline
0
\end{array}
$$

Fractions

A **fraction** is a part of a whole, represented with one number over another number. The number on the bottom, the denominator, shows how many parts there are in the whole in total. The number on the top, the numerator, shows how many parts there are of the whole. To perform operations with fractions, it is necessary to understand some basic concepts.

Simplifying Fractions

To simplify fractions, identify the greatest common factor (GCF) of the numerator and denominator and divide both the numerator and denominator by this number.

Example

Simplify $\frac{16}{24}$

The GCF of 16 and 24 is 8, so divide 16 and 24 each by 8 to simplify the fraction:

$$\frac{16}{24} = \frac{(16 \div 8)}{(24 \div 8)} = \frac{2}{3}$$

Adding and Subtracting Fractions

To add or subtract fractions with like denominators, just add or subtract the numerators and keep the denominator.

Example

$$\frac{1}{7} + \frac{5}{7} = 1 + \frac{5}{7} = \frac{6}{7}$$

To add or subtract fractions with unlike denominators, first find the least common denominator or LCD. The LCD is the smallest number divisible by each of the denominators.

For example, for the denominators 8 and 12, 24 would be the LCD because 24 is the smallest number that is divisible by both 8 and 12: $8 \times 3 = 24$, and $12 \times 2 = 24$.

Using the LCD, convert each fraction to its new form by multiplying both the numerator and denominator by the appropriate factor to get the LCD, and then follow the directions for adding/subtracting fractions with like denominators.

Example

$$\frac{1}{3} + \frac{2}{5} = 1\frac{(5)}{3(5)} + \frac{2(3)}{5(3)}$$
$$= \frac{5}{15} + \frac{6}{15} = \frac{11}{15}$$

Multiplying Fractions

To multiply fractions, simply multiply the numerators and the denominators.

Example

$$\frac{2}{3} \times \frac{1}{4} = \frac{(2 \times 1)}{(3 \times 4)} = \frac{2}{12} = \frac{1}{6}$$

Dividing Fractions

Dividing fractions is similar to multiplying fractions. You just need to flip the numerator and denominator of the divisor, the fraction being divided. Then multiply across, like you would when multiplying fractions.

Example

Solve: $\frac{1}{4} \div \frac{1}{2}$.

Flip the numerator and denominator of the divisor and change the symbol to multiplication.

$$\frac{1}{4} \div \frac{1}{2} = \frac{1}{4} \times \frac{2}{1}$$

Now multiply the numerators and the denominators, and simplify if necessary.

$$\frac{1}{4} \times \frac{2}{1} = \frac{(1 \times 2)}{(4 \times 1)} = \frac{2}{4}$$

Because both the numerator and the denominator of $\frac{2}{4}$ can be divided by 2, the fraction can be reduced.

$$\left(\frac{2}{4}\right) = \frac{(2 \div 2)}{(4 \div 2)} = \left(\frac{1}{2}\right)$$

Comparing Fractions

Sometimes it is necessary to compare the sizes of fractions. This is very simple when the fractions have a common denominator. All you have to do is compare the numerators.

Example

Compare $\frac{3}{8}$ and $\frac{5}{8}$.

Because 3 is smaller than 5, $\frac{3}{8}$ is smaller than $\frac{5}{8}$. Therefore, $\frac{3}{8} < \frac{5}{8}$.

If the fractions do not have a common denominator, multiply the numerator of the first fraction by the denominator of the second fraction. Write this answer under the first fraction. Then multiply the numerator of the second fraction by the denominator of the first one. Write this answer under the second fraction. Compare the two numbers. The larger number represents the larger fraction.

Examples

Which is larger: $\frac{7}{11}$ or $\frac{4}{9}$?

Cross multiply.

$$\frac{7}{11} \times \frac{4}{9}$$

$$7 \times 9 = 63 \qquad 4 \times 11 = 44$$

$63 > 44$; therefore,

$$\frac{7}{11} > \frac{4}{9}$$

Compare $\frac{6}{18}$ and $\frac{2}{6}$.

Cross multiply.

$$\frac{6}{18} = \frac{2}{6}$$

$$6 \times 6 = 36 \qquad 2 \times 18 = 36$$

$36 = 36$; therefore, $\frac{6}{18} = \frac{2}{6}$

Percents

Percents are always "out of 100": 45% means 45 out of 100. Therefore, to write percents as decimals, move the decimal point two places to the left (to the hundredths place).

$45\% = \frac{45}{100} = 0.45$

$3\% = \frac{3}{100} = 0.03$

$124\% = \frac{124}{100} = 1.24$

$0.9\% = \frac{0.9}{100} = 0.009$

Here are some common conversions:

Fraction	Decimal	Percentage
$\frac{1}{2}$	.5	50%
$\frac{1}{4}$	.25	25%
$\frac{1}{3}$	.333 . . .	$33.\overline{3}\%$
$\frac{2}{3}$	.666 . . .	$66.\overline{6}\%$
$\frac{1}{10}$	.1	10%
$\frac{1}{8}$	.125	12.5%
$\frac{1}{6}$	.1666 . . .	$16.\overline{6}\%$
$\frac{1}{5}$	.2	20%

Algebra

There will likely not be too many questions about algebra on the ParaPro Assessment, but you will be expected to solve linear equations and identify how numbers make up a pattern.

Linear Equations

A linear equation contains an unknown value, called a **variable.** The equals sign separates an equation into two sides. You will be asked to find the value of the variable using information in the equation.

The first step is to get all of the variable terms on one side and all of the numbers on the other side. This is accomplished by *undoing* the operations that are attaching numbers to the variable, thereby isolating the variable. The operations are always done in reverse PEMDAS order: start by adding/subtracting, then multiply/divide.

It is very important to remember that whenever an operation is performed on one side, the same operation must be performed on the other side.

Examples

Solve for k in the equation $3k = 33$.

To get k by itself on the left side of the equation, both sides need to be divided by 3.

$$\frac{3k}{3} = \frac{33}{3}$$

$$k = 11$$

The value of k is 11.

Solve for m in the equation $5m + 8 = 48$.

Undo the addition of 8 by subtracting 8 from both sides of the equation. Then undo the multiplication by 5 by dividing by 5 on both sides of the equation.

$$-8 = -8$$
$$\frac{5m}{5} = \frac{40}{5}$$
$$m = 8$$

The variable, m, is now isolated on the left side of the equation, and its value is 8.

Checking Solutions to Equations

To check an equation, substitute the value of the variable into the original equation.

Example

To check the solution of the previous equation, substitute the number 8 for the variable m in $5m + 8 = 48$.

$$5(8) + 8 = 48$$
$$40 + 8 = 48$$
$$48 = 48$$

Because this statement is true, the answer $m = 8$ must be correct.

Patterns

The ability to detect patterns in numbers is a very important mathematical skill. Patterns exist everywhere in nature, business, and finance. When you are asked to find a pattern in a series of numbers, look to see if there is some common number you can add, subtract, multiply, or divide each number in the pattern by to give you the next number in the series.

For example, in the sequence 5, 8, 11, 14 . . . you can add 3 to each number in the sequence to get the next number in the sequence. The next number in the sequence is 17.

Examples

What is the next number in the sequence $\frac{3}{4}$, 3, 12, 48?

Each number in the sequence can be multiplied by the number 4 to get the next number in the sequence: $\frac{3}{4} \times 4 = 3, 3 \times 4 = 12, 12 \times 4 = 48$, so the next number in the sequence is $48 \times 4 = 192$

Sometimes it is not that simple. You may need to look for a combination of multiplying and adding, dividing and subtracting, or some combination of other operations.

What is the next number in the sequence 0, 1, 2, 5, 26?

Keep trying various operations until you find one that works. In this case, the correct procedure is to square the term and add 1: $0^2 + 1 = 1, 1^2 + 1 = 2, 2^2 + 1 = 5, 5^2 + 1 = 26$, so the next number in the sequence is $26^2 + 1 = 677$.

Geometry

The ParaPro Assessment will test your knowledge of basic shapes, such as triangles and circles, and it will also ensure that you remember how to identify points on the coordinate plane.

Polygons

A **polygon** is a two-dimensional object with straight lines that create a closed figure.

- A **regular polygon** has sides with the same lengths, and congruent angles with the same measures.
- An **irregular polygon** does not have sides with the same lengths and congruent angles with the same measures.

You should be prepared to identify the following polygons:

A **triangle** is a polygon with 3 sides.

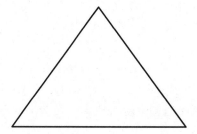

A **quadrilateral** is a polygon with 4 sides.

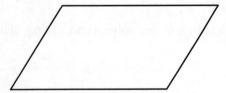

A **pentagon** is a polygon with 5 sides.

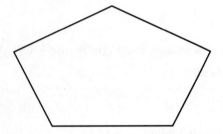

A **hexagon** is a polygon with 6 sides.

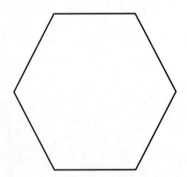

An **octagon** is a polygon with 8 sides.

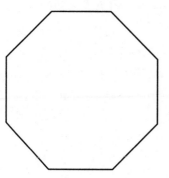

There are special kinds of triangles that are important to know.

An **equilateral** triangle has three sides with the same length.

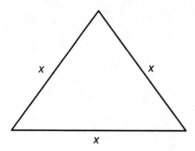

An **isosceles** triangle has two sides with the same length.

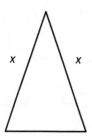

A **scalene** triangle has no sides with the same length.

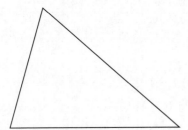

There are also special kinds of quadrilaterals that are important to know.

A **rectangle** is a four-sided polygon with four right angles. All rectangles have two pairs of parallel sides.

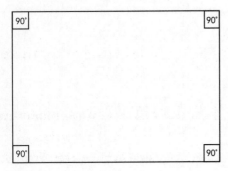

A **square** is a four-sided polygon with four right angles and four equal sides. All squares have two pairs of parallel sides. Note that a square is a specific kind of rectangle.

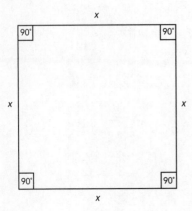

Example

What type of shape is shown below?

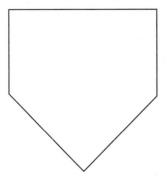

Because the figure has straight lines and makes a closed figure, it is a polygon. Because there are exactly five straight lines, the figure is a polygon.

Circles

A **circle** is a curved, two-dimensional figure where every point on the circle is the same distance from the center. There are several parts of a circle that you should know.

The **diameter** is a line that goes directly through the center of a circle—the longest line segment that can be drawn in a circle.

The **radius** is a line segment from the center of a circle to a point on the circle (half of the diameter).

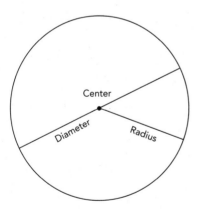

Three-Dimensional Shapes

You may be expected to identify some three-dimensional shapes on the ParaPro Assessment. The two most common types of three-dimensional shapes are shown below.

A **cube** is a three-dimensional figure where each face is the shape of a square.

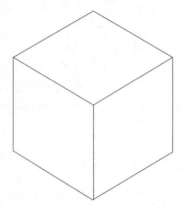

A **rectangular prism** is a three-dimensional figure where each face is the shape of a rectangle. Note that a cube is a specific kind of rectangular prism.

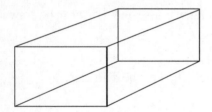

Coordinate Geometry

Coordinate geometry is a form of geometrical operations in relation to a coordinate plane. A **coordinate plane** is a grid created by a horizontal *x*-axis and a vertical *y*-axis.

These two axes intersect at one coordinate point, $(0, 0)$, the **origin**. A **coordinate point**, also called an **ordered pair**, is a specific point on the coordinate plane with the first number representing the horizontal placement and the second number representing the vertical placement. Coordinate points are given in the form of (x, y).

Graphing Ordered Pairs (Points)

The *x*-coordinate is listed first in the ordered pair and tells you how many units to move to either the left or the right. If the *x*-coordinate is positive, move to the right. If the *x*-coordinate is negative, move to the left.

The *y*-coordinate is listed second and tells you how many units to move up or down. If the *y*-coordinate is positive, move up. If the *y*-coordinate is negative, move down.

Example

What is the ordered pair of point *X* on the following coordinate grid?

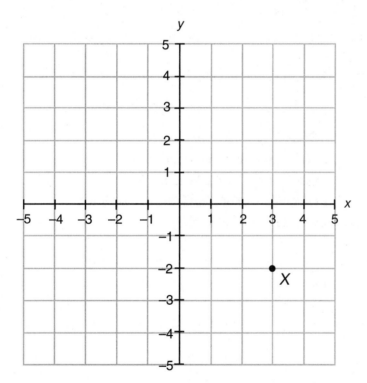

The point on the grid is 3 units to the right of the origin. Therefore, the first number in the ordered pair is 3. The point on the grid is 2 units down from the origin. Therefore, the second number in the ordered pair is –2.

The ordered pair for point *X* is $(3, -2)$.

Perimeter

To find the perimeter of a figure, simply add up the lengths of all of its sides.

Example

What is the perimeter of the following triangle?

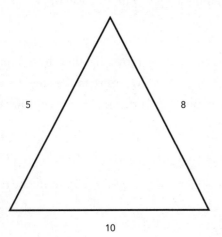

The triangle has side lengths of 5, 8, and 10. The perimeter is therefore the sum of 5 + 8 + 10. The perimeter of the triangle is 23.

Circumference

The **circumference** is the distance around a circle. The circumference can be found by multiplying the diameter of the circle by pi, or π, a special number equal to about 3.14. It can also be found by multiplying the radius of the circle by 2 and then by π. The formulas for the circumference of a circle are circumference = $2\pi r$ and circumference = $d\pi$, where r is the radius and d is the diameter of the circle.

Example

What is the circumference of a circle with a radius of 5?

Following the formula area = $2\pi r$, the circumference is equal to 2(5) π, which is equal to 10π

Area

The **area** is the amount of space inside a two-dimensional shape.

To find the area of a rectangle, you need to multiply the length of the rectangle times the width. The formula is area = length $\times$ width, or area = lw.

To find the area of a triangle, you need to multiply $\frac{1}{2}$ times the base of the triangle times its width. The formula is area = base $\times$ width, or area = $(\frac{1}{2}) lw$.

To find the area of a circle, you need to multiply the radius by itself (or square it), and then multiply it by π. The formula is area = πr^2, where r is the radius of the circle.

Example

What is the area of the following rectangle?

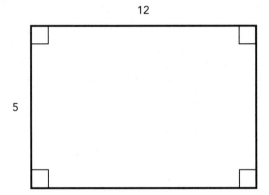

To find the area of a rectangle, multiply the length by the height. Because the length is 12 and the height is 5, the area is therefore 12 × 5, or 60 square units.

Example

What is the area of the following triangle?

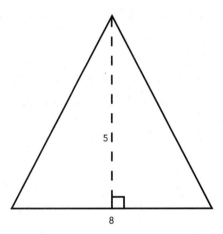

The base of the triangle is 8 and its height is 5. To find the area, just plug in those known values into the formula area = $\frac{1}{2}$ *lw*. You will get area = $\frac{1}{2}$ (8)(5), which is equal to 20. The area is 20 square units.

Example

What is the area of a circle with a radius of 2?

Plug in the value of the radius into the formula for the area of a circle: area = πr^2. You will get area = $\pi 2^2$, which is equal to 4π.

Volume

Volume is the amount of space inside a three-dimensional shape. To find the volume of a rectangular solid, you need to multiply the length times the width times the height.

Example
What is the volume of the following cube?

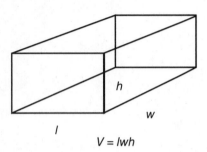

$V = lwh$

To find the volume, you need to multiply the length times the width times the height. Each dimension of the cube is 4, so the volume is $4 \times 4 \times 4$, or 64 cubic units.

Measurement

This section reviews the basics of measurement systems used in the United States (also called the U.S. customary system) and other countries, methods of performing mathematical operations with units of measurement, and the process of converting different units.

The use of measurement enables a connection to be made between mathematics and the real world. To measure any object, assign a number and a unit of measure. For instance, when a fish is caught, it is often weighed in ounces and its length measured in inches. The following lesson will help you become more familiar with the types, conversions, and units of measurement.

Types of Measurements

Length, volume, and weight (or mass) can be measured in either the U.S. customary system or the metric system. It is important to know the U.S. customary measurements.

U.S. Customary Measurements

Units of Length

12 inches (in) = 1 foot (ft)
3 feet = 36 inches = 1 yard (yd)
5,280 feet = 1,760 yards = 1 mile (mi)

Units of Volume

8 ounces* (oz) = 1 cup (c)
2 cups = 16 ounces = 1 pint (pt)
2 pints = 4 cups = 32 ounces = 1 quart (qt)
4 quarts = 8 pints = 16 cups = 128 ounces = 1 gallon (gal)

Units of Weight

16 ounces* (oz) = 1 pound (lb)

2,000 pounds = 1 ton (T)

*Notice that ounces are used to measure the dimensions of both volume and weight.

Converting Units

Metric Measurements

The metric system is an international system of measurement also called the **decimal system**. The unit of length is a meter. The unit of capacity is a liter. The unit of mass is a gram.

Prefixes are attached to the basic metric units to indicate the amount of each unit. For example, the prefix *deci* means one-tenth ($\frac{1}{10}$); therefore, one decigram is one-tenth of a gram, and one decimeter is one-tenth of a meter. The following six prefixes can be used with every metric unit:

Kilo	Hecto	Deka	Deci	Centi	Milli
(k)	(h)	(dk)	(d)	(c)	(m)
1,000	100	10	$\frac{1}{10}$	$\frac{1}{100}$	$\frac{1}{1,000}$

Example

So, for example:

- 1 meter is equivalent to 100 centimeters, or 1,000 millimeters.
- 1 gram is equivalent to 1,000 milligrams, or $\frac{1}{1,000}$ kilogram.
- 1 liter is equivalent to 1,000 millititers, or $\frac{1}{1,000}$ kiloliter.

One way to remember the metric prefixes is to remember the mnemonic: *King Henry Died Of Drinking Chocolate Milk*. The first letter of each word represents a corresponding metric heading from *kilo* down to *milli*: *King—Kilo, Henry—Hecto, Died—Deka, Of—Original Unit, Drinking—Deci, Chocolate—Centi,* and *Milk—Milli.*

Time

Units of Time

60 seconds (sec) = 1 minute (min)

60 minute = 1 hour (hr)

24 hours = 1 day

7 days = 1 week

52 weeks = 1 year (yr)

12 months = 1 year

365 days = 1 year

Converting Units of Measurement

When performing mathematical operations, it may be necessary to convert units to simplify a problem. Units of measure are converted by using either multiplication or division. Note that the ParaPro Assessment may ask you to convert metric units to other metric units *or* U.S. customary units to other U.S. customary units. It will not likely ask you to convert *between* systems, such as converting a number of inches to centimeters.

Converting Units in the U.S. Customary System

To convert from a larger unit into a smaller unit, *multiply* the given number of larger units by the number of smaller units in only one of the larger units.

For example, to find the number of inches in five feet, multiply 5, the number of larger units, by 12, the number of inches in one foot:

5 feet = ? inches

5 feet × 12 (the number of inches in a single foot) = 60 inches:

5 ft = 60 in.

Therefore, there are 60 inches in five feet.

Example
Change 3.5 pounds to ounces.

3.5 pounds = ? ounces
3.5 pounds × 16 ounces per pound = 56 ounces

Therefore, there are 56 ounces in 3.5 pounds.

To change a smaller unit to a larger unit, *divide* the given number of smaller units by the number of smaller units in only one of the larger units.

Example
Find the number of pints in 64 ounces.

64 ounces = ? pints
64 ounces ÷ 16 ounces per pint = 4 pints
Therefore, 64 ounces equals 4 pints.

Converting Units in the Metric System

An easy way to convert within the metric system is to move the decimal point either to the right or to the left, because the conversion factor is always ten or a power of ten. Remember to multiply when changing from a larger unit to a smaller unit. Divide when changing from a smaller unit to a larger unit.

When multiplying by a power of ten, move the decimal point to the right, because the number becomes larger. When dividing by a power of ten, move the decimal point to the left, because the number becomes smaller. Use the table on page 139 to see how many places to move to the left or right.

Example

Change 2 kilometers to meters.

You are changing a larger unit to a smaller unit, so the number must get bigger. You can move the decimal point three places to the right or solve as shown below:

2 kilometers = ? meters
2 × 1,000 meters per km = 2,000 meters

Therefore, 2 kilometers equals 2,000 meters

Example

Change 520 grams to kilograms.

Changing meters to kilometers requires moving from smaller units to larger units and, thus, requires that the decimal point move to the left. Beginning at the ones unit (for grams), note that the kilo heading is three places away. Therefore, the decimal point will move three places to the left. Move the decimal point from the end of 520 to the left three places. That means you need to place the decimal point before the 5: 0.520.

The answer is 520 grams = 0.520 kilograms

Converting Units of Time

The ParaPro Assessment may ask you to convert units of time. Just like converting U.S. customary or metric units, multiply when changing from a larger unit to a smaller unit and divide when changing from a smaller unit to a larger unit.

Example

A teacher creates a lesson plan for the week that will take four hours. How many minutes will the lesson plan take?

Because minutes are a smaller unit than hours, you need to multiply to convert the units. Remember that there are 60 minutes in an hour.

4 hours = ? minutes
4 hours × 60 minutes per hour = 240
Therefore, there are 240 minutes in 4 hours.

Money

In addition to converting between units of length, capacity, weight, mass, and time, you may also be asked to convert between units of money. Remember that one cent is equal to $\frac{1}{100}$ of a dollar, or $0.01. The values of U.S. coins are as follows:

1 penny = 1 cent = 1¢ = $0.01
1 nickel = 5 cents = 5¢ = $0.05
1 dime = 10 cents = 10¢ = $0.10
1 quarter = 25 cents = 25¢ = $0.25
1 dollar = 100 cents = 100¢ = $1.00

Converting Money

As always when converting units, multiply when changing from a larger unit to a smaller unit and divide when changing from a smaller unit to a larger unit. To convert dollars to cents, multiply by 100. To convert cents to dollars, divide by 100.

Example

Jillian has 7 dollars. How many dimes does she have?

To solve this problem, first convert Jillian's dollars to cents. Multiply the number of dollars by 100.

$7 = 7 × 100¢ = 700¢

To convert from cents to dimes, you are going from a smaller unit to a larger unit—which means you have to divide. If Jillian has 700 cents, you need to divide by 10 to find out how many dimes she has.

700¢ ÷ 10 = 70 dimes

Data Organization and Interpretation

To answer the data-based questions on the ParaPro Assessment, you will need to understand how to interpret graphs and tables, as well as find the mean, median, and mode of a data set.

Graphs and Tables

On the ParaPro Assessment you will see graphs, tables, and other graphical forms. You should be able to do the following:

- read and understand graphs, tables, diagrams, charts, figures, etc.
- interpret graphs, tables, diagrams, charts, figures, etc.
- compare and contrast information presented in graphs, tables, diagrams, charts, figures, etc.
- draw conclusions about the information provided
- make predictions about the data

It is important to read tables, charts, and graphs very carefully. Read all of the information presented, paying special attention to headings and units of measure. This section will cover tables and graphs. The most common types of graphs are pictographs, bar graphs, line graphs, and pie graphs. What follows is an explanation of each, with examples for practice.

Tables

All **tables** are composed of **rows** (horizontal) and **columns** (vertical). Entries in a single row of a table usually have something in common, and so do entries in a single column. Look at the table below that shows how many cars, both new and used, were sold during the particular months.

Month	New Cars	Used Cars
June	125	65
July	155	80
August	190	100
September	220	115
October	265	140

Tables are concise ways to convey important information without wasting time and space. Just imagine how many lines of text would be needed to convey the same information. With the table, however, it is easy to refer to a given month and quickly know how many total cars were sold. It is also easy to compare month to month. Practice using tables by comparing the total sales of July with October.

In order to do this, first find out how many cars were sold in each month. There were 235 cars sold in July ($155 + 80 = 235$) and 405 cars sold in October ($265 + 140 = 405$). With a little bit of quick arithmetic, it can be determined quickly that 170 more cars were sold during October ($405 - 235 = 170$).

Bar Graphs

A **bar graph** is a often used to indicate an amount or level of occurrence of a phenomenon for different categories. Consider the following bar graph. It illustrates the number of employees, in two different age groups, who were absent due to illness during a particular week.

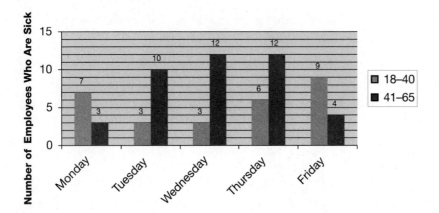

In this bar graph, the categories are the days of the week, and the bars indicate the number of employees who are sick, giving overall data on the frequency of sick days among employees. It can be seen immediately that more of the younger employees are sick before and after the weekend. There is also some inconsistency among the younger employees, with data ranging all over the place. During mid-week, the older crowd tends to stay home more often.

Pictographs

Pictographs are very similar to bar graphs, but instead of bars indicating frequency, small icons are assigned a key value indicating frequency.

Number of Students at the Pep Rally

Freshmen	👤 👤 👤 👤 👤 👤 👤 👤 👤 👤 👤 👤
Sophomores	👤 👤 👤 👤 👤 👤
Juniors	👤 👤 👤 👤 👤
Seniors	👤 👤 👤

Key: 👤 indicates 10 people

In this pictograph, the key indicates that every icon represents 10 people, so it is easy to determine that there were 12 × 10 = 120 freshmen, 5.5 × 10 = 55 sophomores, 5 × 10 = 50 juniors, and 3 × 10 = 30 seniors.

Circle Graphs

Circle graphs are often used to show what percent of a whole is taken up by different components of that whole. This type of graph is representative of a total amount, and is usually divided into percentages. Each section of the chart represents a portion of the whole, and all of these sections added together will equal 100%. The following chart shows the three styles of model homes in a new development, and what percentage of each there is.

Model Homes

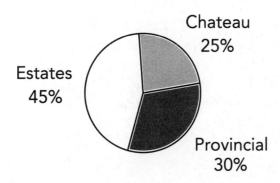

The chart shows the different styles of model homes. The categories add up to 100% (25 + 30 + 45 = 100). To find the percentage of estate homes, you can look at the pie chart and see that 45% of the homes are done in the estate style.

If you know the total number of items in a circle graph, you can calculate how many there are of each component. You just need to multiply the percent by the total.

Example

There are 500 homes in the new development. How many of them are chateaus?

To calculate the number of components (chateaus) out of the total (500), you need to multiply the percent times the total.

$25\% \times 500 = 0.25 \times 500 = 125$

There are 125 chateaus in the development.

Line Graph

A **line graph** is a graph used to show a change over time. The line moves from left to right to show how the data changes over a time period. If a line is slanted up, it represents an increase, whereas a line sloping down represents a decrease. A flat line indicates no change.

In the line graph below, the number of delinquent payments is charted for the first quarter of the year. Each week, the number of customers with outstanding bills is added together and recorded.

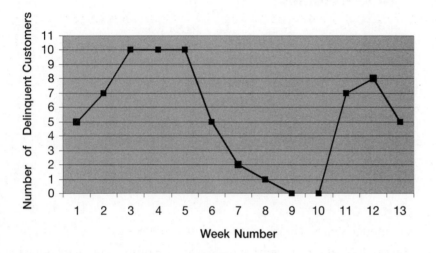

There is an increase in delinquency for the first two weeks, and then the level is maintained for an additional two weeks. There is a steep decrease after week five (initially) until the ninth week, where it levels off again—but this time at 0. The 11th week shows a radical increase followed by a little jump up at week 12, and then a decrease at week 13. It is also interesting to see that the first and last weeks have identical values.

Line graphs are especially useful to identify trends. A trend exists if the data points show a pattern. For example, see the line graph below.

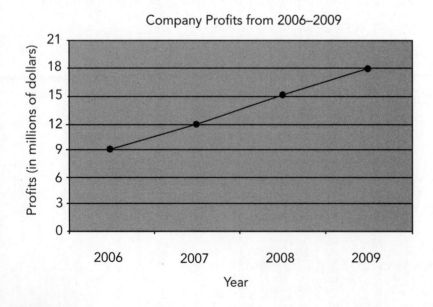

This line graph shows an obvious trend because the points go up as the line moves to the right. That means there is a positive trend. A question on the ParaPro Assessment may ask you to make a prediction based on the trend. Each year, the profits of the company go up by about $3 million. Therefore, if you were asked to predict the profits of the company in 2010, you could add $3 million to the profits in 2009. An appropriate prediction for the company's total profits in 2010, based on the trend in the graph, would be $21 million.

Mean, Median, and Mode

It is important to understand trends in data. To do that, look at where the center of the data lies. There are a number of ways to find the center of a set of data.

Mean

Average usually refers to the **arithmetic mean** (usually just called the **mean**). To find the mean of a set of numbers, add all of the numbers together and divide by the quantity of numbers in the set.

average = (sum of set) ÷ (quantity of set)

Example
Find the average of 9, 4, 7, 6, and 4.

$$\frac{9+4+7+6+4}{5} = 6$$

(Divide by 5 because there are five numbers in the set.) The mean, or average, of the set is 6.

Median

Another center of data is the **median,** which is the number in the center, if you arrange all the data in ascending or descending order. To find the median of a set of numbers, arrange the numbers in ascending or descending order and find the middle value. If the set contains an odd number of elements, then choose the middle value. If the set contains an even number of elements, simply average the two middle values.

Example
Find the median of the number set: 1, 5, 4, 7, 2.

First arrange the set in order—1, 2, 4, 5, 7—and then find the middle value. Because there are five values, the middle value is the third one: 4. The median is 4.

Example
Find the median of the number set: 1, 6, 3, 7, 2, 8.

First arrange the set in order—1, 2, 3, 6, 7, 8—and then find the middle values, 3 and 6.

Find the average of the numbers 3 and 6:

$\frac{3+6}{2} = 4.5$. The median is 4.5.

Mode

The **mode** of a set of numbers is the number that appears the greatest number of times.

Example

Find the mode for the following data set: 1, 2, 5, 9, 4, 2, 9, 6, 9, 7.

For the number set 1, 2, 5, 9, 4, 2, 9, 6, 9, 7, the number 9 is the mode, because it appears the most frequently.

Application of Math Skills and Knowledge to Classroom Instruction

There will be about 12 questions on the ParaPro Assessment that test your ability to apply all of the math skills covered earlier in this chapter toward classroom instruction. That means that the questions will either be related to the classroom or will be connected in some way to the instruction of these skills for students.

Classroom Context

There will be some questions on the math section of the ParaPro Assessment that apply to the classroom. Sometimes these problems will be straightforward, and have only a basic connection to a classroom. Other times these problems will be more complicated, with several steps necessary. The following two questions are examples of these types of problems.

Examples

1. A fish tank in a classroom has a capacity of 32 quarts. How many gallons does the fish tank hold?
   a. 2
   b. 4
   c. 8
   d. 16

   To solve this problem, you need to convert from a smaller unit, quarts, to a larger unit, gallons. That means you need to use division. There are 4 quarts in 1 gallon, so you need to divide by 4.

   32 quarts ÷ 4 quarts per gallon = 8 gallons

   The fish tank holds 8 gallons. The correct answer choice would be **c**.

For the next example, a teacher assigns a different number of pages to be read in a book each day. The table below shows the number per day.

Day of the Week	Pages Assigned to Be Read
Monday	13
Tuesday	15
Wednesday	7
Thursday	10
Friday	15

2. What is the mean (average) number of pages that the teacher assigns per day during the week?
   a. 10
   b. 12
   c. 15
   d. 60

To solve this problem, you need to find the average number in the data set for Monday through Friday. To find the mean requires you to add all of the values in the data set, then divide by the total number of values.

$$\frac{13 + 17 + 7 + 10 + 15}{5} = 12$$

The mean, or average, of the set is 12. The teacher assigned an average of 12 pages per day during the week. The correct answer choice would be **b**.

Instructional Context

As a professional educator, you will often be asked to help students in the classroom. The instructional questions on the ParaPro Assessment will ensure that you have the ability to help students improve their math skills. You may be asked to show that you know the proper steps to solve a problem, or help a student identify why he or she solved a problem incorrectly.

Examples

1. A student has 3 notebooks, each of which has 80 pieces of paper. The student also has 2 packs of printer paper, each of which has 200 pieces of paper. The student wants to figure out how many pieces of paper he has in total. Which expression can the student use to find the answer?
   a. 3(80 + 200)
   b. 2(80) + 3(200)
   c. (3 + 2)(80 + 200)
   d. 3(80) + 2(200)

To solve this problem, you would need to choose the expression that would result in the correct answer. Each notebook has 80 pieces of paper. There are 3 notebooks. Therefore, 80 needs to be multiplied by 3. Each pack has 200 pieces of paper. There are 2 packs of paper. Therefore, 200 needs to be multiplied by 2. The products of each multiplication then need to be added together. The expression in answer choice **d** correctly demonstrates these steps.

2. A student was asked to solve the following equation:
   $4 + 12 \div 2$

   The student adds 12 to 4 to get 16 and then divides 16 by 2 to get 8. The student's final answer was 8. What did the student do incorrectly?
   a. The student should have divided 12 by 2 before adding 4 to the quotient.
   b. The student incorrectly found the sum of 12 and 4.
   c. The student should have divided 4 by 2 before adding 12 to the quotient.
   d. The student incorrectly found the quotient of 16 and 2.

   To solve this problem, you need to identify the student's mistake in the solution. The student did not correctly follow the order of operations, which states that multiplication and division should always be performed before addition and subtraction. Therefore, 12 should have been divided by 2 before any addition was performed. The statement in answer choice **a** is correct.

Math Practice

Directions: Each of the following questions is followed by four answer choices. Choose the best answer choice for each.

1. What is the product of 4 and 3?
 a. 1
 b. $1\frac{1}{3}$
 c. 7
 d. 12

2. A piece of paper has a length of 30 centimeters. What is the length of the paper in millimeters?
 a. 0.3 millimeters
 b. 3 millimeters
 c. 300 millimeters
 d. 3,000 millimeters

3. $\frac{1}{4} + \frac{1}{3} =$
 a. $\frac{2}{12}$
 b. $\frac{2}{7}$
 c. $\frac{7}{12}$
 d. $\frac{2}{3}$

4. A student was asked to calculate 50% of $80. The student multiplied 80 by 50 to find the answer. What should the student have done instead?
 a. multiplied 80 by 0.50
 b. added 80 to 50
 c. multiplied 80 by 0.05
 d. divided 80 by 50

5. What is the value of 3^3?
 a. 6
 b. 9
 c. 18
 d. 27

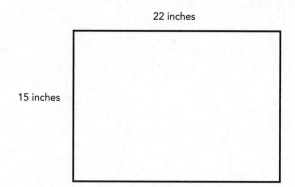

22 inches

15 inches

6. A student is trying to determine how to find the area of a rectangular desk, shown above. Which expression shows how the student can find its area?

   a. (15 inches) (22 inches)

   b. ($\frac{1}{2}$)(15 inches) × (22 inches)

   c. (15 inches) + (22 inches)

   d. (15 inches) + (22 inches) + (15 inches) + (22 inches)

7. Which has the same value as two dollars?

   a. 2 cents

   b. 200 cents

   c. $200

   d. $0.20

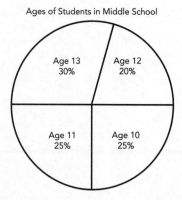

Ages of Students in Middle School

Age 13 30%

Age 12 20%

Age 11 25%

Age 10 25%

8. The circle graph above shows the ages of the students in a middle school. If there are 200 students in the middle school, how many are 12 years old?

   a. 10

   b. 25

   c. 40

   d. 180

9. Which of the following is NOT equal to one-tenth?

    a. 0.1

    b. $\frac{1}{10}$

    c. 0.100

    d. 0.01

10. Which of the following is correct?

    a. $8 + 8 > 17 - 2$

    b. $15 - 2 < 9 + 3$

    c. $19 - 5 > 11 + 6$

    d. $13 + 3 < 12 + 4$

11. The teacher in a classroom orders 12 boxes of crayons for the school year. There are 18 crayons in each box. Which is the best estimate for the total number of crayons that the teacher orders?

    a. 30 crayons

    b. 100 crayons

    c. 200 crayons

    d. 400 crayons

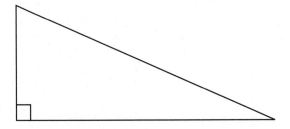

12. What type of triangle is shown above?

    a. equilateral triangle

    b. right triangle

    c. isosceles triangle

    d. obtuse triangle

13. $3,214 + 809 =$

    a. 2,405

    b. 3,023

    c. 4,013

    d. 4,023

14. What is the approximate value of 6.13 ÷ 2.03?

   a. 3

   b. 4

   c. 8

   d. 12

15. A teacher has three 40-minute classes with one group of students every week. How many hours will the teacher have with the group of students during a four-week period?

   a. 2 hours

   b. 6 hours

   c. 7 hours

   d. 8 hours

16. 5, 16, 27, 38, . . .

The first four numbers of a pattern are shown above. If the pattern continues, what will be the 6th number in the pattern?

   a. 49

   b. 50

   c. 59

   d. 60

17. What is the tenths digit in the number 219.74?

   a. 1

   b. 4

   c. 7

   d. 9

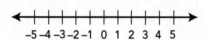

18. A student wants to draw a point for the number −3.5 on the number line above. Between which two integers should the student draw the point?

   a. between −4 and −3

   b. between −3 and −2

   c. between −3 and 3

   d. between 3 and 4

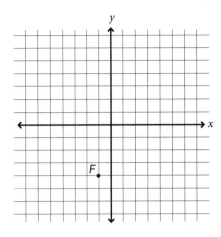

19. What is the ordered pair for point F on the coordinate grid shown above?

   a. $(1, -4)$
   b. $(-1, -4)$
   c. $(1, 4)$
   d. $(-4, -1)$

20. A student is having a hard time solving the following linear equation: $4x = 20$. What step should the student follow to find the value for x?

   a. multiply both sides of the equation by 4
   b. divide both sides of the equation by 4
   c. subtract both sides of the equation by 3
   d. subtract 20 from both sides of the equation

Meal	Snacks	Drinks
Hot Dog: $0.75	Fries: $1.05	Juice: $0.60
Pizza Slice: $0.90	Granola Bar: $0.50	Milk: $0.45
Taco: $1.25	Apple: $0.35	Water: $0.25

21. The prices for different lunch items in the school cafeteria are shown in the table above. A student buys two slices of pizza, one apple, and one milk. How much does the student owe?

   a. $1.70
   b. $1.80
   c. $2.50
   d. $2.60

22. $23 - 3 \times 5 + 2 =$
   a. 6
   b. 10
   c. 102
   d. 140

23. A student is trying to determine the perimeter of an irregular pentagon. Which operation should the student use?
   a. addition
   b. subtraction
   c. multiplication
   d. division

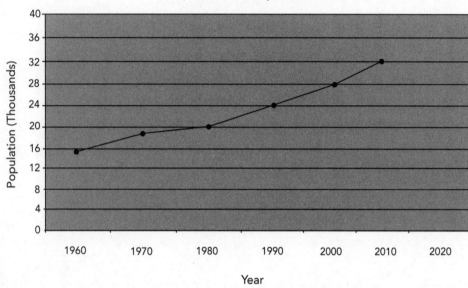

Population of a City, 1960 to 2010

24. The line graph above shows the population of a city every 10 years, from 1960 through 2010. Based on the trend in this graph, which is the best prediction for the population of the city in 2020?
   a. 28,000
   b. 31,000
   c. 35,000
   d. 40,000

25. Which shows the decimals in order from greatest to least?
   a. 1.59, 1.8, 1.88
   b. 1.88, 1.59, 1.8
   c. 1.88, 1.8, 1.59
   d. 1.8, 1.88, 1.59

26. 4.05 − 1.34 =
  a. 2.71
  b. 2.79
  c. 3.71
  d. 5.39

27. The mass of a textbook is 2.5 kilograms. What is the mass of the textbook in grams?
  a. 0.25 grams
  b. 25 grams
  c. 250 grams
  d. 2,500 grams

28. A student is asked to add 13.55 and 4.82. His solution is shown below.

$$
\begin{array}{r}
^{1\,1} \\
13.55 \\
+\ 4.8 \\
\hline
14.03
\end{array}
$$

What mistake did the student make in the solution?
  a. The student made an error when regrouping tenths.
  b. The student did not align by decimal points.
  c. The student used the incorrect operation.
  d. The student made an error when regrouping ones.

29. −25 + (−10) =
  a. −35
  b. −15
  c. 15
  d. 35

Student	Height (in Inches)
Abigail	63
Barry	67
Cat	62
Daryl	67
Erika	66

30. The heights of five students are shown in the table above. What is the median height of the students?
  a. 62 inches
  b. 65 inches
  c. 66 inches
  d. 67 inches

Answers and Explanations

Question Number	Correct Answer	Content Category
1	d	Math Skills: Number sense and basic algebra
2	c	Math Skills: Geometry and measurement
3	c	Math Skills: Number sense and basic algebra
4	a	Math Application: Number sense and basic algebra
5	d	Math Skills: Number sense and basic algebra
6	a	Math Application: Number sense and basic algebra
7	b	Math Skills: Geometry and measurement
8	c	Math Application: Data analysis
9	d	Math Skills: Number sense and basic algebra
10	a	Math Skills: Number sense and basic algebra
11	c	Math Application: Number sense and basic algebra
12	b	Math Skills: Geometry and measurement
13	d	Math Skills: Number sense and basic algebra
14	a	Math Skills: Number sense and basic algebra
15	d	Math Application: Geometry and measurement
16	d	Math Skills: Number sense and basic algebra
17	c	Math Skills: Number sense and basic algebra
18	a	Math Application: Number sense and basic algebra
19	b	Math Skills: Geometry and measurement
20	b	Math Application: Number sense and basic algebra
21	d	Math Application: Data analysis
22	b	Math Skills: Number sense and basic algebra
23	a	Math Application: Geometry and measurement
24	c	Math Skills: Data analysis
25	c	Math Skills: Number sense and basic algebra

Question Number	Correct Answer	Content Category
26	a	Math Skills: Number sense and basic algebra
27	d	Math Application: Geometry and measurement
28	b	Math Application: Number sense and basic algebra
29	a	Math Skills: Number sense and basic algebra
30	c	Math Application: Data analysis

1. d. The product is the result of multiplication. To solve this problem, you need to multiply 4 by 3. The product (and the answer) is 12, choice **d**. Answer choice **a**, 1, is the difference. Choice **b**, $1\frac{1}{3}$, is the quotient. Choice **c**, 7, is the sum.

2. c. Millimeters is a smaller unit of measurement than centimeters. Therefore, you need to use multiplication to convert from centimeters to millimeters. To convert from centimeters to millimeters, you need to multiply by 10. 30 centimeters = 30×10 millimeters, or 300 millimeters, choice **c**.

3. c. To add unlike fractions, you need to find a common denominator. The lowest common denominator or $\frac{1}{4}$ and $\frac{1}{3}$ is 12. To convert $\frac{1}{4}$ so that it has a denominator of 12, multiply the numerator and denominator by 3: $\frac{1}{4} = \frac{1 \times 3}{4 \times 3} = \frac{3}{12}$. To convert $\frac{1}{3}$ so it has a denominator of 12, multiply the numerator and denominator by 4: $\frac{1}{4} = \frac{(1 \times 4)}{(3 \times 4)} = \frac{4}{12}$. Once the fractions have like denominators, you can add them by simply adding the numerators: $\frac{3}{12} + \frac{4}{12} = \frac{7}{12}$.

4. a. Remember that the decimal value of a percent can be found by moving the decimal point two places to the left. So 50% is equivalent to 0.50. The student should not have multiplied 80 by 50, but instead should have multiplied 80 by 0.50, choice **a**.

5. d. To solve for the value of an exponent, multiply the base times itself the number of times in the power. So, to solve for 3^3, you need to multiply 3 by itself 3 times. The product of 3 $\times$ 3 $\times$ 3 is 27, so choice **d** is correct.

6. a. To find the area of a rectangle, a student needs to multiply the length of the rectangle by its width. The expression in answer choice **a** shows this solution correctly.

7. b. There are 100 cents in 1 dollar. Therefore, there are 200 cents in 2 dollars. The only answer choice that has a value equal to 2 dollars is choice **b**, 200 cents.

8. c. There are 200 students in the middle school. The circle graph shows that 20% of the students in the middle school are 12 years old. To find the total number of 12-year-old students in the school, you need to multiply the percent by the total number of students. To multiply a percent, first convert it to a decimal by moving the decimal to places to the left. Because $200 \times 0.20 = 40$, answer choice **c** is correct.

9. d. The value of the decimal 0.1 is one-tenth, because there is a 1 in the tenth column. It does not matter if there are zeros at the end of a decimal; the value does not change. The number 0.1 is equivalent to 0.10, 0.100, or 0.1000. However, 0.01 has a value of one-hundredth, so choice **d** does not represent one-tenth.

10. a. Remember that the symbol > means *is more than* and the symbol < means *is less than*. If you solve for the addition and subtraction on either side of the symbols, only 8 + 8 > 17 − 2 (which is 16 > 15) is correct.

11. c. To find an estimate, you do not need to find an actual answer. You can choose numbers that are easier to work with. Instead of multiplying the 12 boxes of crayons times the 18 crayons in each box, you can round each number to the nearest 10. You can then multiply 10 boxes of crayons by 20 crayons in each box to find an approximate total number of crayons that the teacher ordered. The best estimate for the total number of crayons ordered is 200, choice **c**.

12. b. The small box in the bottom-left corner of the triangle means that the angle is a right angle. Because the triangle has a right angle, it is a right triangle, choice **b**. The triangle has three sides of different lengths, so it is neither equilateral, choice **a**, or isosceles, choice **c**. It does not have an obtuse angle, so it is not an obtuse triangle either.

13. d. The trick to setting up this kind of addition problem is to align the digits properly when stacking them. Make sure to regroup the ten ones to form one more ten, and then regroup the ten hundreds to form one more thousand. The sum is 4,023, answer choice **d**.

14. a. This question asks for the *approximate* value, which means that you to not need to find an exact answer. Because the problem gives you decimals, it would be easier to round each number to a whole number. Instead of dividing 6.13 by 2.03, divide 6 by 2. Now the correct answer, choice **a**, becomes clearer.

15. d. Several steps are required to solve this problem. First, you need to figure out how many minutes a teacher has with a group of students per week. Because the teacher has the group for three classes, and each class is 40 minutes, the amount of time the teacher has each week is 3 × 40 minutes, or 120 minutes. 120 minutes can be converted to two hours because there are 60 minutes in one hour— or 120 minutes in two hours. Last, you need to remember that the question asks for the total number of hours that the teacher has with the group of students during a four-week period. If the teacher has the students for two hours each week for four hours, then the answer is 2 hours × 4 weeks = 8 hours in total.

16. d. The tricky part of this problem is identifying the pattern. If you don't see the pattern right away, try to figure out how to get from the first number (5) to the second number (16). You could multiply by 5 and add 1. Or you could add 11. To go from 16 to 27, however, multiplying by 5 and adding 1 does not work. The number 27 is 11 more than 16, so adding 11 must be the way that the pattern increases. Therefore, the number after 38 will be 49. However, that is only the fifth number in the pattern. The sixth number in the pattern will be 11 more than 49, which is 60, choice **d**.

17. c. The tenths place is the first place directly to the right of the decimal point. In the number 219.74, the digit 7, choice **c**, is in the tenths place.

18. a. A negative number will be to the left of 0 on a number line. The number −3.5 is also smaller than −3, so it will be to the left of −3 on the number line. It will be between −3 and −4, choice **a**.

19. b. Point *F* is one unit to the left of the origin (the point where the *x*-axis and *y*-axis cross). That means its *x*-coordinate is −1. The point is also 4 units down from the origin. That means its *y*-coordinate is −4. The ordered pair for point *F* should be (−1, −4). If you picked choice **d**, you confused the order of the *x* and *y* coordinates in an ordered pair. The *x*-coordinate will always go first.

20. b. To solve this one-step linear equation, a student needs to isolate the variable, *x*, on one side of the equation. Because the left side of the equation has 4*x*, which is the same as 4 times *x*, the student must "undo" the multiplication. To do that, he or she must divide by the number in front of the variable. Whatever is done to one side of the equation must be done to both sides, however. Therefore, the student should divide both sides of the equation by 4, choice **b**.

21. d. The student buys two slices of pizza, which are $0.90 each, one apple, which is $0.35, and one milk, which is $0.45. To solve this problem, add up the prices of each of the items (being sure to count the cost of the pizza twice). $0.90 + $0.90 + $0.35 + $0.45 = 2.60, choice **d**. Be sure to regroup the ten hundredths in your addition, or you may get choice **c** instead.

22. b. You need to remember the order of operations to solve this problem. Multiplication and division always get solved before addition or subtraction (unless there are parentheses). Therefore, the first step is to perform the multiplication:

$$23 - 3 \times 5 + 2 =$$
$$23 - 15 + 2 =$$

Now only subtraction and addition remain. You perform those operations in order from left to right. So subtract the 15 first:

$$23 - 15 + 2 =$$
$$8 + 2 =$$

And finally you can perform the addition:

$$8 + 2 = 10$$

The answer is 10, choice **b**.

23. a. To find the perimeter of any polygon, you must add the lengths of all its sides. If the pentagon were regular, you could multiply the length of one side by 5. But because the pentagon is irregular, the only way to determine its perimeter is to use addition, choice **a**.

24. c. If you follow the line on the graph, you can tell that the population of the city goes up a few thousand every year. The population is a little less than 32,000 in 2010. The question asks for the best prediction for the population of the city in 2020. Therefore, it will most likely be *more* than 32,000, eliminating choices **a** and **b**. It would be a huge jump for the population to reach 40,000—a jump too great for the trend of the line. 35,000, choice **c**, is the best prediction.

25. c. The decimals 1.59, 1.8, and 1.88 all have the digit 1 in the ones place. But because 1.59 has the digit 5 in the tenths place, it is smaller than the other two decimals. The decimals 1.8 and 1.88 both have an 8 in the tenths place. To compare 1.8 and 1.88, it may be helpful to add a zero to the right of 1.8. Changing 1.8 to 1.80 does not change its value. Now you can compare the digits in the hundredths place. Because 8 is greater than 0, 1.88 is greater than 1.8. That means 1.88 is the largest decimal, followed by 1.8, and then 1.59, choice **c**.

26. a. Set up this subtraction problem by aligning the numbers by their decimal points, as shown:

$$\begin{array}{r} 4.05 \\ -\,1.34 \end{array}$$

To subtract in the tenths place, you need to regroup from the ones place.

$$\begin{array}{r} \cancel{4}^{1}.05 \\ -\,1.34 \end{array}$$

Now you can subtract from right to left, and the difference will be 2.71, choice **a**.

27. d. Converting from kilograms to grams involves converting from a larger unit to a smaller unit. That means you must use multiplication to solve. One kilogram is equal to 1,000 grams. Therefore, 2.5 kilograms is equivalent to 2.5 × 1,000 grams per kilogram = 2,500 grams, choice **d**.

28. b. The numbers in the addition problem are aligned to the right. However, decimals must always be added and subtracted with their decimal points aligned. (When multiplying, it is not essential to align by decimal point.) The student found an incorrect sum because he or she failed to align by the decimal point, choice **b**.

29. a. Adding a negative integer is the same as subtracting a positive integer. Therefore, −25 + (−10) is equivalent to −25 − 10. The difference will be smaller (or more negative) than −25. The correct answer is −35, choice **a**.

30. c. To find the median of any data set, you need to put the values in order. The number in the middle will be the median. In the table shown in this problem, the heights are 62, 63, 66, 67, and 67 inches in order from shortest to tallest. The value in the middle of the set is 66 inches, choice **c**. Remember that the values need to be in order. The number 62, choice **a**, may be in the middle of the table, but it is not in the middle when the numbers are in order. The mode is 67 inches, choice **d**, because it appears more often than any other number. The mean of the data set is 65 inches, choice **b**.

6 ▶ WRITING SKILLS AND KNOWLEDGE

CHAPTER SUMMARY

The Writing Skills and Knowledge section of the ParaPro Assessment includes 30 questions. The writing section makes up one-third of the entire test and will always appear last on the test.

Because the Writing Skills and Knowledge section is one-third of the test, you should expect to spend about one-third of the available time on it. That means you will have about 50 minutes to answer the 30 questions. Because it's the last section on the test, you will know how much time you have left to answer the questions on the writing section.

If you spent more than 100 minutes on the math and reading sections, you will have fewer than 50 minutes to complete the writing section. If you spent fewer than 100 minutes in the previous sections, you will have more than 50 minutes. The good news is that the writing section should take less time than the other sections. There are no long passages to read, or complicated math problems to figure out. Therefore, if you finish the writing section with extra time to spare, you will be able to go back and check your answers to the other sections as well.

Of the 30 questions on the writing section, you can expect that about the first 18 will test your writing skills. That means those problems may ask you to recognize the parts of a sentence or identify grammatical or spelling errors. The last 12 questions or so on the writing section will test your ability to apply writing skills to classroom use. That means those problems may ask you to identify the best way to help a student improve an essay or help a teacher perform a writing lesson.

About the Writing Skills and Knowledge Section

Every question on the reading section of the ParaPro Assessment is multiple-choice, with four answer choices. The answer choices will always be **a**, **b**, **c**, and **d**.

About eight of the first problems on the Writing and Knowledge section of the ParaPro will ask you to identify an error in the sentence. The error could be related to grammar, punctuation, or word usage. Four parts of the sentence will be underlined with the letters **a**, **b**, **c**, or **d**. under them. You need to select the part that contains the error. There will always be *exactly* one error in these sentences. Look at the following problem:

1. <u>Although</u> giant squids can <u>grow</u> to be more than 40 feet long, <u>it lives</u> in such deep water that few people
    a   **b**   **c**
<u>have</u> ever seen one.
    d

The subject of the sentence is *giant squids*, which is plural. Therefore, *it lives* should be *they live*. The underlined words *it lives* contain an error, so choice **c** is the correct answer.

Other questions on the test may look like the following problems:

2. Even though it is now the world's largest desert, the Sahara was once home to crocodiles during its wetter past.

    What is the <u>subject</u> of the sentence?
    a. desert
    b. the Sahara
    c. crocodiles
    d. past

This question tests your knowledge of the parts of a sentence. Review the writing glossary beginning on page 166 to ensure that you remember each part. The subject of the sentence is the Sahara, so choice **b** would be correct.

Approximately four questions will test your spelling, as in the following example.

3. Which of the following words is NOT spelled correctly?
    a. poisonous
    b. separate
    c. interior
    d. mamal

For this type of question, you simply need to find the word that is NOT spelled correctly. The word that is NOT spelled correctly is the correct choice. The words in choices **a**, **b**, and **c** are spelled correctly. The word *mamal* should be spelled *mammal*, so choice **d** is correct.

Test-Taking Tips for Writing Skills and Knowledge Questions

Below are a handful of specific tips for the Writing Skills and Knowledge section of the ParaPro Assessment.

Sound It Out!

Don't bother the other test takers, but sometimes sounding out a word or a sentence is the best way to determine the best grammar to use or the proper word to fit the sentence. For example, you may not be sure whether *kick* is in singular or plural form. But if you say to yourself, *The boy kick the ball* and *The boys kick the ball*, you can usually use the one that sounds correct to answer the question. In this case, *kick* sounds better with *boys,* so it is plural.

Look for Simpler Way to Say Something

Can you spot the error in the following sentence?

After she <u>had been running</u> to the library, <u>she</u> realized that <u>it</u> was closed on <u>Mondays</u>.

You may not notice an obvious error in the sentence. You may even try to convince yourself that something is wrong with a part of the sentence that is correct. But the sentence could be written, "After she <u>ran</u> to the library, she realized that it was closed on Mondays." The verbs *ran* and *realized* should be in the same tense. Even if you couldn't put your finger on that reason, the fact that the sentence could be shortened and made to sound better could have tipped you off that something was wrong with the verb tense.

When All Else Fails, Trust Your Instinct

It may be hard to explain why a word looks misspelled. As you'll see later, there are a lot of spelling rules—and just as many exceptions to all those rules. But if you look at a word and something about it seems wrong to you at first glance, trust your initial reaction.

This is a good guide to use throughout the writing section of the ParaPro Assessment. It may be difficult to explain, for example, why one underlined part of a sentence seems like it has an error in it. But if you cannot find any error in the other choices, you should fall back on your instinct. Remember that every sentence with four underlined parts will have one error.

Important Writing Vocabulary

The writing section of the ParaPro Assessment will test your knowledge of important grammatical terms. You will be expected to know many of the bolded words in the following paragraphs. Some, like *subject* or *adjective* will definitely be tested on the ParaPro Assessment. Others, like *clause*, help understand information in this chapter. The best thing to do is to make sure you are familiar with these terms before taking the test.

An **adjective** is a word that describes, or modifies, nouns or pronouns, such as the word *red* in the following sentence: *Jack ran to the red house.*

An **adverb** is a word that describes, or modifies, verbs, adjectives, or other adverbs, such as the word *quickly* in the following sentence: *Jack ran quickly to the red house.*

Agreement refers to the rule of grammar that says parts of a sentence must match, such as whether the words are singular or plural.

An **apostrophe** (') is a grammatical mark used to show possession and contractions.

A **clause** is a group of words with a subject and a verb.

A **colon** (:) is a grammatical mark that introduces elements and shows an equivalent relationship (almost like an equals sign in math).

A **comma** creates a pause, clarifies meaning, and separates different parts of a sentence.

The **complete predicate** in a sentence tells you everything about what the subject is doing.

A **conjunction** is a part of a sentence that joins two words, such as *and* or *or*.

A **dependent clause** is a part of a sentence with its own subject and verb but that cannot stand by itself as its own sentence.

An **independent clause** is a part of a sentence with its own subject and verb that can stand by itself as its own sentence.

A **noun** is a person, place, thing, or idea.

The **predicate** is the action being performed by the subject in the sentence.

A **preposition** is a word that expresses the relationship in time or space between words in a sentence. They are generally short words, such as *in, on, around, above, between, beside, by, before,* or *with,* that introduce prepositional phrases in a sentence.

A **pronoun** is a word that takes the place of a noun or another pronoun.

A **proper noun** is a noun that names a specific person, place, thing, or idea.

A **run-on sentence** is a sentence that should be split into at least two complete sentences, or needs punctuation to separate the two clauses.

A **semicolon** (;) is a grammatical mark that splits two independent clauses.

A **simple predicate** is the verb that describes what the subject is doing in a sentence.

The **subject** is the person, place, or thing in a sentence that is performing the action.

A **verb** is the action word of a sentence.

Writing Skills and Knowledge Review

ETS, the maker of the ParaPro Assessment, says that there are six key skills to know for the Writing Skills and Knowledge questions on the test. The key skills are as follows:

1. know the parts of a sentence, such as a subject
2. know the parts of speech, such as a verb or adverb
3. recognize grammatical mistakes
4. recognize punctuation mistakes
5. use the proper word in a situation, such as *affect* or *effect*
6. recognize spelling mistakes

The next six sections explain each type of skill with examples that show how you might see the concept tested on the ParaPro Assessment.

1. Parts of a Sentence

There are only two basic parts of a sentence: the subject and its predicate. For this question type, you need to be able to identify the parts of a sentence. For example, a question may ask you to find the simple predicate in a given sentence.

The **subject** is the person, place, or thing in a sentence that is performing the action. The subject can be a noun, like in the sentence, *The chair is black*. It can be a pronoun, such as, *He is the vice president*. It can even be a group of nouns or a phrase, such as *Audrey and Anna went to the store* or *The last sip of coffee is the best*.

The **predicate** is the action that is being done by the subject in the sentence. Read the following sentence:

Emma watches the sunrise from her porch.

The subject of the sentence is *Emma*. The action she is performing is *watching the sunrise from her porch*. That entire phrase *watches the sunrise from her porch* is called the **complete predicate.** It tells you about Emma. Usually, you won't need the complete predicate; the **simple predicate** is the main verb in the sentence that tells what Emma is doing. The simple predicate is *watches*.

2. Parts of Speech

A sentence is made up of words. Each word is considered a part of speech. These include six common terms that you must be able to recognize on the ParaPro Assessment: noun, verb, adjective, adverb, pronoun, and preposition.

Nouns

A **noun** is a person, place, thing, or idea. For example, the word *noun* is itself a noun. The words *doctor, bedroom, computer,* and *love* are all nouns as well because they represent a person, place, thing, and idea.

A **proper noun** is a noun that names a specific person, place, thing, or idea. Proper nouns always start with a capital letter. For example, *Roger, Arizona,* and *Empire State Building* are all proper nouns.

Verbs

A **verb** is the action word of a sentence. The three basic verb tenses—present, past, and future—let you know when something is happening, has happened, or will happen. Verbs can appear in many different tenses. For example, *talk, ran, was raining,* and *have slept* are all verbs in different forms.

In its infinitive form, a verb is in the form *to ____*. You can then change this form to a different tense, depending on when the action occurred or whether one or more than one things are involved in the action. These words may look different; the following list shows several common verbs in their past, present, and future tenses.

Infinitive Form	Past	Present	Future
to fall	fell	falls/fall	will fall
to jump	jumped	jumps/jump	will jump

to study	studied	studies/study	will study
to tell	told	tells/tell	will tell
to write	wrote	writes/write	will write

As ironic as it may be, a verb takes on an *–s* if the subject that is performing the action is singular. If the subject is plural, the verb does not have the *–s*. For example, look at the following sentences with the verbs underlined.

Singular: *Madeline <u>helps</u> her friends with her homework.*

The policeman <u>protects</u> the community.

Plural: *Bob and Janet <u>mow</u> the lawn together.*

Her grandparents <u>own</u> the house on the hill.

Adjectives and Adverbs

Adjectives and **adverbs** add spice to writing—they are words that describe, or modify, other words. However, adjectives and adverbs describe different parts of speech. Whereas adjectives modify nouns or pronouns, adverbs modify verbs, adjectives, or other adverbs.

> *We enjoyed the <u>delicious</u> meal.*
> *The chef prepared it <u>perfectly</u>.*

The first sentence uses the adjective *delicious* to modify the noun *meal*. In the second sentence, the adverb *perfectly* describes the verb *prepared*. Adverbs are easy to spot—most end in *-ly*. However, some of the trickiest adverbs do not end in the typical *-ly* form. The following are problem modifiers to look out for:

Good/Well—Writers often confuse the adverb *well* with its adjective counterpart, *good*.

> *Ellie felt <u>good</u> about her test results.*
> (*Good* describes the proper noun, *Ellie*.)

> *Ruben performed <u>well</u> on the test.*
> (*Well* modifies the verb, *performed*.)

Bad/Badly—Similarly, writers confuse the function of these two modifiers. Remember to use the adverb *badly* to describe an action.

> *Henry felt <u>bad</u> after staying up all night before the exam.* (*Bad* describes Henry.)

> *Juliet did <u>badly</u> in her first classroom presentation.* (*Badly* describes the verb form, *did*.)

Fewer/Less—These two adjectives are a common pitfall for writers. To distinguish between them, look carefully at the noun modified in the sentence. *Fewer* describes *plural* nouns, or things that can be counted. *Less* describes *singular* nouns that represent a quantity or a degree.

> *The high school enrolls <u>fewer</u> students than it did a decade ago.*

> *Emilia had <u>less</u> time for studying than Maggie.*

Adjectives that follow verbs can also cause confusion. Although an adjective may come after a verb in a sentence, it may describe a noun or pronoun that comes before the verb. Here is an example:

> *The circumstances surrounding Shakespeare's authorship seemed strange.* (The adjective, *strange*, describes the subject, *circumstances*.)

Take special note of modifiers in sentences that use verbs that deal with the senses: *touch, taste, look, smell,* and *sound.* Here are some examples of sentences that use the same verb, but different modifiers:

> *Sarah felt sick after her performance review.*
> (The adjective, *sick*, modifies *Sarah*.)

> *The archaeologist felt carefully through the loose dirt.* (The adverb, *carefully*, modifies *felt*.)
> *The judge looked skeptical after the witness testified.* (The adjective, *skeptical*, modifies *judge*.)

> *The judge looked skeptically at the flamboyant lawyer.* (The adverb, *skeptically*, modifies *looked*.)

Pronouns

A **pronoun** is a word that takes the place of a noun or another pronoun. For example, the word *his* in the following sentence is a pronoun: *Mark loves his dog*. Without the pronoun, you would have to say *Mark loves Mark's dog*, which sounds pretty redundant. The pronoun *his* stands for *Mark's*.

More examples of pronouns are shown in the following table. Note that some of these words can be used as nouns or pronouns.

all	another	any	anybody	anyone
anything	both	each	either	everyone
everything	few	he	hers	herself
him	himself	his	I	it
its	itself	many	me	mine
my	myself	neither	no one	nobody
nothing	other	ours	ourselves	she
some	somebody	someone	something	their

theirs	them	themselves	they	this
those	us	we	what	which
who	whoever	whom	whomever	whose
you	yours	yourself	yourselves	

Some pronouns are considered **personal pronouns** because they are taking the place of a noun. The pronouns can replace the subject or object in a sentence. Some pronouns are considered **possessive pronouns** because they are simply referring to the noun. See the examples of both types of pronouns in the sentences below. The pronouns are underlined.

Personal Pronouns:
Chase grabbed the microphone and gave <u>it</u> to me.
<u>She</u> ran the marathon in under four hours.

Possessive Pronouns:
Jacqueline read <u>her</u> book in a week.
<u>Mine</u> is the fastest computer in the class.

Prepositions

A **preposition** is a word that expresses the relationship in time or space between words in a sentence. They are generally short words, such as *in, on, around, above, between, beside, by, before,* or *with,* which introduce prepositional phrases in a sentence. See the following examples of prepositions. Some sentences have two or more prepositions. The prepositions are underlined.

The girl ran <u>to</u> her room.
I cannot sleep <u>before</u> 10 o'clock.
Please go to the store <u>with</u> her.
The mouse ran <u>through</u> the hole <u>in</u> the wall.

Other Parts of Speech

You won't be tested on conjunctions, but they are important to know. A **conjunction** is a part of a sentence that joins two words, such as *and* or *or.*

3. Grammar

For the writing section of the ParaPro Assessment, you must be able to identify problems in the grammar of a sentence—you don't need to be a grammar expert. There are only a few aspects of grammar that will likely be tested. For example, you need to be on the lookout for the incorrect use of subject-verb agreement, pronoun agreement, and verb tenses.

Subject-Verb Agreement

They goes together, or *they go together*? You probably don't even have to think about which subject goes with which verb here—your ear discerns easily that the second version is correct. Subject-verb agreement is when the subject of a clause matches the verb *in number*. Singular nouns take singular verbs; plural nouns take plural verbs. However, some instances of subject-verb agreement are tricky. Look out for the following three problem areas on the writing section of the ParaPro Assessment:

- **Phrases Following the Subject**—Pay close attention to the subject of the sentence. Do not be misled by phrases that may follow the subject. These phrases may confuse you into selecting a verb that does not agree with the subject. Try this practice question:

1. Betty Friedan's 1963 book, <u>an exposé</u> of domesticity <u>that challenged</u> long-held American attitudes, <u>remain</u>
                                    a   **b**   **c**
an <u>important contribution</u> to feminism.
      d

The correct answer is choice **c**. The singular subject, *book*, needs a singular verb, *remains*. Don't be confused by the plural noun *attitudes*, which is part of a phrase that follows the subject.

- **Subjects Following the Verb**—Be sure to locate the subject of the sentence. Test makers use subjects that come after the verb to confuse you. Sentence constructions which begin with *there is* or *there are* signal that the subject comes after the verb.

2. <u>Although</u> the Australian government <u>protects</u> the Great Barrier Reef, there <u>is</u> environmental factors
     a   **b**   **c**
that <u>continue</u> to threaten the world's largest coral reef ecosystem.
    d

The correct answer, the underlined section with the error, is choice **c**. The plural subject *factors* requires a plural form of the verb, *are*. Nothing is wrong with the word *although*, so choice **a** is incorrect. The plural verb *protects* matches the singular tense of the word *government*, so choice **b** is incorrect The verb *continue* is in the correct tense to match the plural subject *factors*, so choice **d** is incorrect.

Special Singular Nouns—Some words that end in *s*, like *measles*, *news*, *checkers*, *economics*, *sports*, and *politics*, are often singular despite their plural form, because we think of them as one thing. Watch out for collective nouns—nouns that refer to a number of people or things that form a single unit. These words, such as *audience*, *stuff*, *crowd*, *government*, *group*, and *orchestra*, need a singular verb.

3. That <u>rowdy</u> group of drama students <u>were </u>labeled "the anarchists," <u>because</u> they took over the university
        a   b   c

president's office <u>in a protest </u>against the dress code.
                   d

The correct answer choice is **b**. The collective noun *group* is the singular subject of the sentence. Notice how the position of the prepositional phrase *of drama students* following the subject is misleading.

Pronoun Agreement

Pronouns are words that take the place of a noun. Just as subjects and verbs must agree, pronouns and their antecedents must match. If a noun is singular, the pronoun must be singular. If a noun is plural, the pronoun must be plural. Pronouns also need to match their antecedent in case. Remember that a pronoun can also take the place of another pronoun too. In those cases, the pronouns must agree as well, of course.

A pronoun that takes the place of the subject of a sentence should be in the nominative case (*I, we, he, she, they*), whereas a pronoun that takes the place of the object in a sentence should be in the objective case (*me, us, him, her, them*). Here are some examples.

Matteo is funny, but <u>he</u> can also be very serious. (subject)

Bernadette hired Will, and she also fired <u>him</u>. (object)

In most cases, you will automatically recognize errors in pronoun agreement. The sentence *Me worked on the project with him* is clearly incorrect. However, some instances of pronoun agreement can be tricky. Review these common pronoun problems:

- **indefinite pronouns** like *each, everyone, anybody, no one, one,* and *either* are singular. <u>Each</u> *of the boys presented his science project.*
- **two or more nouns joined by *and*** use a plural pronoun. <u>Andy Warhol and Roy Lichtenstein</u> *engaged popular culture in their art.*
- **two or more singular nouns joined by *or*** use a singular pronoun. <u>Francis or Andrew</u> *will lend you his book.*
- **he or she?** In speech, people often use the pronoun *they* to refer to a single person of unknown gender. However, this is incorrect—a singular noun requires a singular pronoun. <u>A person</u> *has the right to do whatever <u>he or she</u> wants.*

The following table lists some pronouns that are commonly confused with verb contractions or other words. Look out for these errors.

Confusing Word	Quick Definition
its	belonging to it
it's	it is
your	belonging to you
you're	you are
their	belonging to them
they're	they are
there	describes where an action takes place
whose	belonging to whom
who's	who is or who has
who	refers to people
that	refers to things
which	introduces clauses that are not essential to the information in the sentence, unless they refer to people. In that case, use *who*.

Try this practice sentence-correction question:

4. A child <u>who</u> is eager to please <u>will</u> often follow everything that <u>their</u> parents <u>say</u>.
      a   **b**   **c**   **d**

Choice **c** is the correct answer. The subject, *a child*, is singular. Even though you don't know the gender of the child, the possessive pronoun should be *his or her* in order to agree in number.

Pronoun Problem—Unclear Reference

When a pronoun can refer to more than one antecedent in a sentence, it is called an unclear, or ambiguous, reference. Look carefully for this error; a sentence may read smoothly, but may still contain an unclear reference. Look at this practice usage question:

5. A regular feature in American newspapers <u>since</u> the early nineteenth century, <u>they</u> use satirical humor to
                                             a   **b**

<u>visually</u> comment <u>on</u> a current event.
  c   **d**

The answer is choice **b**. Who or what uses satirical humor? You don't know how to answer, because the pronoun *they* does not have an antecedent. If you replace *they* with *political cartoons*, the sentence makes sense.

Shifting Verb Tense

Verb tense should be consistent. If a sentence describes an event in the past, its verbs should all be in the past tense.

Incorrect: *When Kate visited Japan, she sees many Shinto temples.*
Correct: *When Kate visited Japan, she saw many Shinto temples.*

- **Past Tense for Present Conditions:** It's incorrect to describe a present condition in the past tense.
  Incorrect: *My sister met her husband in a cafe. He was very tall.*
  Correct: *My sister met her husband in a cafe. He is very tall.*

- **Incomplete Verbs:** Test makers may trick you by including the *-ing* form, or progressive form, of a verb without a helping verb (*is, has, has been, was, had, had been*, etc.). Make sure that verbs are complete and make sense in the sentence.
  Incorrect: *The major newspapers covering the story throughout the year because of the controversy.*
  Correct: *The major newspapers have been covering the story throughout the year because of the controversy.*

- **Subjunctive Mood:** The subjunctive mood of verbs expresses something that is imagined, wished for, or contrary to fact. The subjunctive of *was* is *were*.
  Incorrect: *If I was a movie star, I would buy a fleet of Rolls-Royces.*
  Correct: *If I were a movie star, I would buy a fleet of Rolls-Royces.*

Now practice answering this usage question.

6. <u>Unhappy</u> about the lack <u>of</u> parking at the old stadium, season ticket holders <u>considering</u> <u>boycotting</u> next
      a   **b**   **c**   **d**
   week's game.

The correct answer is **c**. *Considering* needs a helping verb to be complete and to make sense in this sentence. The clause should read, *season ticket holders are considering boycotting next week's game.*

Correcting Run-On Sentences and Sentence Fragments

While you won't likely be expected to identify run-on sentences or sentence fragments in the error identification part of the writing section, you may be expected to identify these grammatical issues for students—and in a later question on the ParaPro Assessment. What is wrong with the following sentence?

I went to the store I bought some eggs.

There are two separate statements. It is not grammatically correct to combine them without any punctuation. A student could write this as two sentences, separated by a period. Or the student could include some punctuation and a conjunction to combine the thoughts. Those possible solutions are shown in the following rewritten sentences.

I went to the store. I bought some eggs.
I went to the store, and I bought some eggs.

A sentence fragment has the opposite problem of a run-on sentence; it simply does not have enough information to stand on its own as a sentence. As mentioned earlier, the two main parts of a sentence are a subject and a predicate (a verb that tells what the subject is doing). For example, look at the following sentence fragment:

Billy, the tallest student in the class.

The subject is clearly *Billy*. The information after the comma describes him. But nothing is going on—there is no predicate! As a result, this is not a correct sentence. It can be resolved by adding a verb, such as the word "is" in the sentence shown below:

Billy, the tallest student, is my best friend.

What is missing from the sentence fragment below?

Ran the entire way down the street.

There is a verb here—*ran*—but we don't know who ran. The subject is missing! Therefore, this is not a correct sentence. Adding a subject will fix it, such as the word *Tara* in the sentence below:

Tara ran the entire way down the street.

4. Punctuation

Punctuation marks are standardized marks which clarify meaning for your reader, serving as traffic signs that direct the reader to pause, connect, stop, consider, and go. Although you have most likely studied and learned many of the basic rules of punctuation and capitalization, this section will cover some common problem areas that may appear on the ParaPro Assessment—including misuse of commas, semicolons, colons, and apostrophes.

Commas

A comma creates pauses, clarifies meaning, and separates different parts of a sentence. Remember the following six basic rules for using commas:

1. **To separate independent clauses** joined by a coordinating conjunction, such as *and, but, nor, so, for,* or *or.* Use a comma before the conjunction.

   My instinct was to solve the problem slowly and deliberately, but we only had a week before the deadline.

2. **To set off nonessential clauses.** A nonessential clause is one that can be removed from a sentence without changing its meaning.

   My friend Rebecca, who is active in the local labor union, is a fifth-grade teacher.

3. **To set off words or phrases that interrupts** the flow of thought in a sentence.

   The certification program, however, works well for me.

   Elena Alvarez, my adviser and mentor, was present at the meeting.

4. **To set off an introductory element,** such as a word or phrase that comes at the beginning of a sentence.

   Thrilled by the results, Phin presented the study to his colleagues.

5. **To set apart a series of words in a list.** Usually, the last item in a list is preceded by a conjunction. Although a comma is not necessary before the conjunction, it is preferred that you use one.

   Micah, Jose, and Sam attended the conference.

   Micah, Jose and Sam attended the conference.

6. **To separate elements of dates and addresses.** Commas are used to separate dates that include the day, month, and year. Dates that include just the month and year do not need commas. When the name of a city and state are included in an address, set off both with commas.

   Margaret moved to Portsmouth, New Hampshire, for the job.

   Maco came to Greensboro on June 15, 2004, right after she graduated from the program.

   Maco came to Greensboro in June 2004 after she graduated from the program.

Semicolons

A semicolon (;) is a grammatical mark that splits two independent clauses. You may be asked to recognize errors involving the use of semicolons on the ParaPro Assessment. Review how to use this mark correctly in the following guidelines:

1. **Use a semicolon to separate independent clauses** that are not joined by a conjunction.
2. **Use a semicolon to separate independent clauses that contain commas,** even if the clauses are joined by a conjunction.
3. **Use a semicolon to separate independent clauses connected with a conjunctive adverb,** such as *however, therefore, then, thus,* or *moreover.*

Colons

A colon (:) is a grammatical mark that introduces elements and shows an equivalent relationship (almost like an equals sign in math). Follow these guidelines to recognize the correct use of colons:

1. **Use a colon to introduce a list** when the clause before the colon can stand as a complete sentence.

   These are the first-year teachers: Ellen, Ben, and Eliza.

   The first-year teachers are Ellen, Ben, and Eliza. (No colon here.)

2. **Use a colon to introduce a restatement or elaboration** of the previous clause.
   James enjoys teaching Measure for Measure *each spring: it is his favorite play.*

3. **Use a colon to introduce a word, phrase, or clause** that adds emphasis to the main body of the sentence.
   Carrie framed the check: it was the first paycheck she had ever earned.

4. **Use a colon to introduce a formal quotation.**
   Writer Gurney Williams offered this advice to parents: "Teaching creativity to your child isn't like teaching good manners. No one can paint a masterpiece by bowing to another person's precepts about elbows on the table."

Use the punctuation guidelines you have reviewed so far to answer this practice question.

7. Alternative medicine, which includes a range of practices outside of conventional medicine such as herbs,
                 a   **b**
   homeopathy, massage, yoga, and acupuncture; holds increasing appeal for Americans.
                                                   c **d**

Choice **c** is the correct answer. The semicolon does not work because it does not separate two independent clauses. It should be replaced with a comma, setting off the nonessential clause that begins with the word *which*.

Apostrophes

An apostrophe (') is a grammatical mark used to show possession and contractions. Consider these eight rules for using apostrophes:

1. **Add *'s* to form the singular possessive, even when the noun ends in *s*:**
   Mr. Summers's essay convinced me.

2. **Add *'s* to plural words not ending in *s* to show possession.**
   The children's ability to absorb foreign language is astounding.
   The workshops focus on working women's needs.

3. **Add *'* to plural words ending in *s* to show possession.**
   The students' grades improved each semester.

4. **Add *'s* to indefinite pronouns that show ownership.**
   Everyone's ability level should be considered.

5. **Never use apostrophes with possessive pronouns.**
   This experiment must be yours.

6. **Use *'s* to form the plurals of letters, figures, and numbers, as well as expressions of time or money.**
   Mind your p's and q's.
   The project was the result of a year's worth of work.

7. Add *'s* to the last word of a compound noun, compound subject, or name of a business or institution to show possession.

   The president-elect's speech riveted the audience.
   Gabbie and Michael's wedding is in October.
   The National Science Teachers Association's meeting will take place next week.

8. **Use apostrophes to show that letters or words are omitted in contractions.**

   Abby doesn't (does not) work today.
   Who's (who is) on first?

Practice answering this usage question.

8. When Thomas Jefferson sent explorers Lewis and Clark into the West, he patterned their mission on the
                                                                                          a

   <u>Enlightenments'</u> scientific methods: to observe, collect, document, and classify.
   b   **c**   **d**

   The answer is choice **b**. As a proper noun, *the Enlightenment* is correctly capitalized; however, the apostrophe is misplaced. To show possession, add *'s* to a singular noun.

5. Word Usage

A misused word can significantly alter the meaning of a sentence. That's why the ParaPro Assessment will test your ability to recognize misused words. The following list contains some commonly confused words. If you find some that you frequently confuse, study them and practice using them correctly in a sentence.

CONFUSING WORD	QUICK DEFINITION
accept	recognize, receive
except	excluding
affect (verb)	to influence
effect (noun)	result
effect (verb)	to bring about
all ready	totally prepared
already	by this time
allude	make indirect reference to
elude	evade
illusion	unreal appearance
all ways	every method
always	forever

among	in the middle of several
between	in an interval separating (two)
assure	to make certain (assure someone)
ensure	to make certain
insure	to make certain (financial value)
beside	next to
besides	in addition to
complement	match
compliment	praise
continual	constant
continuous	uninterrupted
disinterested	no strong opinion either way
uninterested	don't care
elicit	to stir up
illicit	illegal
eminent	well known
imminent	pending
farther	beyond
further	additional
incredible	beyond belief, astonishing
incredulous	skeptical, disbelieving
loose	not tight
lose	be unable to find
may	be something could possibly be
maybe	perhaps
overdo	do too much
overdue	late
persecute	to mistreat
prosecute	to take legal action
personal	individual
personnel	employees
precede	go before
proceed	continue
proceeds	profits

principal (adjective)	main
principal (noun)	person in charge
principle	standard
stationary	still, not moving
stationery	writing material
than	in contrast to
then	next
to	on the way to
too	also
weather	climate
whether	if

6. Spelling

Approximately four questions on the ParaPro Assessment will test your ability recognize misspelled words. Those questions will ask you to identify the answer choice containing a word that is NOT spelled correctly. All you have to do is point out the misspelled word from the other three correctly spelled words. You do not need to fix the spelling of the misspelled word.

Of course, it would be nearly impossible to memorize the spelling of every word in the English language. But there are a few spelling rules that will help you recognize whether a word is misspelled on the ParaPro Assessment.

Plural Words

Some words are pluralized by adding an –s to the end of the word. Others are pluralized by adding an –es to the end of the word. However, there are other special rules for many words that end with the letter *f*, such as *hoof* or *scarf*. In those words, the letter *f* changes to the letter *v*, and then an –es is added. So *scarf* becomes *scarves* and *hoof* becomes *hooves*. Also remember that nouns that end in –*y* usually change to –*ies* when pluralized. For example, *policy* becomes *policies* and *company* becomes *companies*.

Adding Vowel Suffixes

A lot of common spelling mistakes occur at the ends of words that have suffixes. There are a few rules to remember when looking at the end of a word to see if it is spelled correctly. You need to look at the root word and determine if the suffix is proper.

If a root words ends in with a silent *e*, like *bike*, the vowel should be dropped when added a suffix that starts in a vowel, like *-ing* or *-ed*. Look at the following list of root words and see how the *e* at the end gets dropped when a suffix is added.

Root Word	With Suffix (and e Dropped)
bore	boring
cube	cubic
fame	famous
ice	icicle
move	moving
nose	nosy
sane	sanity

There are exceptions to this handy rule, unfortunately. For example, words that end in *-ce* or *-ge* keep their silent *e* when the suffix begins with *a, o,* or *u*. For example, *change* becomes *changeable* and *courage* becomes *courageous*. The *e* stays on.

If a root word ends in a consonant, then the consonant may have to be repeated when a vowel suffix is added. It depends whether the word ends in a stressed short vowel sound.

Root Word	With Suffix (and Consonant Repeated)
deter	deterrent
occur	occurring
remit	remittance
slip	slipping

A root word that ends in a consonant with a long vowel sound does not need the repeated letter. For example, the word *repeat* can just become *repeated*. And any word with a stress not on the end of the word doesn't need a repeated consonant either. For example, *open* can just become *opening*. Note that the consonants *v, j, k, w,* and *x* are almost never doubled.

When any word that ends in *y* takes on a suffix, the *y* changes to an *i*. See the examples in the following table.

Root Word (with y)	With Suffix (and y turned to i)
body	bodily
fury	furious
happy	happiness
marry	marriage
pity	pitiful

–Sion vs. –tion

When you change some verbs into nouns, they take on a suffix. Some of those words end in -*tion*, like *completion*. Others end in -*sion*, like *extension*. How do you tell whether to use -*tion* or -*sion* at the end of a word? You need to look at the root word. If the root word ends in a *t* sound, use -*tion*. For example *celebrate* becomes *celebration* or *devote* becomes *devotion*. If the root word ends in *s* or *d*, use -*sion*. For example, *extend* becomes *extension* or *decide* becomes *decision*. Any word that ends in -*mit*, however, changes to -*miss*-. That means that *submit* becomes *submission*.

-Ant or -ance vs. -ent or -ence

Many common misspelled words are a result of words that end with -*ent*, -*ence*, -*ant*, or -*ance* suffixes. That's because they sound the same. For example, *innocent* ends with -*ent* while *elegant* ends with -*ant*. How can anyone know the proper spelling? As usual, it helps to look at the root word. Here are some general rules to follow, using the root word as a guide.

Add –*ant* or –*ance* when the root word:

- ends in -*y*: *ally* becomes *alliance* or *rely* becomes *reliant*
- ends in -*ear*: *clear* becomes *clearance*
- ends in -*ure*: *assure* becomes *assurance*
- ends in unstressed -*er*: *hinder* becomes *hinderance*
- begins with *a*: *allow* becomes *allowance*

Add –*ent* or –*ence* when the root word:

- ends in -*ist*: *exist* becomes *existent* or *existence*
- ends in -*ere*: *adhere* becomes *adherence*
- includes -*cid*-: *coincide* becomes *coincidence*
- includes -*fid*-: *confide* becomes *confidence*
- includes -*sid*-: *reside* becomes *residence*
- includes -*vid*: *provide* becomes *providence*
- includes -*flu*-: *affluent* becomes *affluence*
- includes -*qu*-: *frequent* becomes *frequency*
- ends in stressed -*er*: *infer* becomes *inference*

Just like almost every other spelling rule, there are exceptions. For example, *difference* ends in an unstressed -*er*, but it ends in -*ence*.

-Ary vs. -ery

Misspelled words also end in one of these common suffixes. Fortunately, this spelling rule is a bit simpler than some of the others. The truth is that almost all of these words end in -*ary*. For example, *dictionary, evolutionary, necessary, secretary,* and *vocabulary* all end in -*ary*. The best way to know when to use -*ery* is to recognize the exceptions. *Cemetery* and *stationery* (meaning paper) are two of the most commonly misspelled -*ery* words.

Ch vs. tch

Why is it that some words with the same sound use /ch/ while others use /tch/? For example, *beach* and *catch* seem to have the same sound. The rule here is that the /tch/ follows short vowel sounds. The /ch/ follows long vowel sounds. See the following table.

tch (After Short Vowel Sounds)	*ch* (After Long Vowel Sounds)
batch	coach
Dutch	each
kitchen	peach
sketch	speech
witch	teach

Once again, there are a few examples that don't fit this rule. For example, *such, which,* and *much* are all common words that disregard this rule. But this is still a good rule to consider.

I Before E . . .

You've probably heard of this spelling rule. However, there is more to the popular rhyme "*i* before *e*, except after *c*." As with most spelling rules in the English language, there are exceptions. It may be helpful to consider that most words with the *ee* sound tend to fit this rule. See the words with this sound that fit the rule in the table below.

i before *e*	*i* before *e* Except After *c*
believe	ceiling
grief	deceive
piece	receipt
thief	receive

Remember that words that don't make the *ee* sound don't really follow this rule. That's why words like *neighbor* or *weigh* are spelled with *e* before *i*.

Sometimes you simply have to trust your instinct as to whether a word looks right or not. You can sound it out, which helps for some words. For example, if you say *science,* you should hear that the *i* definitely comes after the *e*—even though it follows a *c*. And the word *weird* actually has an *e* sound before the *i* sound, too.

Application of Writing Skills and Knowledge to Classroom Instruction

The last 12 questions on the writing section of the ParaPro Assessment will test your ability to apply writing skills and knowledge to the classroom. That may mean, for example, that you will be asked to show how you would aid students in their writing skills, such as choosing the proper word in a sentence. You may also be asked to show how you would help students organize, draft, and revise their essays in your role as a paraprofessional. These steps for writing an essay are explained in detail in the section called "Aspects of the Writing Process" on page 186.

Other types of questions on the writing skills application section of the test may ask you to help students:

1. Use reference materials
2. Understand the purpose of a piece of writing
3. Understand the importance of the audience of a piece of writing

1. Use Reference Materials

You will likely see a question on your ParaPro Assessment that asks which reference material a student should use to locate specific information. Depending on what the student is looking for, the following reference materials could be used:

- An **atlas** is a book of maps. Students should use an atlas only when trying to find information about geography, such as the capital of California or the countries that share a border with Germany.
- A **dictionary** contains definitions of words. A student would only use a dictionary as a resource if he or she didn't know the meaning of a word.
- An **encyclopedia** contains a wealth of specific information about a subject, both general and specific. For example, an encyclopedia will tell you about Canada, or about where and when a specific person was born.
- A **newspaper** provides up-to-date information about a topic, including current events or issues. Old newspaper articles can also serve as a historical record of an event or issue.
- A **magazine** can also provide up-to-date information about a topic, but magazines tend to go into more detail than newspapers. Look at the name of the magazine or the title of the article to determine whether it suits the student's purpose.
- A **textbook** or a **book** on a specific topic can provide very in-depth information about a topic. For example, a student doing a report on England during the 1800s can turn to a textbook called *Ninteenth Century Europe.*
- A **website** can provide just about any information that can be found in any other resource. For example, some websites will contain general information or details about current events. Whether a website is helpful for the student's purpose depends on the type of website—and whether it is reputable. Students will have to determine whether the Internet site will provide a useful resource.

2. Understand the Purpose of Writing

A piece of writing may serve many possible purposes. It is critical that students understand what a piece of writing is trying to achieve. As a result, students—and paraprofessionals—must be familiar with the following three major types of writing.

Persuasive Writing

Some writing is intended to persuade the reader of something. This type of writing contains an argument and takes a position. For example, a student may write an essay about how the school year should end in April. He or she will attempt to make arguments and *persuade* the reader to agree with the main idea. A common place to find examples of persuasive writing is in the Opinion-Editorial section of a newspaper. Advertisements also contain persuasive writing; they are trying to convince the reader to buy the product!

Instructive Writing

Any piece of writing that contains instructions is an example of instructive writing. Its purpose is simply to tell the reader how to do something. A set of directions or a product manual is an example of instructive writing.

Descriptive Writing

Descriptive writing, as its name implies, is full of descriptions. These descriptions can tell a story and have a great amount of detail. A poem may be an example of descriptive writing. Unlike instructive or persuasive writing, descriptive writing has no motive other than to tell a story. It does not attempt to convince the reader of something or tell the reader how to do a task.

3. Understand the Importance of the Audience

Effective writing pays close attention to its *audience*. Good writers consider their readers: Who are they? What do they know about the subject? What preconceived notions do they have? What will hold their attention?

A student should consider the audience to help make key writing decisions about the level of formality and detail. The level of formality determines whether the student will use slang, an informal tone, technical jargon, or formal language in his or her writing. If a student is writing for a general audience and not for friends or family, for example, the readers may not be familiar with the student's background or experiences. Therefore, in those cases, students should be sure to provide their readers with adequate context.

Aspects of the Writing Process

As classroom educators, paraprofessionals are responsible for helping students develop into strong writers. That involves explaining the steps necessary to build a well-structured essay. The following steps show how a student can create an essay involving a thesis, or a main idea with an argument.

Step 1: Prewriting

The prewriting—or planning—process is essential to developing a clear, organized essay. Prewriting consists of some quick, basic steps: formulating a thesis, brainstorming for examples that will support a student's thesis, and drafting an outline or basic structure for the essay.

A thesis statement should:

- tell the reader what the subject is
- inform the reader what the writer thinks and feels about the subject
- use clear, active language

Students don't have to waste their time making their thesis statement a masterpiece. They will be able to grab the reader's attention by clearly stating the purpose in simple words. For example, a student wants to write an essay about wearing school uniforms.

The following sentences *are not* thesis statements:

- *Many private schools already require school uniforms.*
- *Some students prefer school uniforms, while others detest them.*
- *Why do schools use uniforms?*

The following *are* thesis statements:

- *School uniforms discourage high-school students from learning responsibility and developing individuality.*
- *School uniforms are effective in creating a positive learning environment.*

Step 2: Brainstorm for Ideas

Once a student has decided what he or she wants to write about—or what his or her thesis will be—he or she will begin to brainstorm (think of ideas) for support. Students should try to generate three to five reasons that back up their main idea in a persuasive piece of writing.

Brainstorming is a prewriting process in which you imagine or write down any ideas that come to mind. To brainstorm effectively, students should not judge their ideas initially; they should simply put them down on paper. If they are stuck for ideas, they can try these brainstorming strategies:

- Try the **freewriting** technique, in which you write nonstop for two minutes. Keep your pen to paper and keep your hand moving. Doubtlessly, your ideas will emerge.
- **List** as many ideas as you can. Don't edit for grammar or structure; just write down whatever comes to mind.

Step 3: Outline the Essay

To make sure that a student's essay is well developed and organized, the student must draft an outline. An outline will help students put their ideas into a logical order and identify any gaps in their supporting details. On your ParaPro Assessment, you may see an example of an outline for a student's essay. You may be asked how to help improve the organization of the outline, or fill in the gaps in a student's outline with additional information.

Some essays should follow a specific structure. For example, persuasive essays follow a basic three-part structure:

1. **Introduction:** Present your position to your readers. State your thesis.
2. **Body:** Provide specific support for your thesis.
3. **Conclusion:** Bring closure to your essay and restate your thesis.

Where the introduction and conclusion go is probably obvious. However, a student needs a pattern, or structure, to organize the ideas in the body of the essay. The four most common patterns are **chronological order**, **comparison and contrast**, **cause and effect**, and **order of importance**. The following chart lists each organizing principle's key characteristics and effective uses in writing.

Organizational Pattern	Characteristics	Effective Uses
Chronological order	Uses time as organizing principle; describes events in the order in which they happened	Historical texts, personal narratives, fiction
Order of Importance	Arranges ideas by rank instead of time	Persuasive essays, newspaper articles
Comparison and contrast	Places two or more items side by side to show similarities and differences	Comparative essays
Cause and effect	Explains possible reasons why something took place	Historical analysis, analysis of current events

Step 4: Writing the Essay

First Impression—The Introduction

Once a detailed outline is completed, a student can begin to draft his or her essay. A student must use clear, direct language to introduce the reader to the thesis and focus. A useful technique for creating a strong introduction is to begin with a thesis and then give a summary of the evidence (supporting details) that will be presented in the body of the essay.

Supporting Paragraphs—The Body of the Essay

Working from the detailed outline, a student can begin composing the body of his or her essay.

Each paragraph should be treated like a mini-essay, with its own thesis (a topic sentence that expresses the main idea of the paragraph) and supporting details (examples). Follow these guidelines for creating supporting paragraphs:

- **Avoid introducing several ideas within one paragraph.** By definition, a paragraph is a group of sentences about the *same* idea.
- **Use at least one detail** or example to back up each main supporting idea.
- **Aim for about three or four sentences in each paragraph.** If a student writes more sentences for each paragraph, a reader might lose track of the main idea of the paragraph. If a student writes fewer sentences, he or she may not be developing the idea adequately.
- **Use transitions.** Key words and phrases can help guide readers through an essay. Students can use these common transitions to indicate the order of importance of your material: *first and foremost, most important, first, second, third, moreover, finally,* and *above all.* Remind students not to use "firstly," "secondly," or "thirdly"—these forms are incorrect and awkward.

The Conclusion

The last paragraph of a student's essay should sum up the argument. They should avoid introducing new ideas or topics. Instead, the concluding paragraph should restate the thesis, but in *new words.* The conclusion should demonstrate that the topic was covered fully and should convince readers that they have learned something meaningful from the argument.

Step 5: Revising and Proofreading the Essay

The goal of proofreading is to give a student's essay a final polish, by checking spelling, correcting grammatical errors, and if needed, changing word order or word choice. The following checklist outlines some basic grammatical problems a student should look out for as he or she proofreads. (All of these grammar trouble spots are discussed earlier in the chapter.)

- **Make sure nouns and verbs agree.** The subject of the sentence must match the verb in number. If the subject is singular, the verb is singular. If the subject is plural, the verb is plural.

- **Make sure pronouns and antecedents agree.** Pronouns and the nouns they represent (antecedents) must agree in number. If the antecedent is singular, the pronoun is singular; if the antecedent is plural, the pronoun is plural.
- **Check the modifiers.** Look out for modifiers that are easy to confuse, like *good/well, bad/badly, fewer/less.* Remember: Adjectives modify nouns and pronouns; adverbs describe verbs, adjectives, or other adverbs.
- **Keep the verb tense consistent.** Switching tense within a sentence can change its meaning. Generally, a sentence or paragraph that begins in the present tense should continue in the present tense.
- **Check the sentence structure.** Keep an eye out for sentence fragments, run-on sentences, comma splices, or any other issues that prevent the sentence from being understood.

Writing Practice

Directions: Questions 1–8 each include a sentence with four parts underlined. One of the four underlined parts will contain an error in grammar, punctuation, or word usage. Each sentence will have exactly one error. Select the letter of the answer choice that corresponds to that error.

1. Despite being the world's top polluter; China is also a world leader of green technologies.
     a   b   c   d

2. Theodore Roosevelt was a unique candidate during the 1912 presidential elections because he have been
                              a   b   c   d
   president for two terms already.

3. The Philippines, a country in Southeast Asia, are comprised of thousands of islands in the western Pacific
                 a   b c   d
   Ocean.

4. Athletes can aggravate existing injuries if they overdue their activities at a time when they should be letting
                                            a   b   c
   their bodies heal.
             d

5. While Ohio is called the "birthplace of aviation" because Wilbur and Orville Wright were born there, the
            a   b   c
   state also produce the most astronauts, including Neil Armstrong and John Glenn.
             d

6. Antarctica is the driest continent on Earth, its enormous quantities of snow and ice have built up over
                                        a b   c   d
   millions of years.

7. By working <u>quick</u>, construction workers <u>were able</u> <u>to build</u> the 102-story Empire State Building in <u>less than</u>
               a   **b**   **c**   **d**
one year and two months.

8. Facing the prospect <u>of</u> being impeached, Richard Nixon <u>had resigned</u> in 1974, <u>becoming</u> the first and only
                         a   **b**   **c**
president to step down from the <u>country's</u> highest office.
                                    d

Directions: Answer questions 9–30 by selecting the answer choice that best answers the given question or completes the statement.

9. After a three-year renovation in the late twentieth century, the six-degree tilt of the Leaning Tower of Pisa was reduced <u>by</u> about half a degree.

The underlined word in the sentence above is an example of
a. an adverb.
b. an adjective.
c. a preposition.
d. a verb.

10. Even though he is restricted to a wheelchair and must paint with a brush strapped on his wrist, Chuck Close still creates incredibly realistic images.

What is the <u>subject</u> of the sentence shown above?
a. wheelchair
b. brush
c. Chuck Close
d. realistic images

11. He was born in Connecticut, but George W. Bush <u>moved</u> with his family to Texas when he was only two years old.

The underlined word in the sentence above is an example of
a. a verb.
b. a noun.
c. a preposition.
d. an adjective.

12. Though they were arrested for the act, four bungee jumpers from the Oxford University Dangerous Sports Club inspired a generation of bungee jumpers with their 1979 jump from a 245-foot tall bridge.

What is the <u>subject</u> of the sentence shown above?
a. act
b. four bungee jumpers
c. Oxford University Dangerous Sports Club
d. 245-foot tall bridge

13. Many residents of Washington, D.C. have complained that they do not receive adequate government representation because <u>they</u> do not have a senator in the U.S. senate or any voting member of congress.

The underlined word in the sentence above is an example of
a. a pronoun.
b. a noun.
c. a preposition.
d. an adjective.

14. The inventor of bifocals, the lightning rod, and the Franklin stove, Benjamin Franklin was one of the most creative thinkers in American history.

The <u>simple predicate</u> of the sentence above is
a. invent.
b. was.
c. thinker.
d. history.

15. Which of the following words is NOT spelled properly?
a. changeable
b. confiding
c. detered
d. injuries

16. Which of the following words is NOT spelled properly?
a. acceptence
b. enduring
c. retrieve
d. revolution

17. Which of the following words is NOT spelled properly?
   a. conceive
   b. deleted
   c. independant
   d. unmoving

18. Which of the following words is NOT spelled properly?
   a. antique
   b. global
   c. hibernate
   d. lumpyer

Answer questions 19–20 based on the following essay, written by a fifth-grade student named Gene.

Oscar the dog was unlike any other dog, in the world; Oscar had the ability to talk. When he was just a puppy he could understand everything that his owner, Mr. Thomas was saying. A few years after that the dog was able to talk back with Mr. Thomas. Once his owner knew about the dog's abilities he put him to work for the U.S. government as a secret spy.

19. On which aspect of Gene's writing should the teacher spend the most time working with him?
   a. semicolon usage
   b. verb tense agreement
   c. noun-pronoun agreement
   d. comma usage

20. One of the students in Gene's class said that she did not know who *him* referred to in the last sentence of the story. How could Gene change *him* to make sure that the meaning of the sentence is understood by his readers?
   a. it
   b. Oscar
   c. he
   d. Mr. Thomas

Answer questions 21–23 based on an outline that a student is working on.

Pete wants to write an essay about the career of his favorite professional baseball player. Before he can begin drafting his essay, he puts the notes from brainstorming into the following outline.

Life of My Favorite Professional Baseball Player
  I. Early Life
    A. Family Life
      1. Grandfather played baseball
      2. Father taught him to play
      3. Brother drove him to games
    B. Little League
      1. Learned to pitch
      2. Inspired by coach
      3. Became star of his team
  II. _____
    A. High School
      1. Moved to shortstop
      2. Became friends with other star
    B. College
      1. Chose college over pros
      2. Won college tournament
      3. Got math degree
  III. Professional Career
    A. First years
      1. Drafted by big leagues out of college
      2. First season in rookie league very hard
      3. Hit 30 home runs in minor leagues
    B. Breaking into major leagues
      1. _____
      2. MVP during one season
      3. Won World Series
    C. Final Years and Retirement
      1. Played for 19 seasons
      2. Last at bat a home run
      3. Election to Hall of Fame

21. Pete needs a heading for section II of his outline. Which heading would fit the content best?
   a. Middle School
   b. Won Batting Title Sophomore Year
   c. Sports during Academics
   d. Signed $8 Million Contract

22. One part of section III is left blank. What information about the baseball player could Pete put in that blank part?
   a. Had to take out loans to pay for college
   b. Earned Rookie of the Year Award in first professional season
   c. Coaches his daughters after retirement
   d. Broke his leg when he was 11

23. Once Pete finishes his outline, he wants to begin drafting his essay. Which introductory sentence should he write to sum up the details of his outline?
   a. My favorite baseball player has had a long and successful career.
   b. It isn't fair that baseball players make more money than teachers or doctors.
   c. It takes a lot of practice and hard work to be a professional athlete.
   d. My favorite baseball player won the MVP award one year.

Answer questions 24–26 based on an essay written by a fourth-grade student named Yoshi.

How to Make a Grilled Cheese Sandwich

(1) Use whole wheat or multigrain bread it is much healthier than white bread. (2) Butter one side of two pieces of bread. (3) Put cheese on the other sides of the bread. (4) It will taste better if you use different kinds of cheese. (5) Put the bread with the buttered side down on a pan. (6) Put a cover on the pan. (7) Put the heat on low. (8) When the bottoms of the bread are light brown, put the pieces together. (9) Last but not least, cut the sandwich diagonally.

24. Yoshi needs help creating transitions to improve the meaning of his sentences. Which word could he use after the words "multigrain bread" in sentence 1 to improve the sentence's meaning?
   a. but
   b. and
   c. because
   d. although

25. Yoshi wants to combine sentences 6 and 7 into one new sentence. The new sentence must tell the same information in a way that is easy to understand. Which sentence best combines sentences 6 and 7?
   a. Cover the pan but put the heat on low.
   b. Put a cover on the pan because the heat is on low.
   c. A cover should be put on the pan and then the heat is low.
   d. Cover the pan and put the heat on low.

26. Yoshi wants to add a sentence at the beginning of his essay to tell the main idea. Which sentence would fit best at the beginning of his essay?
   a. Grilled cheese and peanut butter and jelly sandwiches are the best sandwiches there are.
   b. To make a perfect grilled cheese requires following a few simple steps.
   c. Bread is full of carbohydrates, but it is healthy unless you eat too much of it.
   d. If you are hungry for lunch, there are many delicious snacks to make.

Answer questions 27–28 based on the different types of reading materials as explained below.

Students in a classroom are learning how different types of writing may have different purposes. The list below shows a sentence from four different reading materials in the classroom.

   1. To make a model volcano, first you need to get vinegar, baking soda, and dishwasher soap.
   2. The only president to serve two non-consecutive terms was Grover Cleveland.
   3. The cool autumn winds blew strongly, kicking brown and yellow leaves into the air and down the street.
   4. We must hire new police officers immediately to protect the safety of the children in our town.

27. Which sentence looks as if its purpose is to persuade the reader of something?
   a. sentence 1
   b. sentence 2
   c. sentence 3
   d. sentence 4

28. Which sentence seems to have been taken from a source whose purpose is to teach how to do something?
   a. sentence 1
   b. sentence 2
   c. sentence 3
   d. sentence 4

29. A student wants to write a sentence about the home of several rabbits. She is confused by how to show possession of a plural word (more than one rabbit). How should the student write the word?
   a. *rabbit* without an –*s* at the end
   b. *rabbit* with an –*'s* at the end
   c. *rabbit* with an –*s'* at the end
   d. *rabbit* with an –*s's* at the end

30. A student wants to learn which states share a border with Oregon. Which source would be the best place for the student to turn for an answer?
   a. an internet article about California
   b. a dictionary
   c. a news article from Oregon's biggest newspaper
   d. an atlas

Answers and Explanations

Question Number	Correct Answer	Content Category
1	c	Writing Skills: Errors in punctuation
2	d	Writing Skills: Grammatical errors
3	b	Writing Skills: Grammatical errors
4	a	Writing Skills: Error in word usage
5	d	Writing Skills: Grammatical errors
6	a	Writing Skills: Errors in punctuation
7	a	Writing Skills: Grammatical errors
8	b	Writing Skills: Grammatical errors
9	c	Writing Skills: Parts of speech
10	c	Writing Skills: Parts of a sentence
11	a	Writing Skills: Parts of speech
12	b	Writing Skills: Parts of a sentence
13	a	Writing Skills: Parts of speech
14	b	Writing Skills: Parts of a sentence
15	c	Writing Skills: Spelling
16	a	Writing Skills: Spelling
17	c	Writing Skills: Spelling
18	d	Writing Skills: Spelling
19	d	Writing Application: Drafting and revising
20	b	Writing Application: Drafting and revising
21	c	Writing Application: Prewriting
22	b	Writing Application: Prewriting
23	a	Writing Application: Prewriting
24	c	Writing Application: Editing written documents
25	d	Writing Application: Editing written documents

Question Number	Correct Answer	Content Category
26	**b**	Writing Application: Drafting and revising
27	**d**	Writing Application: Writing in different modes and forms
28	**a**	Writing Application: Writing in different modes and forms
29	**c**	Writing Application: Editing written documents
30	**d**	Writing Application: Reference materials

1. c. The semicolon in this sentence should be a colon, choice **c**. Remember that a semicolon separates two independent clauses, so the parts of the sentence on both side of a semicolon must be able to stand alone. The other underlined parts of the sentence are correct as is.

2. d. The verb tense that says *have been* suggests that an action is still going on. Because Roosevelt had been the president before, it would be more appropriate to say that he *had been* president for two terms already. Even if you weren't sure why the verb tense, choice **d**, was wrong, perhaps you were able to identify that it sounded strange.

3. b. The Philippines, although it ends with *–s,* is a singular noun. That is because it is one country. Therefore, every verb about the Philippines must be in agreement and also be singular. The word *are* should be *is.*

4. a. The word *overdue* means *past due,* like a library book could be overdue. The word *overdo* means *go too far,* which is the meaning the sentence is suggesting. Therefore, choice **a** is the correct answer. Word usage problems can be tricky. But if you notice that the other underlined sections do not contain an error, you can be sure that choice **a** must be correct.

5. d. The word *state* is singular. Therefore, every verb about that subject must also be singular. The word *produce* is plural, so there is an error in subject-verb agreement in the underlined section for choice **d**.

6. a. Two independent clauses cannot be separated by a comma. The underlined comma in this sentence could be replaced by a period or a semicolon. The pronoun *its* is possessive and refers to the continent, so choice **b** is correct. The plural verb *have* refers to the quantities of snow and ice, which are also plural—so choice **c** is correct as well.

7. a. The word *quick* is intended to describe how the construction workers were working. It is describing a verb. Therefore, the word is an adverb. Most adverbs end in *-ly.* This is no exception. The word *quick* should be *quickly,* which is why choice **a** is correct.

8. b. All of the action in this sentence occurred in the past, and no other action is being described as taking place at another time. Therefore, you do not need the perfect tense of the verb *had resigned.* You can simply remove the word *had* to put the verb tense in the simple past tense, which would be correct.

9. c. The word *by* is always a preposition, choice **c**. It tells about a relationship between words, such as the degree to which the tilt of the tower was reduced. By itself the word *by* does not describe, or modify, other words, so choices **a** and **b** are wrong. It does not describe an action, so choice **d** is not correct either.

10. c. The word *wheelchair* appears early in the sentence, but the subject can often appear toward the end of a sentence. All of the action in this sentence relates to one person, choice **a**, who must therefore be the subject of the sentence.

11. a. What action did George W. Bush perform? He moved. Therefore, *moved* is the action. A word that describes an action is a verb.

12. b. There are many nouns in this sentence. However, there is only one subject. Don't assume that the subject must appear in the first part of a sentence. Look to see who or what the verbs are referring to. The bungee jumpers were arrested. The bungee jumpers inspired others. It was the bungee jumpers' jump in 1979. The subject is the four bungee jumpers, choice **b**.

13. a. The word *they* is a replacement for *the many residents of Washington, D.C.* That means it is a pronoun. The word *they* is always a pronoun.

14. b. The simple predicate is the verb that tells what the subject did. While it is true that Benjamin Franklin invented many things, the sentence does not use the verb *invent* Therefore, choice **a** is not correct. The sentence says that Franklin *was* one of the most creative thinkers. The simple predicate of the sentence is *was*, choice **b**.

15. c. When a base word ends in an unstressed short vowel sound and a consonant, the consonant must be repeated when a suffix is added. Therefore, the base word *deter* should become *deterred* when in the past tense, choice **c**.

16. a. Almost all words that start with *a* end in *-ance* rather than *-ence*. The word *acceptence* should be spelled *acceptance*, so choice **a** is correct.

17. c. The word *independant* should be spelled *independent,* so choice **c** is correct.

18. d. The word *lumpy* ends in *-y*. Therefore, to add a suffix, the *y* needs to be replaced be an *i*. The correct spelling of the word that means *more lumpy* is *lumpier*, choice **d**.

19. d. Oscar's essay demonstrates correct usage of semicolons, so choice **a** is not correct. There are no agreement errors in either verb tense or noun-pronouns, so choices **b** and **c** are not correct either. Several commas are misused in the essay, so the teacher should spend time reviewing comma usage with the student, choice **d**.

20. b. The word *him* is a pronoun that stands for something else. However, it is unclear whether the word refers to Oscar or Mr. Thomas in the story. The dog's owner put *him* to work, so the pronoun must refer to the dog, Oscar, choice **b**.

21. c. Look at the sub-headers of section II. It mentions high school and college. While "Middle School" may seem like it belongs, the header must cover the information about in the section. "High School" and "College" are not covered by "Middle School," so choice **a** is not correct. The information in choices **b** and **d** are details that do not cover all the information in the section. The best possible heading is "Sports during Academics," choice **c**, because it covers both high school and college.

22. b. The header for section III is "Professional Career," so every bit of information in that section should be about the baseball player's professional career. The information in choices **a**, **c**, and **d** happened either before or after his career. Choice **b** is therefore correct.

23. a. Pete's outline covers the life of a professional baseball player from his childhood through his long career and retirement. You need to find the sentence that provides the best sum-mary. Only the statement in answer choice **a** gives a general enough statement to match all the information in the outline.

24. c. Yoshi is telling his readers to use whole wheat or multigrain bread. Then he says that it is much healthier. You need to figure out which word helps connect those thoughts. Try placing each of the words from the answer choices into the sentences. Yoshi suggests using whole wheat or multigrain bread *because* it is healthier than white bread, choice **c**.

25. d. There are two steps here that Yoshi wants to combine into one step. To connect any two steps, you can use the word *and,* so choices **a** and **b** are not correct. The direction in choice **d** is much easier to understand than in choice **c**, so choice **d** is correct.

26. b. Yoshi's essay shows how to make a grilled cheese sandwich. To find the sentence which would fit best at its beginning, you need to choose the sentence that best sums up what

the essay is about. The sentence in choice **b** does that the best.

27. d. A persuasive piece of writing tries to con-vince a reader of something. Nothing in the first three sentences is trying to convince the reader of anything. The fourth sentence, however, is trying to convince the reader that it is very important to hire new police offi-cers. That means choice **d** is correct.

28. a. To find the sentence that is trying to teach a reader how to do something, look for words that seem like they could be taken from an instruction manual. The first sentence, choice **a**, seems to be trying to teach someone how to make a model volcano, so it is the correct choice.

29. c. Plural nouns that are possessive get an apos-trophe after the -*s*. The student should write about the rabbits' home.

30. d. At atlas contains maps of geographic areas. Therefore, an atlas, choice **d**, would be the best source for a student to learn which states share a border with another state.

Directions: Each of the following questions is followed by four answer choices. Choose the best answer choice by filling in the corresponding answer choice on your answer sheet.

Practice Test

Reading					Mathematics					Writing			
1.	ⓐ	ⓑ	ⓒ	ⓓ	31.	ⓐ	ⓑ	ⓒ	ⓓ	61.	ⓐ	ⓑ	ⓒ	ⓓ
2.	ⓐ	ⓑ	ⓒ	ⓓ	32.	ⓐ	ⓑ	ⓒ	ⓓ	62.	ⓐ	ⓑ	ⓒ	ⓓ
3.	ⓐ	ⓑ	ⓒ	ⓓ	33.	ⓐ	ⓑ	ⓒ	ⓓ	63.	ⓐ	ⓑ	ⓒ	ⓓ
4.	ⓐ	ⓑ	ⓒ	ⓓ	34.	ⓐ	ⓑ	ⓒ	ⓓ	64.	ⓐ	ⓑ	ⓒ	ⓓ
5.	ⓐ	ⓑ	ⓒ	ⓓ	35.	ⓐ	ⓑ	ⓒ	ⓓ	65.	ⓐ	ⓑ	ⓒ	ⓓ
6.	ⓐ	ⓑ	ⓒ	ⓓ	36.	ⓐ	ⓑ	ⓒ	ⓓ	66.	ⓐ	ⓑ	ⓒ	ⓓ
7.	ⓐ	ⓑ	ⓒ	ⓓ	37.	ⓐ	ⓑ	ⓒ	ⓓ	67.	ⓐ	ⓑ	ⓒ	ⓓ
8.	ⓐ	ⓑ	ⓒ	ⓓ	38.	ⓐ	ⓑ	ⓒ	ⓓ	68.	ⓐ	ⓑ	ⓒ	ⓓ
9.	ⓐ	ⓑ	ⓒ	ⓓ	39.	ⓐ	ⓑ	ⓒ	ⓓ	69.	ⓐ	ⓑ	ⓒ	ⓓ
10.	ⓐ	ⓑ	ⓒ	ⓓ	40.	ⓐ	ⓑ	ⓒ	ⓓ	70.	ⓐ	ⓑ	ⓒ	ⓓ
11.	ⓐ	ⓑ	ⓒ	ⓓ	41.	ⓐ	ⓑ	ⓒ	ⓓ	71.	ⓐ	ⓑ	ⓒ	ⓓ
12.	ⓐ	ⓑ	ⓒ	ⓓ	42.	ⓐ	ⓑ	ⓒ	ⓓ	72.	ⓐ	ⓑ	ⓒ	ⓓ
13.	ⓐ	ⓑ	ⓒ	ⓓ	43.	ⓐ	ⓑ	ⓒ	ⓓ	73.	ⓐ	ⓑ	ⓒ	ⓓ
14.	ⓐ	ⓑ	ⓒ	ⓓ	44.	ⓐ	ⓑ	ⓒ	ⓓ	74.	ⓐ	ⓑ	ⓒ	ⓓ
15.	ⓐ	ⓑ	ⓒ	ⓓ	45.	ⓐ	ⓑ	ⓒ	ⓓ	75.	ⓐ	ⓑ	ⓒ	ⓓ
16.	ⓐ	ⓑ	ⓒ	ⓓ	46.	ⓐ	ⓑ	ⓒ	ⓓ	76.	ⓐ	ⓑ	ⓒ	ⓓ
17.	ⓐ	ⓑ	ⓒ	ⓓ	47.	ⓐ	ⓑ	ⓒ	ⓓ	77.	ⓐ	ⓑ	ⓒ	ⓓ
18.	ⓐ	ⓑ	ⓒ	ⓓ	48.	ⓐ	ⓑ	ⓒ	ⓓ	78.	ⓐ	ⓑ	ⓒ	ⓓ
19.	ⓐ	ⓑ	ⓒ	ⓓ	49.	ⓐ	ⓑ	ⓒ	ⓓ	79.	ⓐ	ⓑ	ⓒ	ⓓ
20.	ⓐ	ⓑ	ⓒ	ⓓ	50.	ⓐ	ⓑ	ⓒ	ⓓ	80.	ⓐ	ⓑ	ⓒ	ⓓ
21.	ⓐ	ⓑ	ⓒ	ⓓ	51.	ⓐ	ⓑ	ⓒ	ⓓ	81.	ⓐ	ⓑ	ⓒ	ⓓ
22.	ⓐ	ⓑ	ⓒ	ⓓ	52.	ⓐ	ⓑ	ⓒ	ⓓ	82.	ⓐ	ⓑ	ⓒ	ⓓ
23.	ⓐ	ⓑ	ⓒ	ⓓ	53.	ⓐ	ⓑ	ⓒ	ⓓ	83.	ⓐ	ⓑ	ⓒ	ⓓ
24.	ⓐ	ⓑ	ⓒ	ⓓ	54.	ⓐ	ⓑ	ⓒ	ⓓ	84.	ⓐ	ⓑ	ⓒ	ⓓ
25.	ⓐ	ⓑ	ⓒ	ⓓ	55.	ⓐ	ⓑ	ⓒ	ⓓ	85.	ⓐ	ⓑ	ⓒ	ⓓ
26.	ⓐ	ⓑ	ⓒ	ⓓ	56.	ⓐ	ⓑ	ⓒ	ⓓ	86.	ⓐ	ⓑ	ⓒ	ⓓ
27.	ⓐ	ⓑ	ⓒ	ⓓ	57.	ⓐ	ⓑ	ⓒ	ⓓ	87.	ⓐ	ⓑ	ⓒ	ⓓ
28.	ⓐ	ⓑ	ⓒ	ⓓ	58.	ⓐ	ⓑ	ⓒ	ⓓ	88.	ⓐ	ⓑ	ⓒ	ⓓ
29.	ⓐ	ⓑ	ⓒ	ⓓ	59.	ⓐ	ⓑ	ⓒ	ⓓ	89.	ⓐ	ⓑ	ⓒ	ⓓ
30.	ⓐ	ⓑ	ⓒ	ⓓ	60.	ⓐ	ⓑ	ⓒ	ⓓ	90.	ⓐ	ⓑ	ⓒ	ⓓ

Reading

Directions: Each of the following questions is followed by four answer choices. Choose the best answer choice by filling in the corresponding answer choice on your answer sheet.

1. A sea spider, unlike the land animal that shares its name, does not spin a web to catch its food. Some sea spiders living thousands of feet underwater have developed an interesting technique. Most have eight legs—like land spiders—which they use to catch their food. The long legs have feathers that trap random pieces of food that fall down to the depths of the ocean. Then the sea spider runs its legs across its mouth for a tasty meal.

   What is the primary purpose of this short passage?
   a. to discuss the similarities between land spiders and sea spiders
   b. to describe the unique eating habits of a type of sea spider
   c. to warn people to stay away from dangerous sea spiders
   d. to explain how a land spider uses a web to catch its food

2. It is not always the case that a superior product defeats an inferior product in a technology war. There are many factors that can result in a superior product's defeat, such as marketing or distribution. For example, two video cassette tape companies battled from the mid 1970s to the mid 1980s: Betamax and VHS. Despite the fact that Betamax had a better resolution and less video noise than its competition, VHS became the industry standard and Betamax went out of business.

   The author most likely believes that
   a. Betamax had a better quality than VHS.
   b. watching VHS tapes is better than watching DVDs.
   c. Betamax went out of business because of its high prices.
   d. VHS and Betamax were identical products.

Questions 3–4 are based on the following passage.

   Starfish are among the most widely recognized sea creatures in the world. These fascinating creatures are found in every ocean on the planet, and they live at almost every depth in the water. People usually recognize them as having five arms, but some can have one more, five more, or even 35 more arms. A starfish can also regenerate a new arm if it loses one. But a starfish isn't really even a fish at all. Fish are vertebrates, meaning they have a backbone. Starfish have no backbone, so they are invertebrates. For this reason, it is important to use the name *sea star* instead of *starfish*, and get rid of the word *fish* from the name.

3. The author feels that the term *starfish* is
   a. a good description of the animal's shape.
   b. not accurate and should not be used.
   c. amazing because it can regenerate its arms.
   d. very recognized around the world.

4. According to the passage, a sea star

   a. can regenerate a backbone.

   b. should be called a *starfish.*

   c. can have six arms.

   d. is a type of vertebrate.

Use the following double bar graph to answer question 5.

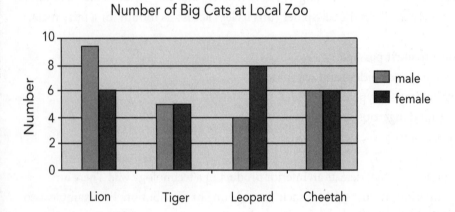

5. Which question could be answered from the data in the graph?

   a. Which is the fastest land animal on Earth?

   b. Why does the local zoo have more cheetahs than tigers?

   c. How much bigger is a male lion than a female lion?

   d. How many female leopards does the local zoo have?

Answer questions 6–9 based on the following passage.

(1) One of Benjamin Franklin's most useful and important inventions was a new stove called, appropriately, the Franklin stove. (2) This invention improved the lives of countless homeowners in the eighteenth century and beyond. (3) Compared to the stoves that were used at the time of his invention, Franklin's stove made keeping a fire inside a home much less dangerous. (4) The design of the stove made it possible to burn less wood and generate more heat than with previous designs. (5) This feature of the stove saved its users considerable amounts of money that would have been needed to buy wood.

(6) As its inventor, Benjamin Franklin was offered the right to patent his stove. (7) That would have meant that only Franklin could have made and sold these useful stoves. (8) It would have made Franklin one of the richest men in the country. (9) However, Franklin turned down the opportunity for the patent. (10) He believed that the stove should be allowed to be used by anyone who wanted to use the safer and more efficient technology. (11) In his autobiography, he wrote, "As we enjoy great advantages from the inventions of others, we should be glad of an opportunity to serve others by any invention of ours; and this we should do freely and generously."

6. The primary purpose of the first paragraph of the passage is to
   a. describe one particularly useful invention of Benjamin Franklin.
   b. point out that Benjamin Franklin was responsible for many great inventions.
   c. explain how a stove works.
   d. discuss the ways that Benjamin Franklin made money from his stoves.

7. According to the passage, Benjamin Franklin was
   a. afraid of making a fire inside his home.
   b. interested primarily in inventing things that would make him money.
   c. one of the richest people in America.
   d. less concerned about making money than helping his fellow humans.

8. The meaning of the word *right* in sentence 6, in context of the passage, most likely means
   a. correct.
   b. good health.
   c. turn.
   d. legal claim.

9. The passage suggests that the Franklin stove was
   a. expensive.
   b. dangerous.
   c. efficient.
   d. small.

10. My knees were muddy from kneeling in the dirt. My back ached from hours spent bending over and digging holes. My gloves were ripped in several places where thorns had torn through the fabric. Clumps of dirt had found their way into my hair. But I was still smiling. Few things bring me greater joy than spending time in the garden. And in a few months, I would be able to enjoy the benefits of all the hard work.

   The author is mostly interested in
   a. pointing out the difficulties in gardening.
   b. explaining that the hardships of gardening have their own rewards.
   c. teaching people how to plant vegetables in the soil.
   d. describing all of the different tools necessary for proper gardening.

11. The United States is one of the most culturally diverse nations on Earth. But is also one of the most climatically diverse nations as well. The climate of the United States ranges from the frigid to the torrid. Some areas of Alaska rarely get warm enough to melt an ice cube! The weather in Hawaii is perfect all year long.

Which of the following sentences from the passage is an example of an opinion?
a. "The United States . . . nations on Earth."
b. "The climate of . . . to the torrid."
c. "Some areas of . . . an ice cube!"
d. "The weather in . . . all year long."

12. The cold winter weather took a break for a day, and so Tameka and I decided to do something about it. It would have been a waste to spend the hours locked inside, like we had been for most of these dark months. Oh, we'd still need our heavy jackets, but maybe we could get away without wearing our gloves. And that meant we could do something like play Frisbee. Or shoot hoops. Or fly a kite. The trick was figuring out what we wanted to do. Tomorrow's forecast called for snow again, so there wasn't much time.

The narrator of the story is primarily concerned with
a. making the most of the day.
b. deciding what clothes to wear.
c. looking for sports equipment.
d. how to stay warm during the winter.

Answer questions 13–16 based on the following passage.

Most people know that George Washington was the first president of the United States. His iconic image appears on the quarter and the $1 bill. Thomas Jefferson is almost as well recognized; the third president can be seen on the nickel and the $2 bill (if you can find one). But between Washington and Jefferson's presidencies served a man who was every bit as influential on his nation even if he is much less recognized today: John Adams.

Born in 1735 in Massachusetts, Adams went to Harvard College at the age of 16. After graduating in 1755, he became a teacher and then a lawyer. As a lawyer, he successfully defended the British soldiers involved in the deadly Boston Massacre. By the 1770s he felt strongly that the United States should be independent from Britain. As a result, he worked with others to draft the Declaration of Independence. Once the United States won the Revolutionary War, Adams was elected to the vice presidency under Washington. After eight years as Washington's vice president, Adams became president in 1797. While his son, John Quincy Adams, was president, Adams passed away on July 4, 1826. That date was the 50th anniversary of the adoption of the Declaration of Independence.

13. In what way is the second paragraph organized?
   a. The events are told in the order in which they happened.
   b. A fact is presented and then followed by several opinions.
   c. Each side of a scientific argument is provided.
   d. A broad statement is offered and then backed up with details.

14. The passage includes all of the following facts about John Adams EXCEPT that he
   a. had a son who became a president.
   b. helped write the Declaration of Independence.
   c. fought in the Civil War.
   d. graduated from Harvard.

15. The author likely mentions the date of Adams's death because it
   a. shows that he was as important as George Washington.
   b. demonstrates a reason why he should be on U.S. currency.
   c. reinforces the notion of him as a U.S. patriot.
   d. presents justification for the nation's entry to the Revolutionary War.

16. It can be inferred in this passage that John Adams
   a. had only one son, John Quincy Adams.
   b. was the second president of the United States.
   c. was a general during the Revolutionary War.
   d. spent eight years as president of the United States.

All about New Jersey

TABLE OF CONTENTS

Answer questions 17–18 based on the table of contents.

17. To which page would a reader turn if he or she wanted to learn about the New Jersey Supreme Court?

   a. 42

   b. 49

   c. 53

   d. 57

18. How is Chapter 2 organized?

   a. area

   b. branch of government

   c. time

   d. importance

Answer questions 19–21 based on the following passage.

(1) Auto racing is one of the most popular sports in America. (2) More than 120,000 people attend each NASCAR race, on average. But at a time when fuel conservation is so important to our planet's health, is automobile racing a responsible sport? (3) The cars in major auto races are driven hundreds of miles for each race. (4) And the cars usually get about four or five miles per gallon, less than even the dirtiest polluter on the highway. The cars' emissions only add to the air pollution. (5) We may need to reexamine our passions in this country and ask whether we can afford to continue them.

19. A paraprofessional asks the students in a class to tell about the main idea of the passage. Which sentence from the student's answers shows that the student understands the passage's main idea?
    a. Automobile racing is the greatest sport.
    b. Automobile racing is harmful for the environment.
    c. It is important to recycle.
    d. NASCAR is more popular than baseball or football.

20. Students in a classroom are learning about words that begin with blended consonant sounds, such as the words *crush* or *tray*. Which word from the passage also has a beginning sound with blended consonants?
    a. auto
    b. sport
    c. race
    d. passions

21. A student in a classroom does not understand the word *reexamine* from sentence 5. Which approach by a paraprofessional would be most effective to help the student comprehend its meaning?
    a. Ask the student to write what he or she thinks the word *reexamine* most likely means on the board.
    b. Provide the student with a synonym for *reexamine*, such as *reevaluate*.
    c. Write out the parts of the word, showing that the prefix *re-* means to do something again.
    d. Show the student each of the letters that are put together to spell the word *reexamine*.

22. A student reads the following sentence in a book:

    "Due in part to the widespread appeal of cats and the variety of its music styles, the play Cats enjoyed an extended *run* on Broadway."

    run (noun). 1. a race; 2. A specific amount of something; 3. an urgent demand for payment; 4. A series or sequence.

    Which dictionary definition should the student use to understand the meaning of the word *run* in context?
    a. dictionary definition 1
    b. dictionary definition 2
    c. dictionary definition 3
    d. dictionary definition 4

Questions 23–26 are based on this excerpt from a book that students are reading.

Mabel's Life in Basketball
Chapter 1: Making the Team

The sun had set at least 15 minutes ago, but there was still a bit of light left in the sky. Mabel took another free throw on the deserted basketball court.

"C'mon, Mabel!" hollered her mother from the living room window of their apartment, across the street from the court. Mabel grabbed the ball, took one more shot at the hoop, and then tucked the ball under her arm. Then she raced home.

"Do you think I'm good enough?" Mabel asked breathlessly as she walked in the front door.

"Good enough for what?" Mabel's mother asked.

"Good enough to make the school basketball team, of course!" replied Mabel.

"Oh, I think so," said Mabel's mom. "But it's not up to me. We'll see what Coach Freeman says tomorrow."

At that moment, Mabel's father brought over some plates of food from the kitchen into the dining room. "If you're going to impress the coach," he said, "you're going to need to be well fed." He made a motion for her to follow him into the dining room table. Mabel and her mother walked in and sat down at the table.

"After dinner we can review some of those plays I taught you," suggested Mabel's mom at the table.

"Thanks, Mom," replied Mabel as she dug into a bowl of pasta. "Tomorrow's basketball team tryouts are going to be difficult, but I know I've done the work to make the team."

23. A student can demonstrate his or her comprehension of a story by predicting an event that will happen later in a story. The student can use clues from the story, as well as the other given information, such as the title or author. Which student's prediction should a paraprofessional use to verify comprehension?
    a. Mabel will miss all of her shots during the tryout.
    b. Mabel will not make the school basketball team.
    c. Mabel will be late for school because she is practicing free throws.
    d. Mabel will make the school basketball team.

24. The events from the story are mixed up in the following list.

I. Mabel's father brings food into the dining room.
II. Mabel eats some potatoes.
III. Mabel's mother calls her from the window.
IV. Mabel practices her free throws.

A student in the class must put the events in the order that they happened in the story. Which shows the correct order?
a. IV, III, I, II
b. III, IV, I, II
c. III, I, IV, II
d. IV, III, II, I

25. It is important that students can recognize compound words. Which word from the excerpt is an example of a compound word?
a. deserted
b. basketball
c. apartment
d. dining

26. The students in the class are learning that a digraph in a word can sound like the letter *f*. For example, *ph*, *ch*, *th*, and *gh* are all digraphs. Which word from the story has a digraph that has the sound like the letter *f*?
a. throw
b. shot
c. enough
d. school

Answer questions 27–29 based on the following teacher-created lesson plan.

Reading Record Lesson Plan

Objective: Students will apply their knowledge of the parts of a book and apply their analyses of the book to a written record.

Explanation: Students will demonstrate that they can recognize the parts of a book by filling out preprinted reading records. Each record will contain a blank space for the title, author, and genre of a book. The paraprofessional will hand out three reading record index cards to the students in the class. The teacher will then request that the students fill out the information on the records for three books of their choosing. The paraprofessional will move around the classroom and help show individual students where to find the information to complete the running record. For example, a student may not know how to find the author of the book. Students will then write a comment or two in the bottom of each reading record to describe whether the book was enjoyable—and why or why not. Once students have filled in all of the information in the running records, the paraprofessional will collect all of the index cards. To help create a library of the reading records for reference, the paraprofessional will organize them alphabetically by the author's last name.

27. The only action that the paraprofessional will NOT be expected to do is
   a. write a comment or two in the bottom of each reading record.
   b. distribute the reading record index cards to the students.
   c. collect all of the index cards from the students at the end of class.
   d. help students locate the title, author, and genre of a book, if needed.

28. The last names of the authors of four books chosen by the students begin with the letter *M.* In which order should the reading records be organized?
   a. Maas, Madison, Mulholland, Mejias
   b. Madison, Maas, Mejias, Mulholland
   c. Maas, Mejias, Madison, Mulholland
   d. Maas, Madison, Mejias, Mulholland

29. One student does not understand the meaning of *genre* in the lesson plan. Which question could a paraprofessional ask to help a student understand the purpose of including it in the reading record?
   a. What important information can be found on the front cover and spine of each book?
   b. How would you describe the type of book so that it can be grouped by similar types of books?
   c. Why does the year that the book was published tell us important information about the book?
   d. If a reader enjoyed reading a book from one specific author, don't you think that he or she would enjoy reading more books from the same author?

30. The students in a class are working on a lesson about antonyms. Four groups of students write two words that they think are antonyms. Which words are antonyms?
a. cold and chilly
b. there and their
c. enormous and tiny
d. peanut and butter

Mathematics

Directions: Each of the following questions is followed by four answer choices. Choose the best answer choice by filling in the corresponding answer choice on your answer sheet. You will NOT be allowed to use a calculator.

31. Which of the following shapes is a right triangle?
a.

b.

c.

d.

32. The closest estimate for the sum of 3.94 + 7.11 + 4.88 is
a. 14.
b. 15.
c. 16.
d. 17.

33. Which inequality is true?

    a. $12 > 8$

    b. $12 = 8$

    c. $12 < 8$

    d. $12 \leq 8$

34. What is another way to show 10^3?

    a. $10 + 10 + 10$

    b. 10×3

    c. 3^{10}

    d. $10 \times 10 \times 10$

> The cost of a marker is \$1.50 and the cost of an eraser is \$2.25. How much must a student pay if she buys 8 markers and 3 erasers?

35. A student in Ms. Owens' class is having difficulty solving the problem shown in the box above. Which expression can Ms. Owens use to help her student solve the problem?

    a. $8(1.50) + 3(2.25)$

    b. $(8 + 3)(1.50 + 2.25)$

    c. $8(2.25) + 3(1.50)$

    d. $8(1.50) \times 3(2.25)$

36. Which fraction or decimal is equivalent to 0.01?

    a. 0.01%

    b. $\frac{100}{1}$

    c. 1%

    d. $\frac{1}{10}$

37.8, 20, 32, 44, 56, 68

37. Each number in the pattern above is 12 more than the previous number. If the pattern continues, what number will be ninth in the list?

    a. 80

    b. 94

    c. 102

    d. 104

38. $\frac{1}{5} + \frac{1}{10} =$

    a. $\frac{2}{15}$

    b. $\frac{2}{10}$

    c. $\frac{3}{15}$

    d. $\frac{3}{10}$

39. A coat is usually sold for $65.75. The coat is on sale for 10% off. Which is the best estimate for the price of the coat during the sale?

    a. $10

    b. $55

    c. $60

    d. $71

40. The height of a classroom door is $2\frac{1}{3}$ yards. How many feet tall is the classroom door?

    a. $6\frac{1}{3}$ feet

    b. 7 feet

    c. $7\frac{1}{3}$ feet

    d. 28 feet

41. Which amount of money is NOT equivalent to five dollars?

    a. 5.00¢

    b. $5

    c. 500¢

    d. $5.00

100 = 10⁰
What number, if placed in the blank box, would make the equation correct?

42. A student in Mr. Martinez's class is having difficulty solving the problem shown in the box above. Which question would best help the student understand how to solve it?
  a. What is the difference in the value of 10 and the value of 100?
  b. How many times do you have to multiply 10 by itself to equal 100?
  c. What will be your answer if you divide the number 100 by 10?
  d. What number multiplied by itself 10 times will be equal to 100?

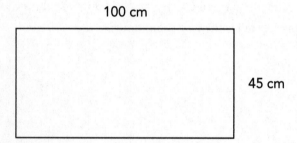

100 cm

45 cm

43. A student in Mrs. Khan's math class measures the dimensions of her rectangular desk, as shown in the diagram above. Which expression shows how the student could correctly find the perimeter of the teacher's desk?
  a. $2(100 + 45)$
  b. 100×45
  c. $2(100) + 45$
  d. $2(100 \times 45)$

Allison's Monthly Allowance Breakdown

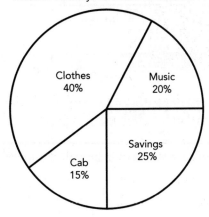

Clothes
40%

Music
20%

Savings
25%

Cab
15%

44. The circle graph above shows how much of Allison's monthly allowance she spends on different things. If her monthly allowance is $40, how much did she save in the last month?

a. $10
b. $12
c. $15
d. $25

45. What digit is in the hundredths place in the number 218.56?

a. 1
b. 2
c. 5
d. 6

46. A school schedule has six classes throughout the day for a total of five hours. If each class is the same length of time, how many minutes long is each class?

a. 11 minutes
b. 45 minutes
c. 50 minutes
d. 72 minutes

Height of Students in Math Group

Student	Height (Inches)
Javier	48
Levi	56
Kaylee	48
Michael	52

47. The table above shows the height of four students in a math group. What is the average (arithmetic mean) height of the four students?
   a. 48 inches
   b. 50 inches
   c. 51 inches
   d. 52 inches

$\frac{2}{1} \times \frac{1}{4}$

48. A student wanted to solve for the problem $\frac{1}{2} \div \frac{1}{4}$ and ended up with the mistaken number sentence above. Which number sentence shows how the student should have solved the problem?
   a. $\frac{1}{2} \times \frac{1}{4}$
   b. $\frac{1}{2} \times \frac{4}{1}$
   c. $\frac{2}{1} \times \frac{4}{1}$
   d. $\frac{1}{2} \div \frac{4}{1}$

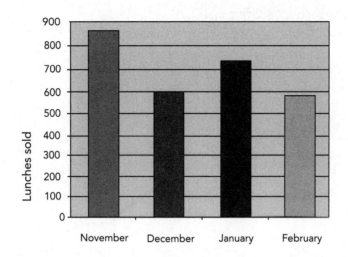

49. The bar graph above shows the number of lunches sold at a cafeteria at an elementary school during the winter months. Which is a true statement about the number of lunches sold in January?

   a. Between 600 and 700 lunches were sold.

   b. More than 800 lunches were sold.

   c. Between 700 and 800 lunches were sold.

   d. More lunches were sold than in any other month.

50. 3,650 − 777 =

   a. 2,873

   b. 2,883

   c. 2,973

   d. 3,983

51. What is the product of 9 and 3?

   a. 3

   b. 6

   c. 12

   d. 27

52. Which number is greater than 1.1 and less than 1.7?

    a. 1.11

    b. 1.07

    c. 1.71

    d. 0.55

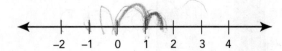

53. Where is $-\frac{1}{4}$ located on the number line shown above?

    a. Between −2 and −1

    b. Between −1 and 0

    c. Between 0 and 1

    d. Between 1 and 2

54. $45.6 + 6.72 =$

    a. 11.28

    b. 51.32

    c. 52.32

    d. 112.8

55. What is the value of y if $y - 4 = 10$?

    a. −6

    b. 6

    c. 14

    d. 40

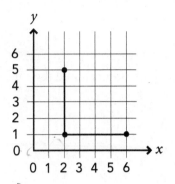

56. The *xy*-plane above shows three points of a square. The fourth point is missing. What must be the coordinates of the missing point?

a. (5, 6)

b. (6, −5)

c. (5, 5)

d. (6, 5)

57. At a school bake sale, 30 brownies were sold at $0.75 each. There were also 18 cookies sold at $0.50 each and 8 muffins sold at $1.50 each. How much money was raised at the school bake sale?

a. $31.50

b. $33.50

c. $43.50

d. $53.50

$$1 \times 1 = 1$$
$$2 \times 2 = 4$$
$$3 \times 3 = 9$$
$$4 \times 4 = 16$$
$$5 \times 5 = 25$$

58. A teacher writes the equations above on the board. Which concept is the teacher likely preparing to teach?

a. exponents

b. order of operations

c. division

d. decimals

$$20 + 2 \times 2 - 9 \div 3$$

59. A student is struggling with solving the problem shown in the box above. In which order should the student solve the operations?

   a. multiplication, division, addition, subtraction

   b. multiplication, division, subtraction, addition

   c. division, multiplication, addition, subtraction

   d. addition, multiplication, subtraction, division

Length of Classroom Turtle Per Month (in Inches)

Month	Sep.	Oct.	Nov.	Dec.
Length (in Inches)	3	3.8	4.6	5.4

60. The table above shows the length of a class turtle at the beginning of each month from September through December, as shown. The turtle grows by the same amount each month. If the pattern continues, what will be the length of the turtle at the beginning of February?

   a. 6 inches

   b. 6.2 inches

   c. 6.8 inches

   d. 7 inches

Writing

Directions: Questions 61–68 each include a sentence with four parts underlined. One of the four underlined parts will contain an error in grammar, punctuation, or word usage. Each sentence will have exactly one error. Select the letter of the answer choice that corresponds to that error.

61. Trail Ridge Road in Colorado, which <u>reach</u> the height of 12,183 feet, <u>is</u> the highest <u>continuously</u> paved

                                                     a   **b**   **c**

road <u>in</u> the United States.

     d

62. A giant <u>muddy</u> swamp in the mid-1800s, Central Park in New York City is now one of the <u>worlds</u> <u>greatest</u>

             a   **b**   **c**

urban <u>parks</u>.

     d

63. A baseball team <u>from</u> New York City <u>won</u> every World Series from 1949 through 1958, <u>accept</u> for 1957

                     a   **b**   **c**

when the Milwaukee Braves <u>were</u> champions.

                          d

64. One of the reasons that manatees <u>are</u> endangered is because <u>it swims</u> near the surface of the water, where

                                   a   **b**

<u>their</u> fins can be <u>damaged</u> by a boat's propellers.

  c   **d**

65. From the northern limits of Alaska near the North Pole <u>to</u> the <u>tropical</u> island of Guam near the Equator<u>;</u>

                                                          a   **b**   **c**

the United States <u>has</u> territories all over the world.

               d

66. <u>Despite</u> <u>being</u> a band for only about a decade, the Beatles <u>influencing</u> popular music perhaps more than

   a   **b**   **c**   **d**

any other band.

67. What makes Old Faithful the most <u>frequent</u> photographed geyser in Yellowstone National Park <u>is</u> not its

                                  a   **b**

height or volume of its spray, but the <u>consistency</u> of <u>its</u> eruptions.

                                    c   **d**

68. Bo Jackson and Deion Sanders <u>were</u> famous for <u>playing</u> two sports professionally<u>;</u> both Jackson and
                                    a   **b**   **c**

Sanders <u>had been playing</u> football and baseball at the highest levels.
         d

Answer questions 69–90 by selecting the answer choice that best answers the given question or completes the statement.

69. Originally included with a few vehicles in the 1970s as a supplement to seatbelts, air bags are now standard in most vehicle manufacturers.

The <u>subject</u> of the sentence above is
a. vehicles.
b. seatbelts.
c. air bags.
d. manufacturers.

70. The lessons learned from the sinking of the *Titanic* helped inspire a new era of safety regulations for ships.

The <u>subject</u> of the sentence above is
a. lessons.
b. *Titanic.*
c. era.
d. regulations.

71. The average storage size of computer hard drives continues to grow at an extraordinary rate each year.

The <u>simple</u> predicate of the sentence above is
a. size.
b. continues.
c. grow.
d. rate.

72. Kilauea, a volcano in Hawaii, may be the world's most active volcano, having <u>continuously</u> spewed lava since 1983.

The underlined word in the sentence above is an example of
a. a pronoun.
b. an adjective.
c. a preposition.
d. an adverb.

73. Pablo Picasso was an artistic <u>prodigy</u> and could paint realistic portraits at a very young age.

The underlined word in the sentence above is an example of
a. a preposition.
b. a pronoun.
c. an adjective.
d. a noun.

74. While the Vatican City is a country, a person could walk <u>from</u> one end to the other in less than 15 minutes.

The underlined word in the sentence above is an example of
a. an adjective.
b. a pronoun.
c. a preposition.
d. a verb.

75. Which of the following words is NOT spelled properly?
a. history
b. permanent
c. believed
d. advantiges

76. Which of the following words is NOT spelled properly?
a. experimants
b. receiving
c. friendly
d. impossible

77. Which of the following words is NOT spelled properly?
a. approximately
b. gravitationol
c. regularly
d. devotion

78. Which of the following words is NOT spelled properly?
a. development
b. activasion
c. arresting
d. extinction

Questions 79–80 are based on the following essay, written by a fifth-grade student named Sadie.

Over my summer vacation I went on a hiking trip with my family. My family love going on hikes. My little brother Jordan and my cousin Mallory especially enjoys long hikes. Together we went to a national park and camped out for several nights. Each day we went for hikes, eating lunch in the middle of the day. Everybody had so much fun except for maybe my mom and aunt; she got a lot of mosquito bites.

79. Which aspect of her writing should the teacher spend the most time with Sadie?
  a. capitalization
  b. semicolon usage
  c. verb tense agreement
  d. comma usage

80. One of the students in Sadie's class said that she did not know who *she* referred to in the last sentence of the story. What could Sadie use to replace *she* so that it would make sense in the essay?
  a. my cousin Mallory
  b. her
  c. they
  d. Jordan

81. A student is writing a school paper about the Italian explorer Christopher Columbus. She wants to know when he took his voyage to America was and what it was like. Which source would be the best place for the student to get her answers quickly?
  a. an Internet article about Columbus Day
  b. a dictionary
  c. a newspaper article from Columbus, Ohio
  d. a history textbook about early explorers

Questions 82–83 are based on the following essay, written by a fourth-grade student named Marco, who is trying to argue for a vegetarian lifestyle in his essay.

(1) It is healthy to be a vegetarian, as long as you make sure you eat healthy foods. (2) There are also the ethical reasons as well. (3) For example, some animals are not treated well before they are killed for food. (4) I believe animals should be cared for. Being a vegetarian is also good for the environment. (5) That is because cows produce lots of methane, methane is a destructive greenhouse gas. (6) If people didn't eat cows, we wouldn't need as many cows, and there would not be as much methane in the atmosphere.

82. Marco wants to add a sentence at the beginning of his essay to state the main idea of his argument. Which sentence would fit best at the beginning of his essay?

   a. There are many reasons to be a vegetarian.
   b. Meat does not taste very good anyway.
   c. It is not easy to become a vegetarian.
   d. Vegetarian foods tend to cost less than meat at the grocery store.

83. Marco needs help creating transitions to improve the meaning of his sentences. Which word could he use after the comma in sentence 5 to improve the sentence's meaning?

   a. but
   b. and
   c. because
   d. although

Questions 84–86 are based on an outline that a student is working on.

Taryn wants to write an essay about the different duties that a book publisher has to do to create and sell a book. Before she can begin drafting her essay, she puts the notes from brainstorming into the following outline.

Duties of a Book Publisher

I. Manuscript Acquisition

    A. Find new manuscripts

        1. Discover new authors

        2. Sort manuscript submissions

        3. Generate new ideas

    B. Secure new products

        1. Negotiate contracts with authors

        2. Set deadlines and schedules

II. _____

    A. Edit manuscript

        1. Edit structure for clarity

        2. Copyedit

        3. Proofread

    B. Lay out book

        1. Format pages with text

        2. Include pictures or graphics

III. Publishing

    A. Promote new book

        1. Prepare press release

        2. Send copies for professional reviews

        3. Advertise in appropriate publications leagues

    B. Distribution

        1. _____

        2. Get book into local libraries

84. Taryn needs a heading for section II of her outline. Which heading would fit the content best?

    a. Prepare for Publication

    b. Give Free Copies Away

    c. Perform Fact Check

    d. List Ads for New Authors

85. One part of section III is left blank. What information about book publishing could Taryn put in that blank part?
  a. Set up author appearance on TV shows
  b. Supply major bookstores with copies
  c. Send author royalty checks
  d. Get second draft from author

86. Once Taryn finishes her outline, she wants to begin drafting the essay. She wants her introductory sentence to sum up the details of his outline. Which would be the best sentence for Taryn to use for this purpose?
  a. To sell a book successfully you must get it sold in all the major booksellers.
  b. It can be very difficult to get your story published, even if it is a wonderful story.
  c. There are three major steps that a publisher must follow to produce a book and get it sold.
  d. Book publishing is an exciting and glamorous industry.

Questions 87–89 are based on a rough draft written by a fifth-grade student who pitches for his little league team.

How to Throw a Fastball

(1) Put your middle and index fingers on top of the seams of the baseball. (2) Then put your thumb on the bottom of the baseball, on the smooth leather between the seams. (3) Hold the ball softly in your fingertips. (4) You can even hold it like an egg. (5) Wind up your body to get power on the pitch. (6) Let go of the pitch from your fingertips that will help you keep control of the ball. (7) Follow through with your body and let the momentum of the pitch push you forward.

87. The student wants to combine sentences 3 and 4 into one new sentence. The new sentence must tell the same information in a way that is easy to understand. Which sentence best combines sentences 3 and 4?
  a. Hold the egg gently in your fingertips.
  b. While holding the ball softly, hold it also like an egg in one's fingertips.
  c. The ball should be held gently, such as an egg in a person's fingertips.
  d. Hold the ball gently like an egg in your fingertips.

88. The student needs help creating transitions to improve the meaning of his sentences. Which word could he use after the word *fingertips* in sentence 6 to improve the sentence's meaning?
  a. however
  b. and
  c. because
  d. but

89. The student needs help creating transitions to improve the overall flow of his directions. Which transition could he use before the word *follow* in sentence 7 to improve the flow of the directions?
   a. Finally,
   b. However,
   c. For example
   d. Even though,

90. Students in a classroom are learning how different types of writing may have different purposes. Which sentence looks like it was taken from a piece of writing whose purpose was to compare two things?
   a. Unlike frogs, toads have dry skin, no teeth, and shorter legs for walking.
   b. While many people fear sharks, the giant fish are responsible for very few human deaths.
   c. I can run for miles and miles and never notice how much time has passed or how much distance I have covered.
   d. James Cameron is one of the most successful directors in Hollywood history, having created *Avatar, Titanic, Terminator,* and many other high-grossing films.

Answers and Explanations

Question Number	Correct Answer	Content Category
1	b	Reading Skills: Main idea/primary purpose
2	a	Reading Skills: Author's purpose
3	b	Reading Skills: Author's purpose
4	c	Reading Skills: Inferences
5	d	Reading Skills: Interpreting graphic text
6	a	Reading Skills: Main idea/primary purpose
7	d	Reading Skills: Supporting ideas
8	d	Reading Skills: Vocabulary in context
9	c	Reading Skills: Inferences
10	b	Reading Skills: Main idea/primary purpose
11	d	Reading Skills: Fact/opinion
12	a	Reading Skills: Main idea/primary purpose
13	a	Reading Skills: Organization
14	c	Reading Skills: Supporting ideas
15	c	Reading Skills: Organization
16	b	Reading Skills: Inferences
17	d	Reading Skills: Interpreting graphic text
18	a	Reading Skills: Interpreting graphic text
19	b	Reading Application: Making accurate observations
20	b	Reading Application: Sounding out words
21	c	Reading Application: Decoding words using context clues
22	d	Reading Application: Using a dictionary
23	d	Reading Application: Making predictions
24	a	Reading Application: Making accurate observations
25	b	Reading Application: Breaking down words into parts

Question Number	Correct Answer	Content Category
26	c	Reading Application: Breaking down words into parts
27	a	Reading Application: Interpreting directions
28	d	Reading Application: Alphabetizing words
29	b	Reading Application: Asking questions
30	c	Reading Application: Synonyms, antonyms, and homonyms
31	b	Math Skills: Geometry and measurement
32	c	Math Skills: Number sense and basic algebra
33	a	Math Skills: Number sense and basic algebra
34	d	Math Skills: Number sense and basic algebra
35	a	Math Application: Number sense and basic algebra
36	c	Math Skills: Number sense and basic algebra
37	d	Math Skills: Number sense and basic algebra
38	d	Math Skills: Number sense and basic algebra
39	c	Math Application: Number sense and basic algebra
40	b	Math Application: Geometry and measurement
41	a	Math Skills: Geometry and measurement
42	b	Math Application: Number sense and basic algebra
43	a	Math Skills: Number sense and basic algebra
44	a	Math Skills: Data analysis
45	d	Math Skills: Number sense and basic algebra
46	c	Math Application: Geometry and measurement
47	c	Math Application: Data analysis
48	b	Math Application: Number sense and basic algebra
49	c	Math Application: Data analysis
50	a	Math Skills: Number sense and basic algebra
51	d	Math Skills: Number sense and basic algebra
52	a	Math Skills: Number sense and basic algebra

Question Number	Correct Answer	Content Category
53	b	Math Skills: Number sense and basic algebra
54	c	Math Skills: Number sense and basic algebra
55	c	Math Skills: Number sense and basic algebra
56	d	Math Skills: Geometry and measurement
57	c	Math Application: Number sense and basic algebra
58	a	Math Application: Number sense and basic algebra
59	a	Math Application: Number sense and basic algebra
60	d	Math Application: Data Analysis
61	a	Writing Skills: Grammatical errors
62	b	Writing Skills: Errors in punctuation
63	c	Writing Skills: Error in word usage
64	b	Writing Skills: Errors in punctuation
65	c	Writing Skills: Grammatical errors
66	d	Writing Skills: Grammatical errors
67	a	Writing Skills: Grammatical errors
68	d	Writing Skills: Grammatical errors
69	c	Writing Skills: Parts of a sentence
70	a	Writing Skills: Parts of a sentence
71	b	Writing Skills: Parts of a sentence
72	d	Writing Skills: Parts of speech
73	d	Writing Skills: Parts of speech
74	c	Writing Skills: Parts of speech
75	d	Writing Skills: Spelling
76	a	Writing Skills: Spelling
77	b	Writing Skills: Spelling
78	b	Writing Skills: Spelling
79	c	Writing Application: Drafting and revising

Question Number	Correct Answer	Content Category
80	c	Writing Application: Drafting and revising
81	d	Writing Application: Reference materials
82	a	Writing Application: Editing written documents
83	b	Writing Application: Editing written documents
84	a	Writing Application: Prewriting
85	b	Writing Application: Prewriting
86	c	Writing Application: Prewriting
87	d	Writing Application: Editing written documents
88	c	Writing Application: Editing written documents
89	a	Writing Application: Editing written documents
90	a	Writing Application: Writing in different modes and forms

1. b. To find the primary purpose, you need to find the statement that best sums up what the entire passage is about. The passage mentions one similarity between land spiders and sea spiders—they both have eight legs—but this is not what the passage is mostly about, so choice **a** is not correct. The passage does not mention any warnings of sea spiders, so choice **c** is not correct. Like the statement in choice **a,** the statement in choice **d** *is* mentioned in the passage—a land spider does use a web—but it is not the focus of the passage. The best description of the passage's primary purpose is that it describes the unique eating habits of a type of sea spider, choice **b.**

2. a. The author states in the passage that Betamax had better resolution and less noise than VHS. The author also uses Betamax as an example where a superior product gets defeated. Therefore, you can conclude that the author believes that Betamax had better quality than VHS, choice **a.** Nothing was mentioned about DVDs or high prices, so choices **b** and **c** are not correct. While VHS and Betamax were both video cassette tape companies, several differences are mentioned, so they are not identical, and choice **d** is not correct.

3. b. While the name *starfish* may be a good description of the animal's shape, that is not mentioned in the passage. The statements in choices **c** and **d** are true, but they do not relate to the name *starfish*. The author states that a starfish isn't even a fish at all. He or she then says that the name should therefore not be used. Therefore, choice **b** is the best description of the author's attitude toward the name.

4. c. The passage mentions that while many starfish (or sea stars) have five arms, some can have one more (or up to 35 more). Therefore, you can infer that a sea star can have six arms, choice **c.** Be careful with the other choices. A sea star has no backbone, so it is an invertebrate; that eliminates choices **a** and **d** And the author states that the name *starfish* should *not* be used.

5. d. The bar graph shows the number of big cats at a local zoo. It is a double-bar graph because it shows the number of male and female cats for each type. Therefore, the question in choice **d** could be answered. The other questions in answer choices **a**, **b**, and **c** might be able to be answered by someone at the zoo, but not from the data in the graph alone.

6. a. The first paragraph of this passage tells about one specific invention created by Benjamin Franklin: the Franklin stove. While Benjamin Franklin *was* responsible for many great inventions, the paragraph does not mention more of his inventions, so choice **b** is not the primary purpose. The paragraph does not tell much about how a stove works, choice **c**, so that is not the primary purpose either. The second paragraph mentions that Franklin *could* have made a lot of money from his stoves, choice **d**, but that he refused to patent it, and so he did not make any money from the invention anyway.

7. d. There is nothing in the passage to suggest that Benjamin Franklin was afraid of making a fire, so choice **a** is not correct. The passage mentions that Franklin *could* have become one of the richest people in America had he patented his stove, but because he did not he was neither extremely rich nor interested primarily in making money. Therefore, choices **b** and **c** are not correct either. In fact, Franklin was less concerned about making money than helping his fellow humans, choice **d**.

8. d. Benjamin Franklin was the inventor of the Franklin stove. Therefore, according to the passage, he was offered "the right to patent his stove." It sounds like he had the ability to patent the stove. You should check the answer choices to see which word or phrase most closely fits the meaning of *right* in the given sentence. In fact, you can even replace the terms in the answer choices with *right*. Only *legal claim*, choice **d**, will make sense. While *turn* may mean *correct*, *good health*, or

turn in other contexts, it refers to a legal claim in the context of the sentence.

9. c. The price or size of the stove was never mentioned in the passage, so the Franklin stove was not likely expensive or small, choices **a** or **d**. The Franklin stove was designed to be much safer than other stoves, so choice **b** is not true. The passage mentions that the Franklin stove burned less wood and generated more heat. This means it was very efficient, choice **c**.

10. b. The author describes the difficulties of gardening. But she also explains that it brings her joy and that she would be able to enjoy its benefits in the future. So the passage is not mostly about pointing out the difficulties in gardening, choice **a**, but in showing that those difficulties have their rewards, choice **b**. The author does not explain how to plant vegetables, choice **c**, and the tools used for gardening, choice **d**, are only a small part of the story.

11. d. An opinion is a statement that cannot be proven. It can be proven that the United States is culturally diverse and that its climate ranges from freezing to hot—and that some areas are so cold that an ice cube will rarely melt. However, "perfect" weather is a matter of opinion. Some people might like cold weather. Some people might like hot weather. That's why the last sentence in the passage is an example of an opinion.

12. a. The narrator of the story talks about all of the things that could be done with the day, such as playing basketball or flying a kite. The author mentions that the trick was "figuring out what we wanted to do." His or her primary concern is what to do—not picking out clothes (choice **b**), looking for sports equipment (choice **c**), or staying warm (choice **d**). All of those concerns are secondary to simply getting outside and enjoying the day—or making the most of the day, choice **a**.

13. a. The second paragraph of the passage begins with the year of John Adams's birth. It ends with the year of his death. In between it lists events in the order in which they happened, so choice **a** is correct.

14. c. To answer this question, you need to find the one piece of information that was NOT given in the passage. The passage mentions that his son was the president in 1826, so choice **a** is not correct. The passage also mentions that Adams graduated from Harvard and that he helped to write the Declaration of Independence, so choices **b** and **d** are not correct either. The Civil War did not happen until the mid 1800s, so John Adams was not involved with that conflict.

15. c. The date of John Adams's death is very interesting. He happened to die on the anniversary of the United States declaring independence. This does not necessarily show that he was as important as George Washington, choice **a**, or demonstrate a reason why he should be on U.S. currency, choice **b**. His death also happened long after the Revolutionary War, so choice **d**. is not correct. The significance of July 4 in U.S. history helps reinforce Adams as a patriot, choice **c**, since even his death was tied in to the history of America.

16. b. An inference is a statement that is not stated explicitly in a passage, but can be deduced from the information given. The passage says that Washington was the first president and that Jefferson was the third president. It also states that Adams served as U.S. president between Washington and Jefferson. Therefore, it can be inferred that Adams was the second president of the United States, choice **b**. None of the other statements in the

answer choices can be inferred from the information, and none of them are correct.

17. d. The Supreme Court is part of the judicial branch of government, so the reader should turn to page 57 to learn about the New Jersey Supreme Court. You can see that the words *judicial*, *judge*, and *jury* all start with the same prefix, and they are all related to the same branch of government.

18. a. Chapter 1 is organized by time. But Chapter 2 is organized by the different geographical areas of New Jersey, so choice **b** is correct.

19. b. The author mentions that auto racing is very popular, but that is not the main idea of the passage. The student should recognize that the author is concerned about the sport's impact on the environment. Therefore, choice **b** best sums up the main idea. A student may choose one of the other answer choices because he or she may feel that the statement is correct. However, be sure that the student understands that the passage must clearly state the main idea for the answer choice to be true.

20. b. The only word from the answer choices that begins with a blended consonant sound is *sport*, choice **b**. Students can sound out the words if it helps them identify the blending sound.

21. c. If a student does not understand the meaning of a word, writing what he or she thinks the word means on the board will not help him or her identify the meaning. Therefore, choice **a** is not correct. The synonym *reevaluate* may not be helpful for a student because the word may actually be more difficult to understand, so choice **b** is not the best choice. Breaking the word into its individual letters will not help a student identify its meaning either, so choice **d** is not correct. Breaking out the word into parts, choice **c**, will be most effective because seeing the parts of the word (*re-* and *examine*) may help a student understand the word's overall meaning.

22. d. The word *run* has many meanings. In the context of the sentence that the student reads, it does not refer to a race, so choice **a** is not correct. It does not refer to a specific amount, choice **b**, or an urgent demand for payment, choice **c**. The "run" on Broadway refers to the series of shows performed. Choice **d** is the best definition for the student to use. If a student is unsure of which word is the best fit, he or she can plug in the given definitions into the sentence to see which provides the best meaning for the context.

23. d. Students should use all of the elements of a story, including the title of a book or a chapter, to make predictions. The name of the chapter is "Making the Team". Therefore, the best prediction that the student can make is that Mabel will make the team. There is no evidence that any of the statements in the other answer choices are likely to happen.

24. a. Mabel is practicing free throws at the beginning of the story. Then her mother calls her from the window. Therefore, the first two steps are IV and III. Then Mabel's father brings food into the dining room, and Mabel digs into a bowl of potatoes. That means that the list of events from choice **a** must be correct.

25. b. A compound word can be separated into two independent words. Of the words in the answer choices, only *basketball* can be separated into two independent words: *basket* and *ball*. Therefore, choice **b** is correct.

26. c. A digraph can make a sound like the letter *f*. But only one of the words in the answer choices contains a word that has that sound. The word *enough* contains the digraph *gh*, which has the *f* sound. Students can sound

out the words to listen for the *f* sounds, if necessary.

27. a. To solve this question, you need to identify the one task that is NOT being requested of a paraprofessional. The lesson plan says that the paraprofessional should distribute the reading records to students, choice **b**; help students locate the parts of a book, choice **d**; and then collect all the cards at the end of class, choice **c**. The students are supposed to write the comments in the reading records, so choice **a** is correct.

28. d. The only list of last names that appear in alphabetical order is the list found in answer choice **d**: Maas, Madison, Mejias, Mulholland.

29. b. A genre is a type of book, such as nonfiction or poetry. It can be helpful to group by genre so that students can sort similar types of books together. The best question to ask to help students understand the purpose of including it in the reading record is therefore listed in choice **b**.

30. c. Antonyms are words that mean opposite things. *Cold* and *chilly* mean the same thing, which means they are synonyms—and choice **a** is incorrect. *There* and *their* are words that sound the same but are spelled differently, so they are homonyms—and choice **b** is correct. *Enormous* and *tiny* mean opposite things, so choice **c** is correct.

31. b. A right triangle is marked with a little square in the corner of one of the angles. That means that the angle has a measure of 90 degrees. A right triangle has one angle with a measure of 90 degrees. Therefore, only the triangle in answer choice **b** is a right triangle.

32. c. The easiest and most accurate way to estimate the sum of these numbers is to round each decimal in the problem to the closest whole number. 3.94 rounds to 4; 7.11 rounds to 7; 4.88 rounds to 5. Now you can just add 4 + 7 + 5. The sum is 16, which is the closest estimate. If you rounded the decimals incorrectly (such as rounding 7.11 to 8 or rounding 4.88 to 4), you would get an incorrect answer.

33. a. Remember that the > symbol means *is greater than*. A helpful way to remember this is to consider that the symbol looks like a mouth that "eats" the larger number. Because 12 is greater than 8, 12 > 8 is a true inequality and choice **a** is correct. The = symbol means *is equal to*, which means choice **b** is not true because 8 and 12 are not equal. The symbol ≤ is a combination of the < symbol (meaning *is less than*) and the = symbol, so it means *is less than or equal to*. Because 12 is *not* less than or equal to 8, choice **d** is not correct.

34. d. The way to solve for an exponent is to multiply the base by itself the number of times shown by the number in the power. In this case, 10 is the base, so it must be multiplied by itself. The power is 3, so 10 must be multiplied by itself 3 times. This is represented by the expression in answer choice **d**.

35. a. The student buys 8 markers at a price of $1.50 per marker. Therefore, 1.50 must be multiplied by 8 to find the total amount of money spent on markers. The student buys 3 erasers at a price of $2.25 per marker. That means that 2.25 must be multiplied by 3 to find the total amount of money spent on erasers. To find the total cost of buying both types of school supplies, the totals must be added together. These steps are represented by the expression in choice **a**. Be careful with the expression in choice **d**; it multiplies the total cost of the markers and the erasers, so it is not correct.

36. c. The decimal 0.01 is one-hundredth of a whole. Remember that a percent also represents one out of 100. Therefore, 1%, choice **c**, is equivalent to 0.01. If you chose **a**, keep in mind that to convert a percent to a decimal you need to move the decimal point two places to the left; that means 0.01% is equivalent to 0.0001. The fractions in choices **b** and **d** are worth 100 and 0.1, respectively.

37. d. The number 68 is the sixth number in the pattern. Each number is 12 greater than the previous number in the pattern. That means the seventh number in the pattern will be 68 + 12, or 80. The eighth number will be 80 + 12, or 92. Finally, the ninth number will be 92 + 12, or 104.

38. d. To add or subtract unlike fractions, you need to find a common denominator (the number on the bottom). The denominator of $\frac{1}{5}$ is 5 and the denominator of $\frac{1}{10}$ is 10. Therefore, a possible common denominator of the two fractions is 10. To convert $\frac{1}{5}$ into a fraction with a denominator of 10, you need to multiply both the top and the bottom by 2: $\frac{1}{5} = \frac{(1 \times 2)}{(5 \times 2)} = \frac{2}{10}$. Now you can add the like fractions $\frac{2}{10}$ and $\frac{1}{10}$ by simply adding the numerators (the numbers on the top) while keeping the denominator the same. $\frac{2}{10} + \frac{1}{10} = \frac{(2+1)}{10} = \frac{3}{10}$.

39. c. You can find the value of 10% of a number by moving its decimal point one place to the left. Or you can multiply it by 0.1. Either way, 10% of $65.75 will end up being about $6. That is the discount for the coat being on sale. Take away that discount from the original price of the jacket to find its price on sale. The best estimate is about $60, choice **c**.

40. b. There are 3 feet in a yard. To find the number of feet in $2\frac{1}{3}$ yards, you can multiply $2\frac{1}{3}$ by 3. Remember that $\frac{1}{3}$ multiplied by 3 will become 1. That means the product will be 7 feet.

41. a. The ¢ symbol means *cents*, or one-hundredth of a dollar. The amount of money listed in choice **c**, 500¢, is therefore equivalent to five dollars. But the amount of money listed in choice **a**, 5.00¢, is still only equivalent to five cents. Since this is the amount of money that is NOT equivalent to five dollars, it is the correct answer choice.

42. b. To solve for an exponent, the base must be multiplied by itself the number of times in the power. In the problem shown, 10 multiplied by itself some number of times is equal to 100. The question that gets students to understand this concept is illustrated in choice **b**. The questions in choices **a** and **c** relate to subtraction and division, so they are incorrect. The question in choice **d.** relates to exponents, but it assumes that 10 is the power—not the base of the exponent.

43. a. The perimeter of any polygon is found by adding the lengths of each side together. For a rectangle, you can simply add the length and the width of the figure and then double its sum. The answer will be the same as adding each side individually. The expression in choice **a** shows this solution. Be careful with choice **b**; this expression would solve for the area of the rectangle instead of its perimeter.

44. a. Allison gets $40 a month for her allowance. According to the circle graph, she saves 25% of her allowance each month. To finds the percent of a number, first find the decimal value of the percent. Because a percent means *out of 100*, 25% is equal to 0.25. Now you can just multiply that decimal by the number in the problem: $40 \times 0.25 = 10$.

45. d. The hundredths place in a number can be found by looking two places to the right of

the decimal point. In the number 218.56, that digit is 6. If you choice **b**, be sure to notice that a place value that ends in *-th* represents a place value to the right of the decimal point.

46. c. To convert hours into minutes, multiply by 60 (because there are 60 minutes in an hour). Now you can see that the school schedule has 60×5, or 300 minutes of class throughout the day. There are six classes during that time. To find the length of each class, in minutes, divide the total time by the number of classes: $300 \div 6 = 50$, so choice **c** is correct.

47. c. The average (arithmetic mean) of any set of numbers can be found by adding all of the numbers together and then dividing the sum by the number of values. In this case you can add $48 + 56 + 48 + 52$. The sum is 204. There were four numbers added, so divide the sum by 4 to find the average: $204 \div 4 = 51$. If you chose choice **a**, you may have confused the definitions of the terms *mean* and *mode*. If you chose choice **b**, you may have confused the definitions of the terms *mean* and *median*.

48. b. To divide fractions requires two important first steps: First, the fraction in the problem must be flipped. In this case, $\frac{1}{4}$ would become $\frac{4}{1}$. Second, the division symbol must be changed to a multiplication symbol. Therefore, the correct number sentence to solve the student's problem is shown in answer choice **b**. The student had originally flipped the wrong fraction.

49. c. The bar for the number of lunches sold during the month of January goes a little beyond the line marking 700 on the scale. It does not reach the line marking 800 on the scale. Therefore, the number of lunches sold during that month must be somewhere between 700 and

800, choice **c**. Choice **d** is incorrect because more school lunches were sold in November than in January.

50. a. This subtraction problem requires several regrouping steps. First, 10 ones must be regrouped from one ten to subtract in the ones place. Then 10 tens must be regrouped from one hundred to subtract in the tens place. Finally 10 hundreds must be regrouped from one thousand to subtract in the hundreds place. If you regrouped carefully, you would end up with the number shown in choice **a**.

51. d. The word *product* means the result of multiplication. The number in choice **a** is the result of division; the number in choice **b** is the result of subtraction; the number in choice **c** is the result of addition. When 9 and 3 are multiplied, the result, or product, is 27, choice **d**. If you got this problem wrong, review the math glossary in Chapter 5; it is very important to remember the meaning of these terms.

52. a. The numbers in choices **b** and **d**, 1.07 and 0.55, are both less than 1.1. The number in choice **c**, 1.71, is greater than 1.7. Therefore, only 1.11, the number in choice **a** is greater than 1.1 and less than 1.7.

53. b. The negative sign in the given number should tell you that the number must be located to the left of zero on the number line. (All numbers to the left of zero are negative; all numbers to the right are positive.) That means you can get rid of choices **c** and **d**. The fraction $-\frac{1}{4}$ is also equivalent to –0.25, which is between 0 and –1.

54. c. To add or subtract decimals, be sure to line up the numbers by their decimal points. If you made a mistake in aligning them, you may have ended up with choice **a** or **d**. If you made an error in regrouping, you would

have gotten choice **b**. The correct sum is 52.32, choice **c**.

55. c. To solve for the value of a variable, y in this case, try to get it alone on one side of the equation. That means getting rid of the – 4 next to it. To do that, you can add 4 to both sides of the equation. You will get $y - 4 + 4 = 10 + 4$. That leaves you with $y = 14$, choice **c**. To check your answer to these types of problems, plug in your number for the variable into the original equation. If it works, the number is correct. If it doesn't work, it must be wrong. Because $14 - 4 = 10$, the value of y is indeed 14, choice **c**.

56. d. The sides of a square must have the same length. If you look at the points on the xy-plane, you will see that the are four units away from each other. The fourth point on the plane must also be four units away from each other. If you're not sure, just draw a point that can be used to form a square. You can even draw lines on the paper to see where the point must be. It should be six units to right and five units up from the corner of the plane, which means the coordinates are $(6, 5)$. If you chose choice **a**, remember that the x-coordinate (the horizontal line) must come first.

57. c. To solve this problem requires several steps. You need to multiply the cost of each baked good by the number sold. Therefore, $30 \times 0.75 = 22.50$; $18 \times 0.50 = 9$; $8 \times 1.50 = 12$. Those products show how much money was made from selling each type of food. Add them together to find the total amount of money raised from the school bake sale. $22.50 + 9 + 12 = \$43.50$, choice **c**. If you chose choice **a**, you may have neglected to add all of the amounts from selling each baked good together. If you chose **b**, you may have made a regrouping error. If you chose **d**, you may have mixed up the prices of the muffins and the cookies.

58. a. The teacher wrote equations that showed the value of some numbers when multiplied by themselves. That is what exponents are about: a number being multiplied by itself. Therefore, the teacher is likely preparing to teach about the concept of exponents. There is no division or decimals involved, so choices **c** and **d** are not correct. Because there is only one operation in each equation, it would not make sense that the teacher is preparing to teach about the order of operations, choice **b**.

59. a. The order of operations state that multiplication and division should always be solved, from left to right, before addition and subtraction. To correctly solve $20 + 2 \times 2 - 9 \div 3$, the multiplication should be solved first, followed by the division. Then the addition and subtraction can be solved from left to right. This order is shown by the list in choice **a**.

60. d. According to the numbers in the table, the turtle is growing at a rate of 0.8 inches per month. That is because the difference between any two consecutive numbers in the table is 0.8. If the pattern continues, the turtle will grow an additional 0.8 inches per month. That means the length of the turtle in January will be equal to 5.4 + 0.8, or 6.2 inches. The question asks for the length of the turtle in February, however. Therefore, the length of the turtle can be found by adding 0.8 to its length in January: 6.2 + 0.8 = 7. Answer choice **d** is correct.

61. a. The subject of this sentence is the Trail Ridge Road. The subject is therefore singular and should have a verb with a matching tense. The verb *reach* is in the plural sense, so it does not match the subject. It should be in the singular tense, *reaches,* so the mistake in the sentence is in the underlined section **a**.

62. b. The word *world* is possessive; therefore, it should contain an -'s at the end. The word *worlds* without an apostrophe simply means more than one world. The error, therefore, is in choice **b**.

63. c. Word usage errors can be difficult to spot. However, the preposition in choice **a**. does not contain an error. The verb *won* is in the correct tense, so there is no error in choice **b**. And Braves is a plural word, so *were* is also a correct verb to use, so choice **d** is not correct. The word *accept* is a verb that means *to allow*. The proper word to use in this context should be *except*, which means *not including*.

64. b. The pronoun *it* is supposed to stand for something else. In the context of this sentence, the something else should be "manatees." Because the noun is plural, the pronoun must be plural as well. The noun and corresponding pronoun must always agree. Because *it swims* should be *they swim*, the error is in choice **b**.

65. c. A semicolon must separate two independent clauses. The first part of the sentence cannot stand alone, so it is not independent. The mistake in the sentence is therefore with the semicolon, making choice **c** the correct answer choice.

66. d. The Beatles, the subject of the sentence, were a band in the past. Therefore, the verbs regarding the actions of the Beatles should also be in the past tense. The Beatles, therefore, *influenced* popular music; the word *influencing* is in the incorrect verb tense, so choice **d** is the correct answer.

67. a. The word *frequent* is being used to describe how often the Old Faithful geyser is photographed. Therefore, it is acting as an adverb and should have -*ly* at the end of the word. Because the word should be *frequently*, choice **a** is correct.

68. d. The verb tense used in the underlined section for choice **d** is called the present perfect progressive tense. That verb tense is used when an action began in the past, continues in the present, and may continue going forward. If you are unsure of whether it is the right tense, see if you can simplify it and have it make sense. You can say that both Jackson and Sanders *played* football and baseball. That matches the simple past tense from earlier in the sentence.

69. c. Air bags were originally included with a few vehicles in the 1970s. Air bags are now standard. Both parts of the sentence refer to air bags, so that is the subject of the sentence.

70. a. It may be tempting to presume that the *Titanic* is the subject of the sentence. But it was not the actual ship that inspired a new era of regulations. It was the lessons learned from the ship's sinking, so choice **a** is correct. You will never find the subject of a sentence within a prepositional phrase. The prepositional phrases in the sentence include *from the sinking, of the Titanic, of safety regulations,* and *for ships.*

71. b. The simple predicate is the verb that relates to the subject of the sentence. The subject is the average storage size. While the sentences says that the storage size "continues to grow at an extraordinary rate each year," that is the complex predicate. The simple predicate is just the verb that begins the complex predicate: *continues,* choice **b.**

72. d. The word *continuously* is being used to describe how the volcano has spewed, so it is describing a verb—and is therefore an adverb, choice **d.** Almost every word that ends in *-ly* is an adverb. The example in this sentence is no exception.

73. d. A noun is a person, place, thing, or idea. A *prodigy,* which is an extremely talented child, fits the descriptions of a noun.

74. c. A preposition links words in a sentence and often describes things like time, place, and direction. In this sentence, the word links the sentence and provides information about the place or direction. It is an example of a preposition, so choice **c** is correct.

75. d. The word *advantiges* should be spelled *advantages.* None of the other words in the answer choices contain spelling errors.

76. a. The word *experimants* should be spelled *experiments.* None of the other words in the answer choices contain spelling errors.

77. b. The word *gravitationol* should be spelled *gravitational.* None of the other words in the answer choices contains spelling errors.

78. b. The word *activasion* should be spelled *activation.* None of the other words in the answer choices contains spelling errors.

79. c. Sadie's essay contains no errors in capitalization (choice **a**), semicolons (choice **b**) or commas (choice **d**). However, there are several instances where the student used an incorrect verb tense. For example, the verb *love* in the second sentence of the essay is plural although the subject, *family,* is singular. Therefore, the teacher should spend the most time reviewing verb tense agreement with Sadie.

80. c. The pronoun *she* is confusing because it is unclear who it is referring to. The last sentence of the story says that everyone had fun except for "maybe my mom and aunt." There are therefore two people that Sadie is writing about. The pronoun should be plural to match the two people. The better preposition would be *they,* choice **c.**

81. d. An Internet article about Columbus Day, choice **a**, may tell a reader about Christopher Columbus, but it is unlikely that it describes his voyage. A dictionary, choice **b** is used to define words and would not describe Columbus's voyage to America either. A newspaper article from Columbus, Ohio, choice **c**, almost certainly would not include information about the voyage. A history textbook, choice **d**, would be the type of resource that would provide information about an early explorer and the journey that he took.

82. a. Marco's argument is that it is good to be a vegetarian. He lists several reasons, including good health, ethics, and the environment. Therefore, the sentence listed in choice **a** would best provide the main idea of his argument, and it would therefore be the best fit at the beginning of his essay.

83. b. Marco makes the statement that cows produce lots of methane. Then he states that methane is a destructive greenhouse gas. These are two separate statements that he is attempting to join. The words *but*, choice **a**, or *although*, choice **d**, are not correct because the direction of the sentence is not changing. And the word *because*, choice **c**, does not work; methane is not destructive *because* cows produce it. Because Marco is simply trying to connect these two thoughts, the word *and*, choice **b**, is the best transition for him to use.

84. a. The subsections of section II are "Edit manuscript" and "Lay out book." These include such steps as copyediting and formatting the pages. The best heading listed in the answer choices to cover both subsections and all of the steps is "Prepare for Publication," choice **a**. The heading listed in choice **c**, "Perform Fact Check," could be a step within section II—but not the heading for the entire section. The headings listed in choices **b** and **d** are steps for other sections but also not appropriate for the title of a whole section.

85. b. Section III is titled "Publishing," and the subsection with the blank line is called "Distribution." Therefore, the steps in that subsection should all be about distributing the books. The best information to go into the blank part is listed in choice **b**, "Supply major bookstores with copies."

86. c. The introductory sentence should sum up the entire outline. Because the outline follows the process of book production from generating ideas through sending out the final books, this introductory sentence must provide a summation of that whole process. The best sentence from the answer choices to do this is listed in choice **c** because it mentions the three major steps listed in the three sections of the outline. The statement in choice **a** is too narrow to sum up the whole outline. It may be difficult to get a story published, **b**, but that is not what the outline was about. There is no evidence in the outline that book publishing is either exciting or glamorous; that is not the point of the outline, so choice **d** is not the best sentence to use.

87. d. The two sentences that the student wants to combine are *Hold the ball softly in your fingertips* and *You can even hold it like an egg*. The combined sentence should explain how to hold the ball in a simple, easy-to-understand way. The sentence in choice **d** combines both the fact that the ball should be held gently in your fingertips and like an egg—and it does it simply and clearly. The sentence in choice **a** tells how to hold an egg, not the ball. The sentences in choices **b** and **c** are unnecessarily complicated and hard to understand.

88. c. The student states that a pitcher should let go of the ball from the fingertips and then states "that will help you keep control of the ball." A word is needed to help provide a transition for that sentence. The direction is suggesting that keeping control of the ball is a result of releasing the ball from your fingertips. This is a cause and effect, which means that *because* would be the best transition word to use.

89. a. Good directions include helpful transitions. While there is nothing technically wrong with the given sentence, it does not flow smoothly. Sentence 7 lists the last step of the directions. Therefore, *finally* would provide a nice way to let the reader know that the last step is about to come. The transitions *however* or *even though* in choices **b** and **d** signal a change in direction. Because there is no change occurring in the directions, these are not appropriate to use.

90. a. The sentence in choice **a** mentions some differences between frogs and toads. That is a comparison of two things. None of the sentences in the other answer choices include a comparison, so choices **b**, **c**, and **d** are not correct.

APPENDIX

The Praxis II: ParaProfessional Assessment has three sections: Reading, Mathematics, and Writing. This appendix lists all of the different skills that will be covered in the three sections of the test. The skills listed are all covered in Chapters 4, 5, and 6 of this book.

Reading

The 30 multiple-choice questions on the reading section of the ParaPro Assessment will test your ability to understand texts and help students develop their reading skills. All of the topics covered in the reading section are covered in Chapter 4.

Reading Skills and Knowledge

About 18 of the 30 questions on the reading section of the ParaPro Assessment will test your general knowledge of reading, including your ability to interpret text and graphs. The subject matter of the texts may vary greatly, from historical passages to poetry. However, the questions will be fairly predictable. They will ensure that you have the ability to:

- understand the main idea or primary purpose
- understand supporting ideas
- understand vocabulary in context
- understand the organization of a passage
- draw inferences or implications from directly stated content
- distinguish between fact and opinion
- interpret graphic text

Application of Reading Skills and Knowledge to Classroom Instruction

About 12 of the 30 questions on the reading section of the ParaPro Assessment will test your ability to help students develop their reading skills in the classroom. These specific questions on the reading section of the ParaPro Assessment assess your ability to help students:

- alphabetize words
- recognize antonyms, homonyms, and synonyms
- use context clues to determine the meaning of a word or phrase
- recognize the parts of a word, such as its prefix, suffix, or root
- identify the sounds that can be used to construct words
- use reading strategies, such as predicting what will come next in a story
- recognize the parts of a word, such as its prefix, suffix, or root
- use a dictionary

Mathematics

The 30 multiple-choice questions on the mathematics section of the ParaPro Assessment will test your understanding of basic math concepts and your ability to help students develop their math skills. You will not be allowed to use a calculator on the ParaPro Assessment, so the level of difficulty will not be too advanced. All of the topics included in the mathematics section are covered in Chapter 5.

Mathematics Skills and Knowledge

About 18 of the 30 questions on the math section of the ParaPro Assessment will test your general knowledge of elementary-level mathematics. Some questions will be straightforward computation, such as 34×18; other questions will present the information in the context of a word problem. The categories of math that will be covered on the ParaPro Assessment are as follows:

Arithmetic

- add, subtract, multiply, and divide whole numbers, fractions, and decimals
- understand the place-value system for both decimals and whole numbers
- recognize the meaning of math terms and symbols, such as *product*, *quotient*, $\div$, $<$, or $>$
- use percentages
- understand that numbers can be expressed in different ways, such as one-hundredth, 0.01, and 1%
- identify the relative value of numbers, such as that 2.5 is between 2 and 3
- use estimation
- demonstrate knowledge of the order of operations

Algebra

- solve single-step linear equations with one variable, such as $x + 1 = 3$
- identify a pattern and the numbers that follow

Geometry

- recognize and name geometric shapes, such as triangles, quadrilaterals, or other polygons
- find the perimeter, area, and volume for shapes
- graph points and identify ordered pairs on a coordinate grid

Measurement

- convert units within the same system, such as 2 feet to 24 inches or 200 centimeters to 2 meters
- understand that information can be demonstrated in multiple ways, such as 1¢, $0.01, and 1 penny

Data

- create and interpret tables, graphs, or charts, including identifying trends
- calculate the mean, median, and mode

Application of Mathematics Skills and Knowledge to Classroom Instruction

About 12 of the 30 questions on the math section of the ParaPro Assessment will test your ability to help students develop their math skills in the classroom. These specific questions assess your ability to help students with the skills in the arithmetic, algebra, geometry, measurement, and data sections.

Writing

The 30 multiple-choice questions on the writing section of the ParaPro Assessment will ensure that you have an adequate level of writing ability and that you can help students develop their own writing skills. There will not be an essay. All of the topics included in the writing section are covered in Chapter 6.

Writing Skills and Knowledge

About 18 of the 30 questions on the writing section of the ParaPro Assessment will check your general knowledge of writing. The questions will test your ability to:

- know the parts of a sentence, such as a *subject* or *predicate*
- know the parts of speech, such as a *verb* or *adverb*
- recognize spelling mistakes
- recognize grammatical mistakes
- recognize punctuation mistakes
- use the proper word in a situation, such as *affect* or *effect*

Application of Writing Skills and Knowledge to Classroom Instruction

About 12 of the 30 questions on the Writing section of the ParaPro Assessment will test your ability to help students develop their writing skills in the classroom. These questions focus not only on the actual drafting of a document but also the entire writing process—from planning through revising. The questions assess your ability to help students:

- use suitable resources to aid them in the writing process
- generate ideas for writing with tools such as prewriting and outlining
- write a thesis statement, supporting paragraphs, and a conclusion
- revise and edit written text by rewriting or removing spelling, grammar, punctuation, or word usage errors

ADDITIONAL ONLINE PRACTICE ▶

Whether you need help building basic skills or preparing for an exam, visit the LearningExpress Practice Center! On this site, you can access additional practice materials. Using the code below, you'll be able to log in and take an additional Praxis II ParaPro practice test. This online practice exam will also provide you with:

- **Immediate scoring**
- **Detailed answer explanations**
- **Personalized recommendations for further practice and study**

Log on to the LearningExpress Practice Center by using the URL: **www.learnatest.com/practice**

This is your Access Code: **7335**

Follow the steps online to redeem your access code. After you've used your access code to register with the site, you will be prompted to create a username and password. For easy reference, record them here:

Username: _____ **Password:** _____

With your username and password, you can log in and answer these practice questions as many times as you like. If you have any questions or problems, please contact LearningExpress customer service at 1-800-295-9556 ext. 2, or e-mail us at **customerservice@learningexpressllc.com**

NOTES

NOTES

NOTES

NOTES

NOTES

NOTES

NOTES